Mussolini's Grandchildren

'To understand the rise of the far right and Meloni, it is necessary to place them in the complex history of Italian fascism in the aftermath of Mussolini's death, and the way in which reactionary positions progressively seeped into the mainstream. This is precisely what David Broder does by guiding the reader through the key events in the "mainstreaming" of the Italian far right, from the nostalgic militancy of the Movimento Sociale Italiano during the "years of Lead" to the progressive push towards the normalisation and pacification of the far right. This culminated in the collaboration of the post-fascist Alleanza Nazionale with Berlusconi, and now with Meloni's Fratelli d'Italia and its combination of strenuous defence of the economic and geopolitical status quo and the pursuit of reactionary policies on migration, identity and education. Meticulously researched and engagingly written by an author with a longstanding knowledge of Italy and interest in its politics and culture, this is a must-read for all those who want to understand what is happening in the country and what may soon happen elsewhere.'
　　　　　—Dr Paolo Gerbaudo, Reader in Digital Politics, Department of
　　　　　　　　　　　　　　　　　　Digital Humanities, King's College London

'Is fascism really a "thing of the past"? Broder shines a light on what the Italian post-fascists keep in the shadows, the ferocity of their syncretic ideology, and their heavy contradictions. A sharp, richly documented survey of the perennial – shameless – rebranding of the Italian far right, from historical fascism to the present.'
　　　　　　　　　　　　　　　　　　　　　　—Carlo Greppi, historian

Mussolini's Grandchildren
Fascism in Contemporary Italy

David Broder

PLUTO  PRESS

First published 2023 by Pluto Press
New Wing, Somerset House, Strand, London WC2R 1LA
and Pluto Press Inc.
1930 Village Center Circle, 3-834, Las Vegas, NV 89134

www.plutobooks.com

British Library Cataloguing in Publication Data
A catalogue record for this book is available from the British Library

ISBN 978 0 7453 4802 5   Paperback
ISBN 978 0 7453 4805 6   PDF
ISBN 978 0 7453 4804 9   EPUB

This book is printed on paper suitable for recycling and made from fully managed and sustained forest sources. Logging, pulping and manufacturing processes are expected to conform to the environmental standards of the country
of origin.

Typeset by Stanford DTP Services, Northampton, England

Simultaneously printed in the United Kingdom and United States of America

Contents

Organisations

Alleanza Nazionale (AN) (postfascist, 1994–2009)

CasaPound Italia (neofascist, 2003–)

Comitati di Liberazione Nazionale (CLN) (Resistance alliance, 1943–5)

Confederazione Generale Italiana del Lavoro (CGIL) (trade union confederation, 1943–)

Democrazia Cristiana (big-tent, 1943–94)

European Conservatives and Reformists (ECR) (right wing to far right, 2009–)

European People's Party (EPP) (Christian-Democratic, 1976–)

Fasci di Azione Rivoluzionaria (neofascist, 1945–7)

Five Star Movement (big-tent populist, 2009–)

Forza Nuova (neofascist, 1997–)

Fratelli d'Italia (postfascist, 2012–)

Fronte della Gioventù (MSI youth wing, 1971–96)

Movimento Politico Ordine Nuovo (neofascist, 1969–73)

Movimento Sociale Italiano (MSI) (neofascist, 1946–95)

Nuclei Armati Rivoluzionari (NAR) (neofascist, 1977–81)

Partito Comunista Italiano (PCI) (1921–91)

Partito Fascista Repubblicano (1943–5)

Partito Nazionale Fascista (1921–43)

Partito Socialista Italiano (1892–1994)

Popolo della Libertà (right wing, Berlusconian, 2009–13)

Radiotelevisione italiana (public broadcaster)

Repubblica Sociale Italiano (1943–5 regime, also known as Salò Republic)

Dramatis Personae

Gianni Alemanno, from 1988 to 1991 the secretary of the MSI's youth front, from 2008 to 2013 mayor of Rome for Popolo della Libertà.

Giorgio Almirante, from 1938 an editor at *La Difesa della Razza*, and chief of staff at the Ministry of Popular Culture in the Salò Republic. In 1946 he was a co-founder of the Movimento Sociale Italiano, of which he was the secretary in 1948–50 and from 1969 to 1987, handing over the reins shortly before his death in 1988.

Enrico Berlinguer, general secretary of the Italian Communist Party from 1972 to 1984.

Silvio Berlusconi, a media tycoon, in 1994 he entered electoral politics with his Forza Italia party and formed the 'centre-right' alliance. Prime minister in 1994–5, 2001–6 and 2008–11.

Junio Valerio Borghese, commander of the Nazi-collaborationist Decima Flottiglia MAS, from 1951 to 1953 honorary president of the MSI, in 1967 founder of the Fronte Nazionale and in 1970 author of a failed coup d'état

Umberto Bossi, founder of the Lega Nord, of which he was the national ('federal') secretary from 1989 to 2012.

Luca Castellini, Hellas Verona football ultra leader and national deputy leader of Forza Nuova. Under house arrest in 2021–2 following the attack on the CGIL trade union's office during a protest against vaccine passes.

Giulio Castellino, a member of a series of neofascist groups including CasaPound and Forza Nuova, currently head of a movement called Italia Libera.

Stefano delle Chiaie, founder of neofascist terrorist group Avanguardia Nazionale and collaborator of South American intelligence services, involved in multiple judicial investigations connected to the strategy of tension. Died 2019.

Francesco Cossiga, Christian Democratic prime minister in 1979–80, and president of the Republic in 1985–1992.

Norma Cossetto, daughter of a local Fascist leader in Visinada (today in Croatia) and herself a student member of the National Fascist Party, famous for being murdered by partisans on the night of 4–5 October 1943. Awarded the Medal of Honour for Civic Merit in 2005.

Bettino Craxi, prime minister in 1983–7, and long-time leader of the Socialist Party, fled to Tunisia in 1994 faced with corruption charges.

Guido Crosetto, from 2001 an MP for Berlusconi's Forza Italia party, in 2012 a co-founder of Fratelli d'Italia. A leading figure in the security industry, in 2022 he became minister of defence.

Gabriele D'Annunzio, nationalist poet and leading champion of Italian intervention in World War I. In September 1919 he led a paramilitary invasion of Fiume (today Rijeka, Croatia) and was ousted by Italian state forces at Christmas 1920. In the early interwar period he was a rival of Mussolini and under the regime was reduced to a peripheral role. He was critical of the alliance with Nazi Germany.

Renzo de Felice, a leading historian of fascism and author of an eight-book biography of Benito Mussolini.

Augusto de Marsanich, a co-founder of the Movimento Sociale Italiano and from 1950 to 1954 its national secretary, after which he became party president. A 'national-conservative' figure, he steered the MSI toward support for NATO membership. Stated at the 1948 MSI congress that it must 'neither restore nor renege on the regime'.

Julius Evola, an esoteric theorist whose anti-modernist works such as *Revolt Against the Modern World* and *Ride the Tiger* were widely influential on the postwar neofascist movement.

Emanuele Fiano, from 2006 to 2022 a member of the Chamber of Deputies, mostly for the Democratic Party. The son of a Holocaust survivor and outspoken antifascist, he was the author of an unsuccessful bill, discussed in 2017, that sought to tighten legislation against fascist apologism and symbols.

Carlo Fidanza, in the 2000s a leading member of the Alleanza Nazionale youth, since 2019 leader of the Fratelli d'Italia group in the European Parliament.

Gianfranco Fini, from 1977 the national secretary of the MSI youth front, he became main leader of the adult party in 1987–90 and again from 1991. He led the 'Fiuggi Turn', dissolving the party into the Alleanza Nazionale in 1995, and became deputy prime minister in 2001 and foreign minister in 2004. In 2009 he led Alleanza Nazionale into Popolo della Libertà, together with Berlusconi's party, but was expelled from its ranks in 2010.

Roberto Fiore, founding leader of Forza Nuova.

Lorenzo Fontana, a leading member of the Lega, who became president of the Chamber of Deputies in 2022.

Maurizio Gasparri, in the 1980s a leading member of the MSI youth, and from 1992 an MP for the party. The minister of communications in the 2001–5 Berlusconi government, he is today a member of Forza Italia and vice-president of the Senate.

Clemente Graziani, a volunteer for the Salò Republic, was among the members of the postwar Fasci di Azione Rivoluzionaria and the founders of the future Centro Studi Ordine Nuovo in 1953. After Rauti rejoined the MSI in 1969, Graziani was the main leader of the continuity Movimento Politico Ordine Nuovo that was banned in 1973.

Rodolfo Graziani, defence minister of the Salò Republic and convicted war criminal. Used mustard gas during the invasion of Ethiopia before becoming its viceroy and then governor of Libya. President of the MSI in 1953–4.

Gianluca Iannone, lead singer of neofascist rock group Zetaze-roalfa and founder of CasaPound.

Roberto Jonghi Lavarini, the self-described 'Black Baron' in Milan, at the centre of various far-right initiatives in the city, including social centre Cuore Nero. In 2018 a Fratelli d'Italia parliamentary candidate, in 2021 he was the focus of a *FanPage* documentary on the party's ties to neofascism.

Ignazio La Russa, the son of a regime-era fascist hierarch in Paternò, Sicily, La Russa was a MSI leader in Milan in the 1970s, and lawyer for the family of Sergio Ramelli. He was an MP from 1992 to 2018, and since then a senator, becoming president of the Senate in 2022. He was the defence minister in Silvio Berlusconi's government in 2008–11 and co-founded Fratelli d'Italia in 2012.

Giorgia Meloni, from 1992 a member of the MSI's youth wing, she became head of the Alleanza Nazionale high-schoolers' organisation Azione Giovani in 2004. From 2006 she was a member of parliament and vice-president of the Chamber of Deputies, and from 2008 the youth minister. A cofounder of Fratelli d'Italia in 2012, she became party president in 2014 and prime minister in 2022.

Arturo Michelini, a Salò veteran in whose office the MSI was founded in 1946. The party's national secretary from 1954 to 1969, his insertion strategy saw the MSI attempt to assert its role as an ally to the Christian Democrats as well as other anticommunist forces.

Alessandra Mussolini, granddaughter of Benito, entered national politics with the MSI in the early 1990s. Quit the Alleanza Nazionale in 2003 to form her own party, but today a member of the European Parliament for Forza Italia.

Giampaolo Pansa, a journalist who in the 2000s became one of the leading representatives of revisionist accounts of World War II, who focused on telling the 'history of the vanquished'.

Erich Priebke, a Nazi war criminal, involved in the Fosse Ardeatine massacre of partisans and Jews in 1944. Brought to justice in Italy in 1996 after being exposed by *ABC News* in Argentina.

Sergio Ramelli, born in 1956, he joined the MSI youth wing while a high schooler. Assaulted by members of far-left Avanguardia Operaia in 1975, he slipped into a seven-week coma and died on 29 April that year.

Fabio Rampelli, an MP for Fratelli d'Italia and current vice-president of the Chamber of Deputies.

Pino Rauti, a volunteer for the Salò Republic and a member of the Fasci di Azione Rivoluzionaria and then MSI. In 1953 a founder of the Ordine Nuovo group, he quit the MSI in 1957 but rejoined in 1969. National secretary of the party in 1990–1, he rejected the 'Fiuggi Turn' and formed his own Movimento Sociale Fiamma Tricolore. Throughout the 1990s a neofascist member of the European Parliament.

Luca Romagnoli, national secretary of Movimento Sociale Fiamma Tricolore from 2002 to 2013, including a five-year spell as a member of the European Parliament.

Pino Romualdi, deputy national secretary of the Salò-era Partito Fascista Repubblicano, and in 1946 co-founder of the Movimento Sociale Italiano.

Matteo Salvini, since 2013 the federal secretary of the Lega, he turned it into an all-Italian nationalist party centred on his own name and image. Interior minister in 2018–19.

Daniela Santanchè, a businesswoman and TV personality, in 2008 prime ministerial candidate for La Destra-Fiamma Tricolore, but from 2010 a Berlusconi ally and, since 2017, a Fratelli d'Italia representative. In 2022 she became tourism minister.

Federico Sboarina, mayor of Verona from 2017 to 2022, from 2021 a member of Fratelli d'Italia.

Mario Scelba, Christian-Democratic prime minister in 1954–5, well-known for his previous stint as interior minister, in which role he put his name to legislation banning the reconstruction of the Fascist Party.

Francesco Storace, Lazio regional president for Alleanza Nazionale from 2000 to 2005 and national health minister from 2005 to 2006. In 2007, split to form La Destra, which he led until its dissolution in 2017.

Giuseppe 'Pinuccio' Tatarella, an MSI 'conservative' who became deputy prime minister in 1994–5. A champion of close relations between the party and Silvio Berlusconi.

Fernando Tambroni, from 1955 to 1959 interior minister in a series of Christian Democratic governments, in 1960 he was prime minister of a short-lived cabinet reliant on MSI votes in parliament.

Palmiro Togliatti, general secretary of the Italian Communist Party from 1926 to 1964, as justice minister in 1945–6 he issued an amnesty for war-era crimes.

Flavio Tosi, mayor of Verona from 2007 to 2017.

Bruno Vespa, TV personality and author of dozens of works of popular history.

Timeline

This is not intended as a complete list of events regarding fascism and its heirs, but a useful guide for issues discussed in this book

4 November 1918	Italian-Austrian armistice in World War I.
12 September 1919	Gabriele d'Annunzio's paramilitaries invade Fiume.
October 1922	March on Rome and appointment of Benito Mussolini as prime minister.
1935–6	Italian invasion and annexation of Ethiopia.
1938	Proclamation of Racial Laws excluding Jews from public functions and banning mixed-race marriages.
10 June 1940	Italy declares war on Britain and France.
6 April 1941	Italy and Germany invade Yugoslavia.
22 June 1941	Axis invasion of Soviet Union.
26 January 1943	End of battle of Nikolayevka.
25 July 1943	King Vittorio Emanuele III sacks Mussolini. Pietro Badoglio appointed prime minister.
8 September 1943	Italian armistice with Allies announced. Nazi Germany invades and occupies north-central Italy.
25 April 1945	Partisan uprising in northern Italy.
28 April 1945	Execution of Mussolini.
26 December 1946	Foundation of Movimento Sociale Italiano.
10 February 1947	Paris Peace Treaty between Italy and Yugoslavia.
June 1948	First congress of MSI.

January 1950	Augusto de Marsanich becomes MSI secretary.
November 1953	Pino Rauti creates Ordine Nuovo group within MSI.
October 1954	Arturo Michelini succeeds De Marsanich as MSI secretary.
26 October 1954	Trieste returned to Italy.
January 1957	Rauti's Centro Studi Ordine Nuovo leaves MSI.
March–July 1960	Period of Fernando Tambroni's Christian Democratic government, reliant on MSI support in parliament.
June 1969	Giorgio Almirante becomes MSI secretary. Pino Rauti rejoins party the following month, co-opted onto its leadership.
December 1969	Formation of Movimento Politico Ordine Nuovo.
12 December 1969	Piazza Fontana bombing.
31 May 1972	Terrorist attack in Peteano kills three *carabinieri*.
12 April 1973	Policeman killed at MSI protest in Milan.
11 September 1973	Coup d'état in Chile.
29 April 1975	MSI activist Sergio Ramelli dies after seven-week coma.
9 May 1978	Red Brigades execute Christian Democrat Aldo Moro.
2 August 1980	Bologna Centrale station bombing kills 85.
22 May 1988	Death of Giorgio Almirante.
February 1991	Dissolution of the Italian Communist Party.
July 1991	Gianfranco Fini takes over from Pino Rauti as MSI leader.
1992–4	'Tangentopoli' scandal destroys Christian Democrat and Socialist parties.
26 January 1994	Silvio Berlusconi announces entry into electoral politics.

April 1994	Right-wing coalition forms government, with MSI in cabinet for first time.
January 1995	Fiuggi congress dissolves MSI into Alleanza Nazionale.
1 January 1999	Italy adopts the euro.
26 December 2003	Occupation of CasaPound.
10 February 2005	First national 'Day of Remembrance' for the *foibe*.
March 2009	Dissolution of Alleanza Nazionale into Popolo della Libertà.
November 2011	Collapse of Berlusconi's fourth government.
December 2012	Foundation of Fratelli d'Italia.
March 2014	Giorgia Meloni becomes president of Fratelli d'Italia.
December 2017	Fratelli d'Italia congress in Trieste.
October 2022	Formation of first government led by Fratelli d'Italia.

Acknowledgements

I originally intended to publish this book in time for an Italian general election planned for spring 2023. However, after the election was brought forward, the work of finishing the book overlapped with the campaign itself, and I owe a particular debt to David Shulman for his patience. I would also like to thank everyone at Pluto Press for their fine work – notably Emily Orford, Amina Darwish, Robert Webb, James Kelly, and Alex Diamond-Rivlin – as well as copy-editor Dan Harding.

In no particular order, I would also like to thank the staff of the Fondazione Gramsci and the Biblioteca di Storia Moderna e Contemporanea, as well as San Lorenzo's Bar Marani, on whose terrace much of the text was actually drafted. Special thanks to Julia Damphouse, including but not only for her indispensable edits.

Introduction
Mussolini's Granddaughters

'I've had to deal with it since I was a kid. They pointed at me at school, but then the real Rachele came through. The person won out over the surname.'[1] Even before Rachele Mussolini began her marketing studies, she knew her brand polarised opinion. She made these comments in October 2021 just after she had topped the poll in Rome's city council elections, as a candidate for the Fratelli d'Italia party. Her father Romano was the dictator's youngest son, making his name as a jazz pianist; but Rachele and her half-sister Alessandra each took to politics. Alessandra entered the fray in 1992 with what was then called a 'postfascist' party, but she quit in protest in 2003 when leader Gianfranco Fini went too far in damning her grandfather's record. Forming her own short-lived party, she then joined Silvio Berlusconi's Forza Italia, before withdrawing from front-line politics after defeat in the 2019 European elections. Both Rachele and her second cousin, Caio Giulio Cesare Mussolini, uphold the family name in Fratelli d'Italia; the candidate named after Julius Caesar even appeared as a 'special guest' at a party event on his great-grandfather's *Doctrine of Fascism*.[2] Taken in isolation, their surname's resurfacing in present-day politics could be considered a curiosity, of a type with another great-grandson's footballing career.[3] But the attention – and many selfie requests – that the Mussolinis draw at Fratelli d'Italia events is also because of the connection between their surname and the party's political lineage.

The 2022 election campaign began with international media reports highlighting this party's ties to fascism – claims which leader Giorgia Meloni was quick to dismiss. She issued a video message in four languages insisting that the 'Italian right has handed over fascism to history for decades now' and had condemned dictatorship and antisemitism.[4] Many pundits sympathised: didn't fascism end decades before she was even born? And hasn't 'fascist' become an overused insult – a way to vilify 'anyone I don't like on the Internet'?[5] It is true: Meloni's party is not rallying Blackshirted militias, will not form a one-party state and is not creating a fascist order. Yet if we want to understand what this party is, we need to know that its family connection with fascism is more than a matter of the Mussolinis. Only occasionally do party representatives speak positively about the regime, but they proudly claim the legacy of the Movimento Sociale Italiano (MSI) founded in 1946. It was founded on the assumption that fascism was not a parenthesis in Italian history, a twenty-year aberration, but a movement, a set of ideas and values, that survived the military defeat. After 1945, many of Mussolini's former supporters did change their colours or become belated antifascists. But the MSI, its historic leader Giorgio Almirante insisted, was something else: a party of 'fascists in a democracy'.[6] Even in the 1980s, he proclaimed that 'fascism is not behind us but ahead of us'.[7] Fratelli d'Italia's leaders, who are mostly veterans of the MSI, today call themselves 'national conservatives'. This book shows that their politics remain entrenched in fascist mythology, ways of talking about the past and visions of national identity.

Founded in 2012, Fratelli d'Italia has always been part of a broader right-wing alliance, including parties not from the fascist tradition.[8] This strategy has some roots in postwar neofascism, but there are also important changes. Upon the MSI's creation in 1946, almost all its leaders were veterans of the Nazi collaborationist Salò Republic, the holdout Fascist regime from whose official name – Repubblica Sociale Italiana – the MSI took its own. Much of this party's history was an attempt to ally itself to other anticommunist forces during the Cold War, whether for electoral ends or in violent confrontations. As late as 1991, its main national leader was a proud fascist and Salò veteran, and when the teenage

Meloni joined it in 1992, there were still many such figures in its top ranks. Yet the generational renewal that followed matters: in terms of the personal biographies of the party leaders and the social context in which they operate. The MSI was founded as a Salò-revivalist party intent on waging war on communism; but by the time Meloni joined in 1992, the Soviet bloc had just collapsed, Italy was on its way into a more closely integrated European Union, and political violence had fallen drastically since its heights in the 1970s. Even insofar as Fratelli d'Italia refers to old ideological traditions, it operates in a society where visions of political change are less ambitious, citizens' trust in institutions is in steep decline, and battles over identity are increasingly paramount. Indicative of the change is the way in which Meloni's memoir alludes to the MSI tricolore flame logo, which is still featured in Fratelli d'Italia's own banner. The epigraph to her first chapter reads: 'If this is to end in fire / Then we should all burn together / Watch the flames climb high into the night.'[9] The words seem to evoke spectres of violence, but they also point to a certain ideological evolution. Meloni cites them not from Il Duce or an esoteric theorist like Julius Evola, but from an Ed Sheeran song for a *Hobbit* movie.

J. R. R. Tolkien became an object of neofascist fascination in the 1970s; today, militants still cite him when they speak of their 'deep roots, not reached by the frost'.[10] But how deep do the roots go? Meloni denies that the flame logo refers to Mussolini himself, claiming that it represents the 'seventy-year tradition of the democratic right'.[11] Yet the mythology of an unbroken tradition, reaching generations further back, is important to party identity. At Fratelli d'Italia's first congress in 2014, Meloni spoke of 'men and women who run from one era to the next, from one generation to the next, carrying with them a fire, a flame that sometimes fades, but which has never gone out entirely',[12] as she explained that 'parties are really parties when they are able to outlive leaders and generations'. Standing before a vast image of the MSI's co-founder, she cited a lesson he had imparted: 'We take up Giorgio Almirante's teaching when he said that "in other times we had to get back on our feet, so that we could pass on the baton ... before it fell from our hands, as it had fallen from others when they were about to pass it on".[13] It seems hard to interpret Almirante's words as anything other than a reference to the creation of the MSI after the defeat of the regime. This family relationship also appears when her memoir refers to her colleague, Ignazio La Russa, as a servant of 'the party', referring to both the MSI and Fratelli d'Italia. She terms him not only 'true to himself' but a guarantor of continuity: 'the heir to a bloodline of sure faith'.[14] During the regime, La Russa's father Antonio was local leader of the Partito Nazionale Fascista in Paternò, Sicily; in postwar decades he became an MP and later a senator for the MSI, giving his son Ignazio the middle name 'Benito'.

This evocation of age-old roots nonetheless has a postmodern hue, its mythical rhetoric divorced from the grand ambitions which once animated historical fascism. Meloni's memoir often refers to postwar neofascist leader Almirante, but not at all to Mussolini's empire, its bloodshed, its genocides or its collapse. She instead harks back to the realms of fantasy, and in particular the Tolkienite spectre of Númenor, a once-great civilisation that fell into godlessness and ruin. Meloni has termed *Lord of the Rings* an 'extraordinary metaphor for man and his world',[15] and often identifies her cause with Tolkien's prince Faramir. She uses his words to summarise her own political creed: 'War must be, while we defend our lives against a destroyer who would devour all; but I do not love the bright sword for its sharpness, nor the arrow for its swiftness, nor the warrior for his glory. I love only that which they defend: the city of the Men of Númenor.'[16] This reference is also typical of a certain preference for a pop vernacular to convey identitarian talking points – with dog whistles to be heard by ideological zealots alongside an ironic or even 'fun' image for mass audiences. Another chapter in her memoir, discussing the tradition of the MSI, alludes to its flame logo via a Maroon 5 lyric, quoted in English; she promises: 'I'll carry these torches for ya that you know I'll never drop.'[17] The memoir's title, *Io Sono Giorgia*, itself refers to a viral 2019 remix of a speech of hers, which had her insisting 'I am Giorgia, I am a woman, I am a mother, I am a Christian' to a catchy disco track. Turning the tables on the attempted satire, the lines in the club anthem, which has over eleven million YouTube views,[18] provide the cue for her chapters.

This branding of Meloni as an 'ordinary Italian mother' bears parallels with French far-right leader Marine Le Pen. In each case, a decades-old party steeped in both historical fascism and modern-day identity politics uses the face and Christian name of its leader to reach voters who have no bond with the party itself. This also helps to frame its agenda as 'common sense' rather than 'ideological'. This was apparent in the rhetorical posture that Meloni took during Mario Draghi's government in 2021–2, a cross-party cabinet which itself claimed to transcend political divides. The only major opposition leader, Meloni emphasised that her approach to former European Central Bank chief Draghi's policies would be 'constructive' rather than 'party-political'. Yet, even beyond the fact that it voted down almost all its concrete measures, Fratelli d'Italia also painted this government as the latest expression of an unelected left-wing establishment.[19] In the 2022 election campaign, she claimed to embody democracy itself, promising a government of 'free people who haven't been bought by anyone', an end to the dominant 'power system' and a moment of liberation which would 'allow normal Italians to raise their head after decades'. Yet the war on her domestic opponents, the 'LGBT lobbies', 'migrant NGOs' (non-governmental organisation) and the 'violent and extremist left' was allied with a message of stability: a pro-business stance, a commitment to reforming rather than breaking up the European Union and demonstrating Italian allegiance to NATO. Many commentators saw in this as evidence that Meloni had 'gone mainstream' or even 'grown up':[20] the prime-minister-in-waiting no longer looked like the teenager who once appeared on French TV praising Mussolini.[21]

Yet sometimes the symbols of the past seem much more obvious in the present. What name other than 'fascist' is appropriate for

Fratelli d'Italia activists in Civitavecchia who decorated a party office with the banners of Salò-era paramilitaries?[22] How about the much more senior members who unveiled a mausoleum to Mussolini's defence minister Rodolfo Graziani?[23] What about the party's head in the European Parliament Roman saluting in the company of a prominent Milan neofascist?[24] What about those leaders who say that the name of fascist is a 'compliment' or have even claimed it for themselves?[25] Meloni has in recent times denounced 'pantomime nostalgics' as 'traitors', who hand weapons to her party's enemies.[26] But is this only a matter of 'nostalgia' – and for what? It seems unlikely that this question can be answered simply by talking about what distinguishes our own time from the world of 1945. Even in postwar years, the MSI formally accepted Italy's place within a US-led military alliance, took part in elections and sought a place for itself within broader right-wing and anticommunist alliances. These choices brought many splits and changes, but they did not stop the MSI calling itself fascist. Up to his death in 1988, Almirante routinely insisted that fascism did not die with Mussolini but continued as a 'movement' once the regime was over. There are also more modern political positions that raise questions. Is there a fascist connection in the conspiracy theories, repeatedly spread by Meloni, that accuse 'usurers' of plotting with the left to plan the 'ethnic replacement' of Europeans? Without doubt, Fratelli d'Italia is a creature of our own time and not the 1940s. For this reason, this book tries to explain what it is by reconstructing its genealogy, from its roots to its more modern partners.

HYBRID TRADITIONS

So, is fascism making a comeback? Ahead of the 2022 general election, as international media predicted Italy's most right-wing government since 1945, many pundits complained that there was too much hype. Veteran newspaperman Paolo Mieli pleaded for a 'two-month [campaign] where we don't talk about history'.[27]

Meloni almost never publicly mentions Mussolini, still less as a model: she often cites neofascists like Almirante, but also claims inspiration from conservative traditionalists like Roger Scruton and even liberal critics of Islam like journalist Oriana Fallaci. In short, Fratelli d'Italia has integrated the neofascist tradition into a broader nationalist identity politics, and is able to draw on influences from other sources and even other countries. This process has allowed a fascist-derived party to find a place for itself within an international conservative movement which is ever more preoccupied with civilisational decline. But this movement's radicalisation is contradictory: it takes the form of an aggressive nationalist identity politics but also takes for granted the long-term weakening of European nation states and their inability to cope with the crises of globalisation. Fratelli d'Italia is markedly less interested in confronting threats to humanity such as climate change or the pandemic as what Meloni calls the 'extinction of the Italian people'[28] due to falling birth rates. These traditions share the assumption that national decline is a reality. Fratelli d'Italia often derives its language to describe this from US and French sources, notably when it sees former colonised peoples taking over the West. Yet it still bears unmistakable fascist influences: a legacy apparent in its victim narrative of World War II history, its celebration of postwar neofascist leaders and its recasting of regime-era ideologues as generic Italian patriots.[29]

This combination of influences is not new: it is in fact typical of the MSI tradition and has roots even in the Mussolini era. Historian Robert Paxton reminds us that fascists do not '*invent* their myths and symbols'; they draw on elements of national culture without any 'inherent or necessary link to fascism' and repurpose them for their own ends.[30] Fascism's ideological strength has historically lain in its ability to fuse various influences and political forces under its own direction. Mussolini built his own cult of the Risorgimento and World War I, of Dante as well as Cicero; even what Il Duce labelled his 'totalitarian' fascist regime integrated many different and competing trends. Mussolinian fascism was a terroristic revolt against the revolutionary 'ideas of 1789' but also a mobilisation of the masses; it was a promise to assert Italy's place in industrial modernity and also an exterminationist colonialism; it was the veneration of aristocracy, but also a vehicle for the social rise of middle-class youth. It was what Renzo de Felice called 'fascism movement', with its myth of remoulding society and mankind, and 'fascism regime', the relations which Mussolinism established with the institutions and elites inherited from liberal Italy. Such currents were reflected in postwar neofascism: from self-styled 'left-fascists' who saw Salò as a lost revolution, to spiritualists who yearned for the premodern past, 'national conservatives' who built alliances with right-wing anticommunists and those who did all these things at once. The more classically right wing of these trends is most hegemonic in today's Fratelli d'Italia, but it is an organic continuation of part of the MSI tradition rather than a break from the past.

Historian Roger Griffin pointed to this process in a study of the 1990s development of what he called 'constitutional fascism'. His essay responded to the MSI congress at the spa town of Fiuggi in January 1995, held just after it entered government for the first time as a junior ally in Silvio Berlusconi's coalition. Griffin noted that while the MSI had stood in elections since its creation in 1946, it had never sincerely committed itself to liberal democracy. It had instead bristled at the antifascist parties that dominated the Republic; in denouncing the ruling 'partyocracy', it sharply condemned the new 'regime' but remained rather more ambiguous about whether it accepted democracy on principle.[31] The congress held at Fiuggi thus marked a change: the party formally embraced liberal democracy as against violent, revolutionary or totalitarian projects, and moreover it condemned the Mussolini regime's antisemitism. Yet it retained elements of a fascist worldview, including through its vision of a homogeneous national community. It thus produced a 'hybrid', 'constitutional' fascism: what Griffin called an unstable 'compound [of] components taken from two ideologies with theoretically incompatible ineliminable cores: the palingenetic ultra-nationalism of generic fascism' – as per his famous definition – and 'the commitment to the party-political rules of the game of liberal democracy'.[32] The MSI did not mount a critical rejection of fascism, exploring the connection between its ideological premises and its final outcome, but simply purged it of its most disreputable elements: the congress theses could thus speak of a right-wing tradition that endured before, during and after the 1920s.

The MSI's ability to proclaim such a change was also indebted to a new political context. From the outset, it had been bound together by its fascist identity but also sought to break itself from isolation.[33] It repeatedly sought collaboration with other right-wing forces, and even attempted to sell itself to US Republicans as a bulwark against communism.[34] Yet the strength of antifascist mobilisation ensured it never gained a foothold in national government, and in a context of growing prosperity and social liberalisation its reactionary recipes were never called upon. Only when the old party system collapsed at the beginning of the 1990s, exploding the relationship between citizens and the Republic's institutions, would it get its chance to enter government. This decisively relied on a realignment on the right wing of politics, as Silvio Berlusconi formed a new coalition in which the old antifascist barriers no longer applied. As we shall see in Chapter 3, the MSI's now much greater opportunities for electoral advance provided Gianfranco Fini with an opportunity to renew his party, changing its name and even proclaiming it part of the 'European centre-right'. Yet this process also brought many tensions within the party, and Fratelli d'Italia was created in 2012 by cadres who had broken with Fini, establishing an ambiguous relationship with his reform process. Compared to the Fini era, the refounded party is markedly less interested in a critical approach to the fascist tradition: rather, it uses the mantra that Mussolini has been 'consigned to history' to shut down critical discussion of the fascist forces and ideas active in the present.

POSTMODERN POSTFASCISM

'We are children of our history. Of all our history. As with any nation, the path we have taken is complex, much more so than some would like to say.'[35] In her memoir, Meloni speaks of complexities of national history, adding that the contradictions are themselves something all Italians share. This approach to history speaks the language of 'pacification': making peace among Italians by lowering 'ideological' tensions, and in particular stripping out the antifascist parts of the Republic's foundational myths in favour of an acceptance of all sides. Yet, the problem with creating a pacified national story is that compatriots rarely agree what the basis of the common identity is meant to be, and any proposal for one is asserted in opposition to other rival candidates. One great national myth is built on the history of disunity among different territories, encapsulated in liberal leader Massimo D'Azeglio's claim that only in having 'made Italy', the unified state formed in 1861, was it possible to 'make Italians', a single people; *Io Sono Giorgia* cites these words in order to push back against them. 'From time to time', Meloni admits, Italians may not have believed in national 'homogeneity'; yet, faced with 'the great challenges of History with a capital H, they have demonstrated with their own bodies that they have a very strong sense of national community'. As well as 'the Risorgimento itself, this is testified by the trenches of World War I, where the blood of Italians mixed to become one and indissoluble', and by 'the heroes of El Alamein' in 1942.[36] This story of 'national community' is thus simplified in the name of integrating its more 'complex' elements: it celebrates Italian military heroism in World War II while removing this history from its intimate connection to Mussolini's war, which itself goes unmentioned.

This language of 'pacifying' history also refers to a general lowering of the stakes of political combat. The fact that Rachele and Ciao Giulio Cesare Mussolini take part in elections is symbolic of important changes in the context in which the far right operates. Italy has left behind the intense political violence that punctuated the twentieth century, from the March on Rome to the terrorism of the 1970s; today's far right acts in a context of reduced social strife and, even at the level of ideas, the ebbing of grand projects for reorganising society. These trends affect all political forces, including the various ones drawing on the neofascist tradition: it is most apparent in those involved in electoral politics, but also in smaller militant groups who more explicitly assert their continuity with the Mussolinian past. Even they no longer plan to create a one-party state or build a new Roman Empire as in the days of the interwar regime. Yet, retracing their political lineage from fascism, and its influence on their contemporary politics, is also important if we are to discover who these people are and what they want in the present. When the Brigate Rosse (BR) kidnapped former prime minister Aldo Moro in 1978, earning this ultra-left terrorist group condemnation by the left-wing parties, Rossana Rossanda insisted that it hadn't come from nowhere: BR's violent tactics and Stalinist jargon set it at odds with most of the contemporary left but belonged to its 'family album'.[37] A group portrait of Fratelli d'Italia would include countless Fascist ancestors, many divorces and not a few old flames.

Why 'postfascists'? Fratelli d'Italia calls itself a conservative party: when pushed to explain cases of members glorifying historical fascists, its leaders usually change the subject to talk about antifascist crimes, or else claim that the party has 'consigned the regime to history'. What this never amounts to is any general criticism of fascism as a political culture – a move which would raise questions over the MSI and not just the regime itself.[38] The awkward expression 'consign to history' itself points to this difficulty: it does not mean 'make fascism a focus of historical scrutiny', critically investigating it in order to draw lessons from it, but rather banishing the word 'fascism' from contemporary politics and circumscribing its relevance to the interwar era. This has elements of plausibility: Fratelli d'Italia will not restore the Mussolini regime or one like it. Yet the claim that fascism only amounts to the world of 1922, or indeed to the dictator alone, is jarring in the mouths of a party descended from the MSI. While, from 1922 to 1945, the various strands of fascism were bound together by Mussolini personally, its ideas, its rituals and most of its personnel outlived him, and the MSI openly asserted that fascism had not disappeared with Il Duce. This insistence – its 'neofascism' – surely faced strong hostility in postwar Italy, partly because of the disaster into to which its leaders had taken the country. Yet, 1945 was not a unanimous or total condemnation of fascism, ensuring that it could never survive or have a resurgence. Rather, the MSI remained weak in postwar decades because other forces resisted it, drawing on the tools of history – their critical understanding of what fascism had been and still could be – to mobilise against it. When the MSI did reach government in 1994, this was not because it had cut all ties with fascism. Rather, it was able to find space for itself thanks to the collapse of the political order that had long restrained it.

At a rally on 25 April 1992, the anniversary of liberation from Nazi-Fascist rule, MSI MP Franco Servello spoke of a watershed: his party could celebrate 'the end of the Republic born of the Resistance'.[39] He did not mean the end of parliamentary democracy or a return to Fascism but the demise of the mass parties that had led the Resistance, with the self-dissolution of the Communist Party in 1991 and then the corruption scandals that engulfed the Christian Democrats and Socialists. It was in the attempt to take advantage of this moment, to reshape the new 'Second Republic', that the MSI turned itself into a broader, 'postfascist' party called the 'National Alliance'. It was a creature of a new era: the new party was allied to Berlusconi, the TV tycoon-politician who foreshadowed Donald Trump; but this was also the moment of Italy's integration into a European single currency, the discrediting of political institutions in the eyes of large swathes of the population and, connected to this, the call for figures from outside the electoral arena, from celebrities to judges and technocrats, to replace them. Where post-World War I Fascism arose in the context of expanding suffrage, revolutionary mobilisations and the lowering of the thresholds of violence, postfascism made its breakthrough in a society in which the historic boulders of mass organisation had been shattered into heaps of pebbles. If Almirante organised 'fascists in a democracy', postfascists have established their presence in an ever more postdemocratic context, in which citizens feel increasingly unable to change the course of events through political action. It would be an era of technocracy, historically low levels of democratic mobilisation and conspiracy theories more likely to be spread by online media than by revived street movements.

Fratelli d'Italia's recent electoral breakthrough in the land of Fascism's birth surely lends itself to evocative analogies: at the time of writing, Italy faced not just a postfascist becoming prime minister but the centenary of the March on Rome, a coincidence which invited myriad comparisons ahead of the election. There have even been recent instances of Fratelli d'Italia officials, including one regional president, celebrating the anniversary of the Fascist seizure of power in October 1922.[40] The history that Italians choose to honour, despise or lament remains highly political: the regime era still evokes pain and admiration, disgust and pride, fear and what Italian media often indulgently call 'nostalgism'. Yet this does not mean that Mussolini's heirs repeat the past in the present. This book argues that the political culture of Italian postfascism helps us to understand the future. For Italy's recent history encapsulates essential dynamics – visible in different forms and in other Western democracies – which point to wider developments in right-wing politics. These trends include the sense of permanent national decline and economic crisis; the collapse of the mass, class-based political parties that once mediated popular demands; and the rise of national-populist leaders who furiously denounce 'globalist' conspiracies even as they integrate themselves into the dominant international institutions. Their nativism, demonisation of opponents, exclusivist conception of the nation and family and postmodern approach towards truth and historical fact all pose many dangers. Yet they draw on a different spirit of the times than the regenerative violence of the past.

From Orbán to Trump and Le Pen to Putin, the rise of new ethnonationalist leaders and parties in recent years has pushed the word 'fascism' back into everyday use. Scholars, pundits and activists are often divided as to the appropriate use of this term: we live in an age of sharp rhetorical polarisation, even in countries where the main parties agree on central planks of economic and foreign policy; in this sense, symbols from the past can often provide recognisable markers of political identity yet obscure the real substance of politics. Yet this debate need not run aground on the question of whether a given party or movement reproduces the fascism of the 1930s. The broader interest in studying what Meloni calls 'the seventy-year tradition of the Italian right' since World War II is precisely that it includes a clear fascist genealogy, which continued even through its metamorphosis into an electoral party that rejects political violence. From MSI to Alleanza Nazionale to Fratelli d'Italia, this tradition has adapted to Italy's junior role in the international order, the fragmentation of Italians' relationship to work and family and even many trends towards social liberalisation. It is thus not a turn back to the past. It is the recomposition of this tradition in the present, setting specifically fascist ideas and historical references within a nationalist identity politics geared to postmodern times. This is not only a prolongation of an Italian experience or the regime itself; it has integrated the lessons of currents from other countries, from 'great replacement theory' to US evangelicals. Examining the interaction between these trends helps us understand how this postfascist tradition has managed to insert itself into the mainstream of right-wing politics.

Chapter 1 examines the resentful Italian nationalism promoted by Fratelli d'Italia and its relations with changing narratives on World War II history in contemporary public life. The story begins from the party's ideological platform developed at its national congress held in Trieste in December 2017, and the identification this document draws between this borderland city's history and Italy's supposedly besieged national identity. It explains how, far from wanting to 'leave history to the past', postfascists have become increasingly successful at shaping public history to their liking. Exploring how public debate around World War II has increasingly focused on the crimes committed by Yugoslav partisans against Italians, rather than the victims of Fascism itself, it shows how postfascists use this memory to frame their narrative of a 'cultural genocide' against Italians waged in the present.

Chapter 2 turns to the origins of Meloni's Fratelli d'Italia party, in the MSI founded by defeated lieutenants of Mussolini in 1946. It shows how a party which rejected the legitimacy of the new antifascist state nonetheless became an established part of the postwar Republic's life. This was a history marked by a continual ambiguity, as the MSI foregrounded its anticommunism in order to try to forge alliances either with Christian Democrats or other right-wing forces. Under long-time leader Giorgio Almirante's guidance, this was a party that stood in elections but called itself 'anti-systemic', retained its fascist identity and maintained close ties with both terrorists and repressive far-right dictatorships in the Mediterranean and Latin America.

Chapter 3 starts from the end of the 'First Republic' and the early 1990s political moment in which the MSI entered national government for the first time. It shows how Gianfranco Fini led the party increasingly to distance itself from its fascist identity in favour of a pro-European conservatism. Yet it also highlights the contradictions of this process, at a time when antifascist narratives of Italian identity were becoming weaker and anti-immigration politics were becoming a more prominent part of the Italian political debate. It shows how the moves to dissolve the former MSI's identity in turn produced a mounting backlash within party ranks, ultimately leading to the creation of Fratelli d'Italia.

Chapter 4 looks beyond national-level politics to examine more closely the forms of neofascist political organisation, and the activity of the extraparliamentary far right in Rome, Milan and Verona. It shows how the 'centre-right' parties have acted as a conveyor belt for ideas and militants from radical circles, who are routinely integrated into its electoral lists. To this end, it shows how explicitly fascist movements have been able to build their presence in mainstream political debate, including thanks to collaboration with the larger right-wing parties and their use of spectacular forms of mobilisation.

Chapter 5 takes us to the current moment, Fratelli d'Italia's plans for government and the policies that animate both its base and the right-wing voters to which it appeals. In particular, it draws out the policy influences it has drawn from right-wing parties without fascist roots, such as Poland's Law and Justice, Hungary's Fidesz and allies on the white nationalist fringe of the US Republican Party. This chapter, moreover, argues that the party's 'strategy of insertion' is now succeeding on an international level, as it combines a reactionary civilisational politics with an effort to transform the European Union from within.

1

The Victims of History

Tightly hugged by Italy's north-eastern border, the port city of Trieste has long been a focus of nationalist ambitions. For five centuries a subject of the Habsburg crown, upon the proclamation of the Kingdom of Italy in 1861 it remained part of Austria-Hungary, 'unredeemed' even after the Italian territorial gains when the two states went to war in 1866. Trieste entered the twentieth century as a cosmopolitan sea outlet for a multinational empire: it had a nearly two-thirds Italian-speaking majority, a growing Slovene minority and smaller German, Croat and Hungarian populations. Yet, as Europe sank into conflict in 1914, the liberation of Trieste became a rallying cry for the proponents of Italian intervention, and they got their way in May 1915 when Antonio Salandra's government entered the war on the British-French side. The initial Italian offensive faltered, and defeat in the Battle of Caporetto in November 1917 drew the front over a hundred miles into its own territory. But the Italian army held the line at the river Piave, and in October 1918 it won a famous victory over the Austrian-led forces at Vittorio Veneto. Both imperial Germany and the multi-national Habsburg empire were beginning to unravel, and Vienna sued for peace. On 3 November 1918, the same day the armistice was signed, Italian marines crossed the Gulf of Venice and disembarked in Trieste. Irredentists could claim a major victory. Yet this proved to be just one moment in a decades-long struggle to define the border in this multiethnic region, with effects on Italian political life even today.

The Paris Peace Conference in 1919 repartitioned the Adriatic coastline; it confirmed Italy's ownership of Trieste but left other claims disappointed. London and Paris had drawn Rome onto their side in 1915 with the promise of gains along the eastern flank of the Adriatic. These were the lands which nineteenth-century irredentists had labelled Venezia Giulia, including parts of the old Venetian Republic which had collapsed in 1797. Yet Italian forces did not occupy this region during World War I itself, and the newly established Kingdom of Serbs, Croats and Slovenes – the state later renamed Yugoslavia – also made competing claims. Especially in dispute was the port city known to Italians as Fiume. When the Paris Peace Conference failed to cede it to Italy, the flamboyant nationalist poet Gabriele d'Annunzio complained that his country had been left with a 'mutilated victory', and in September 1919 he forced the issue, leading bands of irregular troops into Fiume and declaring a 'Regency of Carnaro' that would prepare the ground for Italian rule.[1] This heralded a major trend in both Italy and postwar Europe: the imposition, through paramilitary force, of state order and state borders. Over Christmas 1920, in accordance with international treaties, the Italian army ousted D'Annunzio's forces and created a Free State of Fiume, but in 1924 new prime minister, Benito Mussolini, annexed it to Italy. Irredentist propaganda termed the two newly conquered port cities *italianissime*: 'most Italian'. Yet, especially in the hinterland, Venezia Giulia remained a patchwork of nationalities: as of 1921, only around 52 per cent of its population was Italian speaking.[2]

From the armistice onward, the new borders imposed harder separations between populations, a process which radicalised with the rise of Fascism. From late 1918, Venezia Giulia was ruled by military authorities, which began to forcibly Italianise schoolrooms and surnames. The region's creation brought a sizeable influx of migrants from other Italian regions, including tens of thousands of officials; but there were also around 100,000 Slovenes and Croats who departed for Yugoslavia.[3] Trieste soon became a crucible of racialised Fascism. Nationalist street violence had already broken out before the war,[4] and it reached new heights in July 1920, with first fighting in Spalato (later Split, Croatia) and then the Fascist arson attack which destroyed Trieste's foremost Slovene cultural centre, the Narodni Dom. Even before taking power, Mussolini repeatedly visited the city to extol the rebirth of Italian national consciousness in its borderlands,[5] and with Fascism's turn to biological antisemitism, in September 1938 he again came to Trieste – home of Italy's third-largest Jewish community – to proclaim the segregationist Racial Laws. The ethnic reordering of this region accelerated in April 1941, as Mussolini launched a full-scale invasion of Yugoslavia. The Italian invaders, joined by Nazi Germany, partitioned the entire Balkans: Italy directly annexed southern Slovenia, Montenegro and much of the Dalmatian coast while helping to create an Axis-puppet fascist Croatia. The occupation forces decimated the local populations, killing around a million Yugoslavs in a series of pogroms, round-ups and anti-insurgency operations.

Yet Mussolini's Balkan empire proved short-lived. One reason was the partisan resistance led by Josip Broz Tito's Communists, a multinational movement which captured large swathes of land from occupation forces and local collaborationists. This was one of several fronts where Mussolini faced setbacks, and as Allied forces threatened the Italian mainland, military leaders in Rome began to turn against him. On the night of 24–5 July 1943, the Fascist Grand Council voted to hand control of the war effort to the king, who then had Mussolini arrested, appointing Marshal Pietro Badoglio prime minister in the interest of seeking an armistice with the Allies. But even this was not enough to end the war: Adolf Hitler ordered an immediate occupation of the former ally, restoring Mussolini to power in northern-central Italy – but also imposing direct German rule in the border zone, including Venezia Giulia. Here, the armistice produced a short-lived uprising against the Fascist authorities, but the anti-partisan war now proceeded under German command, with Italian-Fascist volunteer battalions as auxiliaries. It was now that the Fascist-controlled Italian press introduced readers to a peculiar geological phenomenon of the region, known as the *foibe*; the sinkholes where, they reported, Tito's Communists dumped the bodies of the Italians they killed. The *Corriere della Sera* of 20 January 1944 spoke of Fascist federations commemorating the '471 Fallen in the "foibe" in Istria-Dalmatia', including women, children and workers but mostly 'squadrists and Fascists, the greater number who gave their lives in this holocaust'.[6]

Yet there would also be a second wave of *foibe* killings. In the final days of April 1945, as Nazi Europe headed towards its final collapse, New Zealander troops, Italian antifascists and Yugoslav partisans raced to liberate Trieste first. Until early June, the city in fact fell under competing administrations. There was also continued fighting around Venezia Giulia, as Tito's forces imposed their control even in some areas which Italy had held before the initial invasion. While the numbers are disputed, most historians estimate that the Yugoslav Communists killed a few thousand people, from Fascist personnel to policemen, civilians and even some Italian partisans. Trieste was becoming a Cold War front line; in March 1946, Winston Churchill termed it the southern end of an 'Iron Curtain' falling across Europe.[7] Venezia Giulia was itself divided, and in February 1947, another Paris Peace Conference granted Yugoslavia control of Fiume (today Rijeka), Zara (Zadar) and Istria, while making Trieste part of an independent 'Free Territory'. The Communist takeover also fuelled an 'exodus' of Italians, at least 200,000 of whom left the region by the late 1950s, as well as tens of thousands of local fascists, collaborationists and other opponents of the new authorities. A 1954 treaty redrew the frontier, returning Trieste to Italy while making most of its hinterland Yugoslav. Yet some in the city continued to mobilise, staging militant protests against official bilingualism (in 1961) and Tito's planned official visit to Italy (in 1970). These protests were a particular mobilising focus for the neofascist MSI, which rejected all postwar peace treaties.[8] When Giorgia Meloni joined the MSI in 1992, she became active in a local section in Rome named after Italian refugees from now-Yugoslav Istria and Dalmatia.

The defence of the border remains central to the way Meloni's party talks about both twentieth-century history and national identity today. We can see this in the ideological platform issued by the Fratelli d'Italia national congress held in Trieste in December 2017, whose preamble takes up an old refrain as it labels this the 'most Italian' of cities.[9] The second conference held under Meloni's leadership, it provided historical grounding to the party's present-day agenda, focused on defending an embattled national identity. The preamble centres Italian nationhood on the borderland: it is special because its annexation in 1918 brought the 'real baptism of a united Italy', through the patriotism that was stirred 'deep in the population thanks to the threat to its freedom and the energies this could unleash'.[10] This idea of completing the Risorgimento is well established in antifascist historiography to refer to the World War II-era partisan Resistance, a movement based on stronger popular mobilisation than the unification of the nineteenth century.[11] The *Trieste Theses* displace this judgement back onto World War I, as it deems the border populations to be the 'first Italian partisans'.[12] The *Theses* connect this to a judgement on 1945: the people of Trieste again fought 'with great sacrifice to return to Italy',[13] resisting the Yugoslav Communists and then holding firm even in the shadow of the Iron Curtain.[14] Yet this potted history erases one period entirely: National Fascist Party rule. Mussolini's efforts are airbrushed out of the story, which is instead fought between Italians and the foreigners who threaten their borders.

Reframing Italy's experience in both world wars in terms of the defence of a besieged national identity, the *Trieste Theses* explain how this informs its 'Philosophy of Identity' in the present. Fascism and its colonial endeavours go entirely unmentioned. Rather, Italians are cast as the victims of racism – of a globalist empire that destroys Italianness in the name of an 'abstract multiculturalism'. Hence, having been 'blinded by the self-flagellating condemnation of the *hatred toward foreigners* supposedly shown by indigenous Europeans against migrants ... the dominant castes and their ideology fail to notice the *hatred from foreigners*.[15] Worse, the decades-long 'repression, negation and debasement of the concept of *Patria*'[16] – a word meaning 'fatherland' or, less belligerently, 'homeland' – has left Italians defenceless against the 'indiscriminate, uncontrolled access by people from other continents', said to be arriving 'in numbers which herald an outright ethnic substitution'.[17] The document ventures that contemporary immigration is producing 'scenes akin to the troubling prophesies in Jean Raspail's *The Camp of the Saints*'.[18] Here, it refers to a 1973 French novel[19] famed in white nationalist circles and promoted internationally in recent years by former Trump aide Steve Bannon; Raspail foretells a dystopian near future in which Western civilisation is overwhelmed by an influx of Third World immigrants, spurred along by leftist agitators and liberals. In this perspective, 'mass Muslim immigration' threatens 'the national belonging and the very existence of the peoples of Europe': the *Trieste Theses* darkly insist that the 'denial of *Patrie* has always formed the deep foundation of physical and cultural genocides'.[20]

The document makes no reference to Mussolini, but its celebration of 'the values of the *Patria*' draws on classic Fascist references. Its use of Giovanni Gentile – the regime's most important ideologue, assassinated by Communist partisans in 1944 – is telling. A neoidealist philosopher renowned even before the regime, the co-author of the *Doctrine of Fascism* is respectably discussed far outside the fascist tradition; yet the *Theses* draw on him in a classically fascist key, in its call for the political mobilisation needed to mould national consciousness.[21] Hence, while 'soil, common life, [and the] commonality of customs, language and tradition' provide the 'material' out of which the nation is moulded, for the nation to exist as such it must be formed into a political subject: 'conscious ... of the constituent content of its own spiritual essence, the object of its own will'.[22] The Fratelli d'Italia congress document also cites futurist poet and art critic Filippo Tommaso Marinetti, from whom we learn that not all peoples are equal: Italians' role in the world is to be 'a most brilliant minority species', 'superior to the human mean'.[23] The document's focus on the borderland struggle after World War I also gestures towards other fascists who had tumultuous relations with Mussolini like D'Annunzio, whose efforts in Fiume party leaders praise as a foundational moment of Italian identity.[24] Yet it also inserts these historic Fascist references within a broader and even international array of nationalist thinkers. For instance, along with *Camp of the Saints* author Raspail, the French figures positively cited here include white nationalist pundit Éric Zemmour, the theorist of nationalism Ernest Renan, counter-Enlightenment thinker Joseph de Maistre and Charles de Gaulle, here painted as the defender of a 'Europe of Nations'.

These figures are upheld as the defenders of 'patriotism' and hailed as the antidote to outmoded 'theories of the supremacy of the white race'. The fight is not posed in terms of biological racism but of ideology and culture: a patriotic resistance against the 'radical universalist' project to uproot individuals from ties of nation, tradition and family. There is a 'concentric attack against our civilisation's constituent structures, waged in the name of the fight against *prejudice*, with the same ideological schema that the Enlightenment created in its crusade in the name of *reason* against the *authority* of tradition'.[25] Such claims may sound reminiscent of the Mussolini who denounced the 'ideas of 1789';[26] yet the words chosen owe more to English conservative Roger Scruton, who theorised the defence of tradition against an 'abstract' universalism. Indeed, this party's references are not *only* fascist. It raises the regime-era slogan 'God, Fatherland and Family', but insists that it was originally inspired by Risorgimento leader Giuseppe Mazzini;[27] its warnings about the dangers to Europe echo the cultural pessimism of nonfascist 'conservative revolutionaries' like Oswald Spengler, but also modern French and US conspiracy theories about non-whites imposing a 'reverse colonialism' on the metropole.[28] There is an obsessive conspiratorial drive: the *Trieste Theses* do not speak, like Spengler, of a long twilight of Western hegemony as this civilisation 'ages'. Italy is the victim of a political project for its destruction: the fusion of 'old-school-communist internationalist utopia, pauperist Third Worldism and globalist commerce'.[29]

This telling of history thus ties together the defence of Italy's borders in 1918 and 1945, the Slavic-Communist assault against Italians and the present-day threat to Italianness posed by the supposed 'plan for ethnic substitution'. No longer concerned to defend Mussolini – or, in fact, even to mention him – this version of events rescues Italian history and even certain Fascist reference points from their association with Nazism, while casting both Yugoslav partisans and contemporary progressives as the totalitarian architects of an anti-Italian 'genocide'. Such a combination of claims is, in part, a reaction against antifascist attacks on the party tradition; Fratelli d'Italia leaders often complain that they 'consigned Fascism to the past' decades ago and no longer need to talk about it. Yet, while it does not claim Mussolini's legacy, Fratelli d'Italia surely does want to talk about World War II, in order to challenge the patriotism and the moral superiority of the antifascist parties in the present. This becomes clear when we see its leaders claim that, just as the historical left defended Tito's Communists, today it is again siding with Italy's enemies. As Fratelli d'Italia co-founder Ignazio La Russa put it in 2018, during that year's general election campaign: 'Today like yesterday, the worst racism is the ideological racism against Italians. Yesterday it was in favour of Stalin and Tito, today against the Italians who ask for controls on immigration and the Islamic threat.'[30] The combination of these themes is central to a story of national victimhood and the fight to defend Italian identity in the present.

RETURNING TO THE BORDER

La Russa wrote these words in a post regarding the National Day of Remembrance of the Exiles and Foibe, an annual commemoration of the events that followed Italy's military defeat in Yugoslavia. The initiative for the day, first held in 2005 under Silvio Berlusconi's government, came from La Russa together with Roberto Menia, a 1980s MSI youth leader in Trieste whose father was a postwar exile from Istria. This proposal gained near-unanimous backing in parliament – the sign of a remarkable refocusing of public memory on these events, which are today habitually considered one of the central moments of Italy's World War II history. Political initiatives to make this into a sacred object of collective piety have gone beyond the Day of Remembrance. In February 2021, at Fratelli d'Italia's instigation, the Veneto region joined neighbouring Friuli-Venezia Giulia in condemning 'foibe denialism, minimisation or apologism', promising to strip public funds from bodies who deny the assertion that Yugoslav Communists 'murdered over 12,000 Italians because they were considered "ethnically different"'.[31] The legislation drew explicit parallels with Holocaust denial, and three months later Fratelli d'Italia tabled a bill to amend the penal code's existing ban on the 'denial, grave minimisation or apologism for the Shoah' to also include the words 'and of the foibe';[32] hence, to 'deny or minimise' these killings would be tantamount to Holocaust denial and punishable by a prison sentence. This concern to respect 'victims on both sides' has definite limits. While recognising those killed 'in both the foibe and the Holocaust', it pays no attention to the millions killed by Fascist Italy's bullets, bombs and mustard gas in Ethiopia, Eritrea, Somalia, Libya, Albania, Yugoslavia, Greece, the USSR, Spain or France.

To be a victim of the foibe – an infoibato – means, literally, to have been thrown into one of the sinkholes that pockmark the borderland region. Some of these natural shafts were used to dump the bodies of people who had already been shot, as well as dead soldiers, horses and various kinds of debris. Yet the verb evokes something much more vivid and atavistic than this: the practice of throwing victims to their deaths. There are witness accounts of a few dozen cases of this happening, yet the term is commonly used more broadly to refer to the killing of Italians by Yugoslavs. It can thus even refer to war criminals being sentenced to death by regular courts and executed in jail.[33] The effect is to create an image of a brutal destruction of the Italian population by Yugoslav Communists, which, according to the Veneto region motion, is an act comparable to the Holocaust whose history deserves similar protection. Again though, what is notable is what this narrative remains silent about. Even after 1918, the Italianisation of much of this region had been strongly repressive; the Axis occupation starting in 1941 meant massive round-ups of Jews, travellers and forced labourers; a vast series of killings and collective punishment designed to crush the partisan movement; and a civilian death toll well above half a million. As historian Eric Gobetti insists in his discussion of public memory culture,[34] these preconditions are glibly overlooked by a narrative which start the clock at the armistice in September 1943[35] – the moment when, it is imagined, Italians stopped being perpetrators of violence and became victims.

But even if the Italian occupation brought violence to the region first, did Yugoslavs conduct 'ethnic cleansing'? Since the first major studies in the early 1980s, pioneered by the Resistance institute in Trieste,[36] historians have generally agreed that Yugoslav partisans (and some Italian ones and other individuals who were not partisans at all) killed some thousands of people in this period, most of them Italian, mainly in the wake of September 1943 and then in a larger wave after April 1945.[37] Beyond piecing together the often limited evidence on individual cases, scholarly discussion has sought to trace the motives behind these events in relation to the Italian-German invasion, the breakdown of the previous social order and the wider Communist takeover. Most agree that the killings had varied motives and were not the unfolding of a premeditated plan: they cannot be understood as a mechanical 'response' to Nazi-Fascist atrocities, but nor was there a concerted attempt to destroy or expel the Italian population. The main forces driving events were the overthrow of holdout Italian authorities, a peasant rebellion against landowners and, simultaneously, the formation of a new Communist-led state apparatus involving elements of terror, interpersonal vendettas and wider social violence.[38] The claim that Italians were killed because they belonged to a different ethnicity is incapable of explaining the vast predominance among the victims of soldiers, policeman and Slavic collaborators – that is, representatives of political and economic power. All such distinctions are lost in a narrative of 'ethnic cleansing', which suppresses real historical understanding.

Such claims often draw on the language of 'pacification' – a term used to present the idea of freeing history from the ideological polarisation of Fascism and Resistance. This also means removing the moral difference between the sides in the name of what is called a 'serene' reflection on historical facts which can recognise all crimes. At a historical level, the investigation of Allied crimes is neither new nor specific to Italy: even staunchly antifascist historians have explored the rapes committed by Soviet soldiers in Germany, Britain's role in the Bengal Famine and the bombing of civilian districts. In this sense, it is equally right that professional historians have studied violence on the Yugoslav-Italian border, establishing the facts about what happened. At the level of individual human dignity, it can surely be agreed that no specific instance of suffering or injustice is justified by the general preferability of the Allied victory. Yet a far-right politician like Matteo Salvini does something else when, year after year, he insists on Remembrance Day that from the *foiba* at 'Basovizza to Auschwitz, there are no Serie A and Serie B martyrs'.[39] Such a claim is outwardly about honouring all victims, regardless of their sides in the political conflict. Yet it establishes an equivalence between groups – the Italians killed in the *foibe* and Jews murdered at Auschwitz – regardless of who they were, why they were killed and indeed whether or not their political action contributed to their deaths. Particularly striking here is the way that the specific role of Italian Fascism in either history is suppressed.[40] This is necessarily the case when it comes to talking about the role of Italian Fascism in the events that led up to the *foibe*, which must be silenced in order to avoid 'relativist' – even 'whataboutist' – comparisons. Such an approach is incompatible with stating even basic facts about Italy's wartime record never mind advancing any kind of shared reflection on history.

'Pacification' has often meant a zealous revisionism. Ahead of Remembrance Day 2019, the researcher who had drawn most attention to the *foibe* in the 1980s, Raoul Pupo, was among three historians to co-write a short booklet for the Friuli-Venezia Giulia Resistance institute. It characterised the killings as driven by the assault on Italian-Fascist political authorities, not 'ethnic cleansing'. The regional government then passed a motion which counted this text among recent examples of '*foibe* reductionism', which it explicitly compared to Holocaust denial and 'hate speech' which disturbs 'civil coexistence in society'.[41] The political character of the killings is, in fact, indirectly raised in the 2004 law that allows relatives to request medals in honour of the dead. It bars from recognition those who 'volunteered for formations that did not serve Italy'.[42] This phrase seems designed to avoid judgement on whether Fascist militias or the Salò Republic as a (de facto) state were indeed able to 'serve Italy'. This is important when we consider that after the armistice in September 1943, Venezia Giulia was under direct German rule: the mention of 'volunteering' might thus distinguish between established police officials and Salò-era militiamen. Yet these latter also feature heavily among the medal recipients.[43] The fact that medals are issued upon request means that the recipients cannot be assumed to be *representative* of all those who died. Even so, Fratelli d'Italia figures and media close to the party do defend honouring Fascist volunteers. One telling case in 2015 involved Paride Mori, a volunteer for the Mussolini Battalion from September 1943, who was killed during anti-partisan operations in Slovenia in February 1944. When he was granted a medal in February 2015, prompting protests, *Secolo d'Italia* termed Mori both a 'fascist' and 'valiant fighter for Italy' who was victimised by the 'decrepit antifascism' that forbids historical 'pacification'.[44] In April 2015, the honour was withdrawn on the grounds that Mori had died in combat.[45]

THE MEMORY OF THE DEFEATED

The call for 'pacification' often relies on the idea of liberating Italian history from the political codes of the postwar Republic, including their 'antifascist prejudices'. Responding to the Mori case, the federation of exiles' associations insisted that he should be judged in the spirit of 'national pacification, following the fall of the Berlin Wall', rather than the 'political instrumentalisations' of history.[46] The fight over the border had surely remained a live political question in the aftermath of 1945 when faced with the spectacle of the Italian exodus from the region: this situation was especially embarrassing for the Italian Communists, given their still ostensibly close ties with Tito's party,[47] whereas leading Christian Democrats in Trieste resisted all territorial concessions (see Chapter 2). Yet the city's return to Italy under a Christian Democratic government in 1954 and the formal abandonment of territorial claims in 1975 did much to marginalise this issue, and its peaceful settlement could also be taken as a token of good relations with Belgrade. The real exception, as well as exiles' associations, was the MSI, which adamantly rejected all border treaties. The collapse of Yugoslavia and the Balkan Wars of the early 1990s rekindled its mobilisation around this theme. In July 1991, leader Gianfranco Fini, Robert Menia and Mirko Tremaglia went to Belgrade to consult with the new Serb authorities about their claims to the territory. In November 1992, Fini headed out by boat from Trieste, launching 350 bottles into the sea to reassert Italy's claim. The message read 'Istria, Fiume, Dalmatia – Roman, Venetian, Italic lands. Yugoslavia is dying, torn apart by war: the unjust, shameful treaties of 1947 and 1975 no longer apply ... Istria, Fiume, Dalmatia, we swear, we will return!'[48]

While there was no serious prospect of Italy reclaiming the border territories, events in central-eastern Europe were redrawing Italy's political map. The Communists had long been one of the main champions of antifascist memory culture, but in 1991 the party dissolved: and historians of the Resistance now faced a massive revisionist wave, largely arriving from outside the realm of scholarship.[49] One contributor was TV anchorman Bruno Vespa, host of Rai talkshow *Porta a Porta* and since the 1990s a prolific author. He also saw the end of the Cold War as an opening, claiming that up till 1991 'in books and textbooks there had been no trace' of anything other than 'the Communist thesis' regarding the Resistance,[50] thus imposing a 'monolithic' narrative of Communist heroism.[51] This was a ludicrous claim in a country where the Communists had been banished from government for over four decades, and showed his lack of knowledge of the body of research he dismissed. Yet the promise to push back against a Communist-dominated narrative of the Resistance helped his books sell hundreds of thousands of copies, as did works by fellow pundit Giampaolo Pansa, whom Vespa credited with 'giving the dignity of memory to the blood of the vanquished'.[52] A veteran journalist, in 2003 Pansa began a series of pseudo-historical works which purported to reintegrate the losing, Fascist side into the historical narrative.[53] He marketed them on the basis that only the left-wing winners of World War II, the 'gendarmes of memory', had ever been 'allowed' to write its history.[54] While his books dispensed with the scholarly apparatus of footnotes and evidence, and in some cases were novelised, their force lay in their promise to highlight forgotten victims.

Pansa's promise to expose partisan criminality received a vast platform, connecting the *foibe* to extrajudicial killings in Italy. Pansa's books regurgitated the narrative of the 'defeated' – neofascist memoirs – to tell the tale of a civil war in which partisans used the Allies' arrival to exact vengeance on their enemies. He particularly echoed the claims of postwar MSI senator Giorgio Pisanò, a veteran of the Nazi collaborationist Xᵃ Flottiglia MAS who had written a *History of the Italian Civil War* in the 1960s.[55] Pisanò's writings had hitherto drawn little attention outside of neofascist ranks and scholars working on the far right itself; even the term 'civil war' was rarely used by historians, partly because antifascist accounts often identified the German and Italian foes in a fused *nazifascismo*. Yet there were other challenges to the anathema regarding this term, most notably from historian Claudio Pavone's 1991 *Una guerra civile*.[56] A vast portrait of 'morality in the Resistance', Pavone's study wove together the combined strands of class, civil and patriotic war, whose interaction varied between different parties, the phases of the struggle in different regions and even individual experience. His use of the term 'civil war' was controversial and would have been difficult for a historian without his record as a partisan to launch into mainstream debate.[57] Yet, far from writing a work of moral relativism, Pavone drew out the different ideals and drives to action that animated his dramatis personae and the *necessity* of fighting a civil war in order to refound Italian democracy.[58] Pansa's approach did the opposite, insisting on the humanity of all victims and casting the men of the Salò Republic as a different kind of patriots.[59]

The narratives advanced by Pansa and Vespa enjoyed a visibility out of all proportion to their historical merits, overshadowing historians like Raoul Pupo and Jože Pirjevec who have worked on the *foibe*. Yet, while their books had wide media echoes, this shift towards relativising fascism and antifascism is not just a matter of sensationist literature. In the early 2000s, Italy was riven by polemics over official 'days of memory', outwardly aimed at forming a consensual basis for a republican patriotism. In practice, these events illustrate the opposite: that in an era in which antifascism is no longer assumed to be the foundation of democratic politics, the common reference points on which Italians could build a shared reflection on the past are ever less unanimous. The most important republican commemoration remains Liberation Day, the holiday held on 25 April since 1946. Marking the anniversary of the partisan uprising that liberated the main northern cities, rather than the final evacuation of German troops a few days later, it specifically celebrates the Italian partisans' role in freeing the country from *nazifascismo*. While this occasion is often still used by centre-left and institutional figures to invoke a spirit of 'national unity', the main right-wing leaders openly mock and refuse to celebrate it. Two more recent official days are at least intended to be more palatable. In 2000, centrist President Carlo Azeglio Ciampi signed into law a bill to mark a Day of Memory upon the 27 January anniversary of the liberation of Auschwitz. In 2001, he restored Republic Day's status as a bank holiday; held on 2 June, this is the anniversary of the referendum that put an end to the monarchy in 1946 but is more defined by military pageantry than Liberation Day.

From 1977 to 2000, Republic Day had been downgraded on grounds of cost, and the new memory days created in the new millennium multiplied all the more easily once it was agreed that they would not be bank holidays. Such was the case of the Day of Remembrance for the *foibe*, first held in 2005. Held on 10 February, the date of the 1947 Peace Treaty, it falls two weeks after the day marking the liberation of Auschwitz. It has routinely been marked by attempts to set the events in parallel, through political speeches, fictional works and even classroom materials claiming that Italians suffered a Holocaust-style genocide;[60] but many local councils hold one set of events to mark both – or created plaques and renamed parks in homage to 'the victims of the foibe and the Holocaust'. Such relativism is not just a far-right phenomenon, but is widespread among ex-Communists attempting to distance themselves from the Stalinist past. Notably, President Giorgio Napolitano set the two anniversaries in parallel during a 2007 speech on *foibe* Remembrance Day, in which he further denounced the 'wave of hate and bloodthirsty fury and a Slavic annexationist plan which prevailed first in the 1947 Peace Treaty and assumed the sinister contours of "ethnic cleansing"'. Today a member of the centrist Democrats, he condemned the 'ideological blindness' that had suppressed recognition of the killings, in a seeming reference to his old party's difficulties in reckoning with this history.[61] But he also conferred medals of honour on victims, from little-known civilians to Vincenzo Serrentino, the World War II-era police prefect in Zara, and a war criminal executed by Yugoslavia in 1947.

The Balkan Wars of the 1990s saw not only the worst conflict in Europe since 1945 but what now became called 'ethnic cleansing', and Italian politicians recast World War II in light of these events. This was also apparent in the fictional portrayals which reached the largest mass audiences. In 2002, communications minister Maurizio Gasparri, a former MSI leader, called for evocative fictional works to relate the drama of the *foibe*,[62] and on 6–7 February 2005, ahead of the first Remembrance Day, public broadcaster Rai delivered the miniseries *Il cuore nel pozzo*, in which bloodthirsty Yugoslav partisans hunt down Italian orphans. Receiving primetime billing – and scathing reviews from historians[63] – it has enjoyed repeated reruns. The idea of Italians as pure victims again appears in 2019's *Red Land*, which dramatises the death of Norma Cossetto,[64] a 23-year-old student whose father was a local Fascist leader. Partisans arrested her, raped her and threw her into a *foiba* on the night of 4–5 October 1943.[65] Though she was a member of the Fascist Party, she was not an important one; and given her youth, the cruel sexual violence against her and her lack of personal responsibility for the regime's repressive apparatus, Cossetto has today become a leading icon of the *foibe*. In 1944, Mussolini's Salò Republic named a women's paramilitary unit in homage to her, and upon the first Remembrance Day in 2005, President Ciampi awarded her a medal for civil merit. In 2019, at the instigation of Fratelli d'Italia's regional education minister, the Veneto region issued a graphic novel to hundreds of schools entitled *Norma Cossetto, the History of an Italian Woman*. The publisher was Altaforte, run by neofascist social centre CasaPound.[66]

POST-ANTIFASCISM

We earlier cited Ignazio La Russa's claim that the 'worst racism' is 'racism against Italians'. Posting these words on *foibe* Remembrance Day 2018, he paired them with a 1946 quote from Communist daily *l'Unità*. The cropped text appears as a sharp attack on the refugees from the borderlands: it seems *l'Unità* deemed them 'unwelcome' in Italy because they were 'not driven by the enemy on its heels but fearful of the wind of freedom'.[67] Citing such an old article from a defunct party's newspaper may seem a rather anachronistic account of contemporary left-wing opinion. But a closer look at the whole article has more to tell about La Russa's agenda. As the Nicoletta Bourbaki historians' collective notes, the 1946 piece's author draws a sharp distinction between some refugees – 'thousands and thousands of honest Italians, our true brothers and sisters, [whose] dramatic situation moves us and demands reflection' – and other, unwelcome ones, the 'criminals who do not want to pay the price for their crimes'.[68] This latter group included thousands of Croatian fascist collaborators who sought refuge in Italy, as well as the Fascist 'hierarchs, black brigaders, torturers and profiteers'.[69] The article's claim that 'honest Italian' refugees fled only because of 'spectres of a terrorism that does not exist' is barely credible; surely many did not want to live in Yugoslavia, or under a Communist-led state, and the terror was no mere invention. Yet the meme misrepresents the article by collapsing the difference it establishes between Fascist personnel and civilians.[70] Only by erasing this point can the article be used as a scandalous illustration of antifascist criminality and 'anti-Italian racism'.

Even relativism over the killings on the north-eastern border rarely amounts to explicit and fulsome praise for Mussolini's regime, preferring instead to bury its history; pressed on the issue, Fratelli d'Italia leaders often narrowly frame its criminality in terms of the alliance with Nazi Germany. Gianfranco Fini, leader of the postfascist party's predecessors in the 1990s and 2000s, had in fact gone further in denouncing the regime's specific guilt. In 2003, speaking at the Yad Vashem Holocaust Museum on an official visit to Jerusalem, then Deputy Prime Minister Fini denounced Mussolini's antisemitic Racial Laws; when asked if fascism was the 'absolute evil', he replied that such a term could be applied to 'all that led to the extermination of the Jews'.[71] Widely reported as a blanket condemnation of fascism, Fini's statement provoked uproar in his party, prompting Alessandra Mussolini to quit its ranks. Yet, whereas Fini ultimately admitted the need for the right to have an anticommunist antifascism of its own – acknowledging that in 1945 'all democrats were antifascists, even if not all antifascists were democrats'[72] – the Fratelli d'Italia party created in 2012 has consistently avoided doing this. Rather, it insists that the Racial Laws and the alliance with Hitler have 'already been apologised for', and efforts to engage in further discussion of the subject are mere attempts to demonise and disqualify it.[73] When writer Tomaso Montanari criticised the granting of medals honouring Fascists killed by Yugoslav partisans, Meloni claimed that this amounted to a justification for 'violent and unconstitutional' actions against Fratelli d'Italia members akin to the Taliban.[74]

The dismissal of the relevance of antifascism is not only a tendentious argument promoted by far-right politicians. It gains from a broader cultural shift, diagnosed in historian Sergio Luzzatto's 2004 work on Italy's turn to 'post-antifascism'. For Luzzatto, in the postmodern era antifascism suffers an 'inevitable condition of senility':[75] its importance has declined with the passing of the generations who directly experienced this history, but it also faces a 'grave credibility deficit' fuelled by the political collapse of the Communist side and of grand ideological narratives in general.[76] This also owes to a decline in the sense of fascist threat. Telling in this sense were the reactions to neofascist group Forza Nuova's October 2021 attack on the offices of the Confederazione Generale Italiana del Lavoro (CGIL) union during a violent protest against vaccine passes. The assault led to the banning of the group; Fratelli d'Italia abstained in the parliamentary vote and limited its criticisms to generic denunciations of all totalitarianisms.[77] Yet, while the attack prompted a trade union rally under the title 'Never Again Fascism', historian Emilio Gentile intervened to criticise the overuse of this word. 'Fascism', he insisted, 'no longer means anything when it is applied to everything'.[78] He explained: 'I don't wonder whether the danger of fascism is returning. How many people were there: ten thousand? Twenty thousand? ... The past is closed and can be studied. But the present remains to be understood and explained.'[79]

Journalist and TV pundit Paolo Mieli agreed that given the rhetorical inflation of the term, 'if you tell your daughter to come home at 11.30 not midnight, you are a fascist'.[80]

Gentile and Mieli occupy different positions in Italian public life. The former is Italy's most authoritative living historian of fascism; Mieli has spent over half a century as editor of major national newspapers like *Corriere della Sera*, in a career marked by a combination of historical essays and decidedly more lowbrow journalistic interests. Yet despite their different paths, both have one thing in common: they are both former students of Renzo de Felice, the late professor at Rome's La Sapienza university whose eight-book, 7,000-page biography of Benito Mussolini represents a landmark in historical reflection on the Fascist era and its presence in public memory culture. With its first volume issued in 1965 and its last in 1997, shortly after De Felice's death, the monumental *Mussolini* was widely seen as a challenge to a dominant antifascist paradigm. It stood apart both on account of its discussion of the 'years of consent' – the 1930s period in which, De Felice argued, the regime had achieved real popular support through means other than sheer repression – and its effort to unpick the typical antifascist identification between German Nazism and Italian Fascism. De Felice claimed to approach his subject in more neutral and scholarly terms, including through a minute reconstruction of day-to-day decision making, which drew heavily on Mussolini's correspondence.[81] Nonetheless, other historians accused De Felice of ignoring important elements of differentness: his *Mussolini* did not mention crucial questions such as the use of mustard gas in Ethiopia and the ideological radicalisation of institutions such as the military even before the formation of the Rome–Berlin Axis.

De Felice surely had no interest in rehabilitating Fascism. Yet his research was seized upon by neofascists who wanted to find cracks in the edifice of historical condemnation.[82] Francesco Germinario, an important scholar of the way neofascists talk about their own past, explains that comments on his work in the MSI press were generally less concerned with the literal content of De Felice's writing as the broad perception that the history of fascism could be relativised and broken out of its subordination to Nazism. This often required a paradoxical interpretation of *Mussolini*. De Felice had drawn a distinction between the Fascist movement's revolutionary and totalitarian aspirations and the reality of Fascism-as-regime; in particular, he questioned whether Mussolini had mounted a radical break with the realpolitik of earlier Italian governments. De Felice emphasised more conservative dimensions of Fascist rule before the alliance with Hitler, especially with regard to its foreign and economic policies. Such a perspective could be taken as a less total moral condemnation of Mussolini's record. This was, however, certainly a paradoxical judgement in a party founded by cadres of the holdout Salò Republic, who often venerated its final struggles as the purest and most radical incarnation of Fascism. Yet Germinario also tells us that this past was venerated in a contradictory way: whereas more anti-bourgeois elements of the MSI posed Salò as a moment of revolution, other forces within the MSI presented it as a less 'ideological' endeavour' – a resistance against Anglo-American invasion in which patriots fought to the last, despite knowing it was a lost cause.[83]

Beyond *Mussolini*, De Felice's interventions in public debate challenged the use of antifascism as a unifying national myth. He sharply criticised the pretence – common in official commemorations, but also much history-writing in the first postwar decades – that the political breadth of the Resistance, which had included Christian Democrats, liberals and even monarchists as well as Communists and Socialists, meant that it could claim the at least passive support of most Italians.[84] Emphasising the minoritarianism of both sides, whose military units mobilised numbers in the low hundreds of thousands (with strikes and other forms of resistance involving some millions), De Felice focused on the 'grey zone' of Italians who identified with neither Fascism nor the Resistance. Their behaviour, he argued, was governed more by their own personal interests, or even mere survival, and was sceptical of ideological causes or leadership by politicised minorities.[85] Moreover, while in the postwar period the victorious Resistance camp, and in particular the Communist Party, could evoke the fight against *nazifascismo* as the heart of its constitutional patriotism, De Felice argued that this point of reference was in any case bound to decline over time, as the protagonists of the war era faded from public life. In an interview with *Corriere della Sera* published on 27 December 1987,[86] De Felice suggested that while Italians who had experienced fascism would likely hand down this memory to their children, the offspring of those born in the postwar Republic would no longer consider antifascism as central to their own identity. Yet, as we shall see, the weakening of antifascism was not only due to the dying away of the World War II generation.

PRIVATE GRIEF

Memory is not only a matter of subjective feelings and personal recollection. As historian John Foot reminds us, it can also mean a public, collective processing of the past, even when this memory is divided or does not represent everyone. Foot cites the wartime stories that do not fit the epic of a unanimous Resistance movement: the clashes among partisans, the victims of Allied bombings and the communities left permanently devastated by Nazi reprisals.[87] Yet, he adds, memory also produces hierarchies, even among groups of victims. In a discussion of the novelist Italo Calvino, literary critic Alberto Asor Rosa argued that even the crimes of the two sides were not the same: 'Behind the most honest, good-faith, idealistic' fighter in a Fascist militia were 'the round-ups, the torture chambers, deportations, the Holocaust; behind the most ignorant, thieving, cut-throat partisan was the struggle for a peaceful and democratic society.'[88] Yet, if Liberation Day celebrates a collective moment, in which all are meant to find their place, postfascists insist that they are excluded; and across recent decades the republican epic has given ever more room to what Pansa termed 'accepting the narrative of the defeated'. This means not quite embracing it but at least respecting it, in the manner that one prominent centre-left parliamentarian said it was important to understand the rationale of the 'young men of Salò'.[89] This is a country where public broadcaster Rai's control board is made up of political appointees: in 2002, its president, Antonio Baldassare, told the Alleanza Nazionale's congress that where the 'old Rai' 'offered one-sided interpretations' of the Resistance,[90] this would now change. The sharing of political control over Rai is widely termed *lottizzazione*, literally the parcelling-out of land; today, in postmodern, 'post-antifascist Italy', it seems that a similar fragmentation is also becoming the norm in public memory culture.

Indeed, even as it insists that others must 'accept' its truths, the historical memory cultivated by a political minority can also become self-referential and intolerant of outside interference. A dispute over a 2017 TV report from Mussolini's tomb, his final resting place in his Predappio hometown, was illustrative of this. The crypt remains a major site of neofascist pilgrimage, with shops in the town selling fridge magnets, T-shirts and busts celebrating the dictator and even the paramilitaries of the Salò Republic. The shrine-like decoration of the tomb, including an eternal flame, blatantly makes Mussolini an object of veneration rather than historical judgement. In the footage shot at the crypt by RaiTre's *Agorà*, journalist Serena Bortone claimed that the existence of such a monument to a dictator in a democracy 'marks the real difference between us and other European countries', where such a display would not be allowed.[91] The broadcast also noted the presence of open praise of the regime in the crypt's guestbook, including calls for Mussolini's 'return'.[92] However, not everyone was outraged. The tabloidesque daily *Libero*, which comes from a right-wing but nonfascist tradition, slammed the reporters for 'profaning' the grave by entering with filming equipment, and insisted that guestbook comments were 'irrelevant' given that there had, 'thankfully, been no more Marches on Rome'.[93] Interviewed on the controversy, Alessandra Mussolini insisted that the tomb is a site of familial mourning and thus deserving of respect from all political sides – comparing this to the criticism she might face if she visited the grave of a victim of her grandfather's, such as murdered socialist MP Giacomo Matteotti.[94] It would thus seem that discussion of Il Duce is a matter of private grief.

It is surely true that 'Marches on Rome' are unlikely to recur in the present, and that neither Fratelli d'Italia nor smaller and more explicitly fascist and regime-apologist militant organisations plan to restore the dictatorship. Coup plots are far less of a threat today than in postwar decades when neofascist military officers bristled at rising Communist strength (see Chapter 2). Yet this hardly means that symbolic references to historical fascism are part of a merely private honouring of the past. To draw a loose analogy with the United States, it is quite possible that someone who flies a Confederate battle flag at a Trump rally does not literally expect to restore chattel slavery or even rerun the Secession. This would hardly lead us to the conclusion that by waving the Southern Cross he is honouring young soldiers who died serving their home states. Rather, the historical reference symbolises a rebellion against the current Constitution and its political avatars, aimed at a rollback of civil rights which does not require the intervention of slaveowner generals on horseback. Equally, in the Italian case, the relitigation of World War II history is about the present more than the past; it is a fight to determine the boundaries of patriotism and political legitimacy and of who gets to define them. This is precisely what informs the memory laws and even constitutional changes today proposed by Fratelli d'Italia, which seeks to sideline official antifascism by tarnishing its enemies with the charges 'foibe minimisation' and 'apologism for communist totalitarianism'.[95] As with our Dixie-commemorating Trump supporter, the invasion of present-day politics by references to the past should not be mistaken for its simple recurrence.

Commentators who emphasise Fratelli d'Italia's political moderation often dismiss evidence of its members using fascist symbolism, claiming this is a trivial residue of its origins: a 'nostalgic' reference to the past, with little real bearing on present-day politics. Those who wave the banners of Salò-era paramilitaries, or Roman salute at neofascist cadres' funerals, are not forming real militias to crush their opponents. Meloni has sometimes warned militants to cut out their antics with Salò-era banners and SS memorabilia.[96] Indeed, Fratelli d'Italia's way of talking about history is much less focused on building up fascist heroes than on honouring fascist victims. This often manifests itself in the claim that 'the Italian right' is the victim of a kind of discrimination, comparable even to racism and 'hate speech'. As historic MSI figure Giano Accame put it in 2003: 'There is only one category of the different that the Left has not only overlooked for over five decades, but even helped marginalise: ex-fascists, now reduced into a sort of psychosis as a persecuted ethno-religious minority. Toward which it even became a habit to proclaim that "killing a fascist is no crime".'[97] Meloni, who grew up politically in the 1990s, habitually diverts discussions about historical fascism into warnings against the dangers of modern-day antifascism. For instance, in her October 2022 speech seeking confidence from the Chamber of Deputies, she referred to the 'innocent youths killed with metal tools in the name of antifascism' in postwar decades, a reference to the MSI activist Sergio Ramelli who was killed in 1975 (see Chapter 2). The violent danger is not from fascism but those who claim to be rooting it out.

In this sense, it is clearly not the case that Fratelli d'Italia has gained mainstream status by embracing an antifascist reading of history. Rather, its rhetorical strategy consistently denies that such a thing should be necessary. Telling in this regard was a 2019 interview with party co-founder Ignazio La Russa upon the thirtieth anniversary of the fall of the Berlin Wall. Explaining how the MSI had become a party of government in the 1990s, La Russa made no mention of efforts to change its culture, and denied that it should thank its ally Silvio Berlusconi for bestowing legitimacy upon it. Rather, it was simply 'History itself' that had freed this party from the position to which it was reduced in the antifascist Republic: the end of the Cold War 'ended our delegitimisation, unbinding us from the system that had existed since the end of World War

II'.[98] In this reading, the collapse of the Eastern Bloc was a final condemnation of communism and all it stood for, including the zombified antifascist ideology it used to sustain itself: the continuation of antifascism in postwar decades, La Russa insisted, was an artefact of the division of Europe in 1945, which had only illegitimately outlived the end of Mussolini's regime. In this same interview, La Russa insisted that his party had reckoned with the past by condemning the regime's antisemitic Racial Laws, unlike a left that refused to exorcise its demons. Yet also notable was the fact that he painted Fratelli d'Italia in close continuity with the MSI of the past.[99] In this interview, he described the postwar MSI simply as an 'anticommunist' force, oppressed by the 'partyocracy'; he has elsewhere claimed it moved on from the Mussolini era in 1970 when it 'removed regime symbols from its offices'.[100]

Hence, rather than answer antifascist criticism through a purposeful rejection of fascism and its values, Fratelli d'Italia overcomes this problem by delegitimising antifascism as stained by its association with the *foibe*, the Soviet Union and postwar leftist violence. This is the spirit in which it insists that public holidays rooted in the Resistance such as Liberation Day and even Republic Day are 'factious' occasions which glorify violence against Italian patriots, even as it damns others for not marking the *foibe* Remembrance Day.[101] From Rachele Mussolini to Giorgia Meloni, Fratelli d'Italia representatives proudly refuse to celebrate antifascist anniversaries: democracy, they insist, cannot be based on 'only one side'. On Liberation Day 2021, Meloni made her annual statement that she would not be marking the anniversary, in this case because the liberation which Italians needed was an end to Covid-19 curfews.[102] The following year, given the opportunity to leave the house, she again promised not to celebrate 25 April: she insisted that she would instead defend freedom by preparing her speech for the forthcoming Fratelli d'Italia programmatic conference.[103] She has called for its replacement with celebrations of World War I. La Russa has likewise proposed that this celebration of the Resistance be replaced, albeit indicating the possibility of a commemoration of the 'victims of all wars and of the coronavirus'.[104] Such a move to recast Liberation Day in terms unrelated to anti-fascism is surely an infantile rhetorical trick, at the level of angry social media posts insisting that 'the Left are the real fascists'. Yet the angry accusations of progressive 'totalitarianism' are also bound up with a conspiratorial worldview and not only drawn from the Mussolini regime.

THEY SHALL NOT PASS

While Meloni has criticised the 'pantomime nostalgists' decked out in regime-era flags and uniforms, her attempt to leap over the Mussolinian past also involves the embrace of other, modern theories of anti-Italian conspiracy. This is especially clear in her polemical focus on the 'extinction of Italians' and a supposed 'plan for the ethnic substitution' of white Europeans with Africans and/ or Muslims. Today, this is a common trope used by white nation-alist movements internationally, often speaking, as per French conspiracy theorist Renaud Camus, of an elite-orchestrated 'great replacement'. While Camus' compatriot Éric Zemmour repeatedly adopted this wording in the long build-up to his 2022 presidential campaign, comparable reference points like Raspail's *Camp of the Saints* popularise a roughly analogous connection between left-wing agitation, mass immigration and civilisational destruction. While Camus insists that he rejects violence, many have taken his words as a call to arms: *Great Replacement* provided the title of the manifesto by Brenton Tarrant, the Australian terrorist who murdered 51 people in the Christchurch mosque attacks in March 2019.[105] While great replacement theory echoes older narratives of the eclipse of the West, and more American ideas like 'white genocide', it is also notable for its specific focus on elite conspir-acy: the 'replacist power' which aims to substitute whites. Even in Camus' version, there is a certain interplay between the work of 'replacist' plotters – ranging from the Pope to liberal politicians – and more impersonal processes driven by capital's drive for consumers and cheap labour.[106] The versions of the theory espoused by Meloni have routinely combined these elements, from its specific 'ethnic' dimension to the forces behind it.[107]

Tarrant cited among his inspirations Luca Traini,[108] author of a racially motivated terrorist attack in Macerata, in the Marche region, on 3 February 2018. Traini drove through the town, shooting from the window at black people in the street, before firing on the local office of the Democratic Party. Six people – migrants from Mali, Nigeria, Gambia and Ghana – were injured. Traini was found by police with an Italian flag draped over his shoulders while fascist saluting. This took place a month before the general election and reports soon centred on the fact that Traini had earlier been a council candidate for the Lega. He claimed that his attack was in 'revenge' for 18-year-old Pamela Mastropietro – the victim of a murder in Rome the previous week, for which a Nigerian man was charged. While Mastropietro's family denounced the political use of the murder to demonise minorities, Traini's attack made it even more sharply contested. Antifascist groups called a demonstration in the city, but neofascist group Forza Nuova, which claimed Traini was 'driven to despair', organised their own protest two days before.[109] The antifascist march was massively larger, attracting around 30,000 marchers, but Meloni and Salvini strongly criticised this focus. Meloni called the shooting the act of someone 'unbalanced, but not reducible to a clear political connotation'.[110] On the day of the antifascist march, she told Tg24 that 'in Italy there is a plan for ethnic replacement', yet 'this election campaign doesn't manage to talk about it, preferring to talk about fascism. Today's demonstration in Macerata did nothing but create yet another rift in the country.'[111] She added that neither CasaPound or Forza Nuova are 'xenophobic parties'; this latter group, which offered Traini legal support, had mobilised only a few dozen marchers, who fascist saluted as they chanted 'Forza – Nuova – national pride'.[112]

The 'ethnic replacement' narrative is often attached to warlike rhetoric and the language of 'invasion'. A Fratelli d'Italia video in November 2018 marked a century since the end of World War I, echoing the *Trieste Theses'* identification of contemporary migration policy with the historical defence of the border. Meloni tweeted the clip together with a slogan from the war era: 'Today like yesterday, the foreigner will not pass. 100 years on we remember [the soldiers'] sacrifice by fighting the same battle, against fresh invaders.'[113] The video devoted special ire to the 'speculator' George Soros, a Hungarian-born supporter of migrant rescue NGOs and a frequent target of Viktor Orbán's government in Budapest. Meloni has attacked Soros as the 'financier who supports and finances mass immigration and the plan for ethnic substitution worldwide'[114] and a 'usurer' allied to the left against 'the Italian people'.[115] What is important here is the conspiracist idea of the hidden hand behind the immigrant masses: Meloni has denounced the 'invasion of Europe and project of ethnic substitution willed by grand capital and international speculators', facilitated by Italian liberals in EU institutions.[116] This 'plan for the ethnic substitution of European citizens'[117] is specifically associated with *ius soli*, proposed legislation by the centre-left which would grant citizenship to children born in Italy even if their parents are non-citizens. At a June 2017 rally against a Senate bill on this measure,[118] Meloni told reporters: '100,000 Italians were driven abroad last year whereas 500,000 asylum seekers were brought into Italy in the last three. Yes, I think there is a plan for ethnic substitution'.[119] In December, the *Trieste Theses* returned to the idea, claiming that Raspail's dystopia had come to Italy.[120]

In a country where non-white immigrant populations have begun to lay down roots, the claim that Italy is subject to an 'invasion' – one specifically aimed to bring in 'people not like us'[121] – finds increasingly fertile ground across the right. Like Meloni, the Lega leader, Matteo Salvini, has repeatedly spoken of the 'plan for ethnic substitution', claiming that Soros 'would like Italy to be a giant refugee camp because he wants slaves'.[122] The opening sections of Fratelli d'Italia's 2018 election manifesto focused on the means of avoiding national 'extinction',[123] with proposals which echo the Fascist past but also modern US identity politics. In this document we read that a Meloni government would launch 'the most powerful plan for supporting birthrates and families in Italian history', allied with a fight against 'gender ideology', a term used to refer to all manner of feminist and LGBT rights demands. Defending Western civilisation also means authoritarian measures like the 'militarisation of Europe's borders' and, in defiance of international maritime law, the sinking of migrant boats and NGO rescue ships. In this sense, it seems that the party would like to go beyond even existing EU structures for suppressing migration such as border agency Frontex and the outsourcing of migration control to authoritarian regimes in Libya, Morocco and Turkey. The *Trieste Theses* even aired the idea of military intervention to this effect: an 'international ground mission to take control of the ports the boats leave from' in North Africa, albeit with the consent of the local regimes.[124] In Trieste itself, in November 2018 the right-wing parties in charge of the local council passed an ingenious measure to govern migration: a cap on the number of foreign children in classrooms.[125]

2

Exiles in Their Own Fatherland

When fascists honour a fallen comrade, they proclaim that this *camerata* is still present in their ranks. The tribute was perhaps fitting for an icon of the MSI tradition like Assunta Almirante, and as her coffin emerged into Rome's Piazza del Popolo on 28 April 2022, a dozen or so voices cried out '*camerata* Almirante, presente!'[1] The salute, duly accompanied by outstretched palms,[2] was devoted to a woman who had been both wife to the MSI's co-founder Giorgio Almirante and, after his death in 1988, an unyielding defender of his record. Also present among the hundreds gathered at the Chiesa degli Artisti was Giorgia Meloni: she, like most of the mourners, did not join with the saluting and shouting. Yet, even in its guise as a 'conservative' party, Fratelli d'Italia strongly claims the legacy of the MSI's main historic leader. Typifying the party's integration of the fascist tradition into a broader nationalist frame, in one section of Meloni's memoir he appears as a defender of Europe and critic of European federalism. In one sentence, Meloni proclaims herself to be a supporter of 'De Gaulle's "Europe of Nations" and the Europe which, as Giorgio Almirante loved to repeat, must turn to the right, or else it will not be'.[3] Upon the 2022 anniversary of his death, she specified that his greatness lay in his 'ability to transmit ideas, values, traditions and an infinite love of our Nation to the next generations'.[4]

This link is deeply felt. Meloni's memoir relates the morning in 2019 when Fratelli d'Italia moved into the MSI's old headquarters on Rome's Via Scrofa. Her 'heart was racing' as she got to her office occupied by its historic leaders:

I remain silent, and suddenly I realize the enormous responsibility I have taken on. I picked up the baton of a seventy-year-long history, I carried on my shoulders the dreams and hopes of a people who had found themselves without a party, without a leader, who had risked going astray. It's as if those millions of people are all here, all those fighting with me today and those who are no longer here. As if they were looking at me, silently, asking, 'are you up to the task'.[5]

There passed before her eyes 'a history of tragedies, betrayals, victories, defeats, dreams, a whole world that never ceased to believe, or to fight'.[6] But what experiences were these? And if this party has consigned 'fascism to history', but upholds the 'glorious tradition of the Italian right',[7] is there so simple a break between the regime and the world after 1945? Almirante based himself on an almost opposite claim: that fascism could be renewed. One famous expression of this came in his 1986 address to MSI members at Milan's *Lirico* theatre, site of Il Duce's final speech. Forty years since the MSI's foundation, Almirante argued that while it would be an 'offence against fascism' to see the regime only nostalgically, as an 'absolute model', to disavow it would be a 'shameful betrayal'.[8] For Almirante, the party's 'roots' must be 'attentively cared for' and 'projected toward the future'; without this there is 'no possibility of a present or a future worthy of the name'.[9]

Ignazio La Russa made a telling allusion to Almirante's attachment to fascism in 2016 when he praised the MSI co-founder for bringing the unwanted 'stepchildren' of postwar Italy into 'democratic participation'.[10] In the new situation following 1945, many of Mussolini's supporters either withdrew from the public gaze or changed their political colours; in these same comments, made as he lay flowers to 'the fallen' of the Salò Republic, La Russa complained that only 'those who were not coherent [in their choices] were allowed to forget' their pasts.[11] In this sense his comments also echoed a judgement by Almirante, who termed the MSI the party of 'fascists in a democracy', or what one militant legend called 'exiles in their own fatherland'.[12] During the regime, all fascism had revolved around Mussolini; but those who wanted to keep a fascist movement alive had to proceed without him. The MSI, too, had to find its way in the postwar world, not only in a democracy, but in a Cold War context in which Italy was a relatively junior force in the Western camp. This was surely humiliating for Salò veterans who had fought alongside Nazi Germany to defend Italian soil from the US-led forces. Yet the Cold War also presented opportunities for the MSI, which repeatedly tried to form anticommunist fronts able to supplant the Republic's foundational antifascism.[13] This did not mean abandoning the fascist tradition, but making it the cutting edge of a wider mobilisation.

MSI co-founder Pino Romualdi had an even stronger fascist pedigree: in Salò he was a leading member of the Partito Fascista Repubblicano, and he even promoted rumours that he was Mussolini's biological son. He was a delegate to the Verona Congress in November 1943, which decreed that Jews were enemies of the Italian nation, and in the final months of the war he became the Partito Fascista Repubblicano's vice-president. In the immediate postwar period, he created a circle of veterans, including Pino Rauti, which mounted small-scale terrorist attacks against the new Republic. But from the MSI's foundation he insisted on its place in a broader right-wing bloc. He insisted that there was no point in neofascists isolating themselves from the postwar Western alliance: one could keep 'throwing bombs at the Republic' or, as he preferred, change it from within.[14] Yet, from the 1960s, neofascist militants impatient with the electoral process would indeed plant bombs in train stations and throw grenades at police, and this, too, changed the Republic in lasting ways. As Romualdi's son Adriano put it, fascism was not a two-decade parenthesis, limited to the regime period alone, for its ideas had become part of European culture. We cannot know if Adriano Romualdi was only the son of Pino, or Mussolini's grandson too. But his observation has much to tell us about how the MSI understood its place in the new Italy.

THE DEFENCE OF THE RACE

If Almirante is today an icon for 'postfascists', his own fascism was precocious and enduring. Born in 1914, he began his career as a propagandist in 1933, writing for Telesio Interlandi's Rome newspaper *Il Tevere*. Interlandi admired Nazi antisemitism and in 1938 founded the journal *La Difesa della Razza* ('The Defence of the Race').[15] Initially backed by the Ministry of Popular Culture, it claimed to give scientific justification to Mussolini's turn to explicit biological racism, following the conquest of Ethiopia in 1935–6, the proclamation of the Italian Empire and the Racial Laws which excluded Jews from many jobs, positions and even classrooms. From its first issue, it combined this antisemitism with a brutalisation of Blacks, gypsies and other 'non-Aryans'; an approach inspired by the July 1938 Manifesto on Race[16] and confirmed in the November 1938 ban on interracial marriages. In September 1938, the 24-year-old Almirante became chief editor under Interlandi, committing famous words to *La Difesa della Razza*'s pages. In 1942, Almirante summarised his racial creed: he spoke of the need to thwart the 'agenda of Jews and half-castes', to make 'racism into our common fuel', a 'living racial consciousness', a 'racism which must be that of the blood flowing in my veins, which I feel flowing back into me, and can see, analyse and compare with the blood of others'.[17] After Italy declared war on Britain and France (later followed by similar declarations against Greece, Yugoslavia, the Soviet Union and the United States), Almirante reported from the front line in Libya and Egypt.

Fascism's defeats soon troubled this budding journalistic career. As the Western Allies closed in on Italy, pressures grew within the leadership, and on 24–5 July 1943, Fascist hierarchs removed Mussolini from power. In September, Nazi Germany invaded Italy to shore up its military position, reinstalling Mussolini at the head of the Salò Republic. The Allied-occupied south had a rival royalist government, which later integrated antifascist representatives of the National Liberation Committee (CLN). For the young Almirante, the choice between the two Italies was clear. He enrolled in the Mussolinian National Republican Guard, and on 30 April 1944 became chief of staff at the Ministry of Popular Culture. While the ministry was based in Salò, on Lake Garda, Almirante was present in Rome at the start of June 1944 as Allied troops moved into the outskirts of the capital. When Mussolini telephoned him for the latest information, Almirante only had bad news to give. Yet the young official himself felt deflated. When, at the end of one update, Mussolini politely asked his subordinate 'may I call you back later?' Almirante knew that this was no longer the great dictator of old. As he remembered, 'this "may I?" was the end of a man and the end of a great illusion'.[18] Almirante continued to serve under Minister of Popular Culture Ferdinando Mezzasoma until the final defeat in the north in April 1945.

This raised problems of self-preservation. Even before the defeat, Mezzasoma had joined plans to create a neofascist party[19] that would be able to survive the regime's collapse. Yet Almirante reports that at their final meeting, the minister told him he had embraced Il Duce's fate as his own: 'I am heading off to die with Mussolini.'[20] On this point, Mezzasoma was correct, and he was shot together with Mussolini at Dongo on 28 April 1945. With the CLN parties now forming an antifascist government, Almirante headed into a self-imposed 'clandestinity', seemingly for fear of being punished for his role in Salò. A less famous face than Mezzasoma, Almirante was never actually indicted, but he had reason to be fearful at a time when the boundaries of *epurazione* were undefined, amid both trials of war criminals and extrajudicial reprisals. A key turning point came in June 1946, when justice minister Palmiro Togliatti granted an amnesty for a swathe of wartime crimes, including 'collaborationism'. This call for 'social peace' in turn allowed Almirante to raise his head. In September 1946, Almirante ended his 'clandestinity' and joined Romualdi's Fasci di Azione Rivoluzionaria. Founded in the aftermath of the defeat, this was one of many groups which sought to show that the Fascists had not disappeared: before Almirante joined, it had already marked the first anniversary of Mussolini's death by breaking into a radio station and playing the regime-era anthem 'Giovinezza'.[21]

The pacification process allowed more open organising efforts. On 26 December 1946, Romualdi, Almirante and others met in Arturo Michelini's office to proclaim the MSI.[22] It claimed to uphold the political heritage of the Salò Republic, and to provide a common party for the various existing neofascist initiatives. Romualdi's project was to resume public political activity: what historian Giuseppe Parlato calls not just a '"party for veterans" but one that could be politically effective'; not a 'nostalgic party, though it would programmatically refer to institutions and concepts typical of fascism'.[23] While the MSI resented what it called the 'CLN regime' – in fact, a multiparty democracy – and denounced even timid purges of the state apparatus, it began to contest elections. In the autumn 1947 campaign for Rome city council, its rallies were regularly broken up by opponents, but a minority of residents in the capital did support it: in this first contest it scored 4 per cent and elected three councillors.[24] When city hall met, the MSI representatives' votes proved decisive in the narrow re-election of the Christian Democratic mayor, Salvatore Rebecchini. Hence, from early on it faced in two directions: what Parlato calls a 'double line', 'anti-Communist and philo-Christian Democratic in institutional settings', while also 'extremist and asserting itself as a third force in its public-square rallies and its programmes'.[25] At a time when other militants were organising armed cells, the MSI instead worked to secure an institutional footing for an openly fascist party.

Almirante soon became the MSI's main leader, proclaiming it to be an 'anti-systemic' force within the democratic institutions. It was not the largest party opposed to the new Republic: major contingents of ex-regime supporters joined the royalist Partito Nazionale Monarchico and the self-styled 'anti-political' Fronte dell'Uomo Qualunque ('Everyman's Front'). Yet the MSI created in 1946 had a difference: it was self-consciously bound to the experience of Salò, even barring from membership those fascists who had 'betrayed the Patria' by splitting with Mussolini in July 1943. Yet the MSI could not command the allegiance of all Salò veterans, and there were divisions even among those who continued to organise as fascists. Some, such as Augusto de Marsanich, joined the MSI in the hope of forming a 'national conservative' force to the right of the Christian Democrats. In contrast, a circle around Stanis Ruinas promoted a 'left-fascist' project outside of MSI ranks, which promised to reclaim Salò's 'anti-bourgeois' and anti-American spirit. In its initial phase, part-funded by the Communist Party through linkman Giancarlo Pajetta,[26] it was known after its bimonthly journal *Il Pensiero Nazionale*, which vehemently attacked the MSI's alignment with other right-wing forces and accused it of subordination to Christian Democracy. Similar criticisms were aired within MSI ranks at the first congress, but De Marsanich concluded proceedings with a speech that was well designed to hold together different currents: his call to 'neither restore nor renege on the regime' sought to define the party as the bearer of the Fascist past, while leaving open its future strategy.

INSERTION

One Salò veteran in the MSI was long-time Fascist hierarch, Carlo Emanuele Basile. Joining Mussolini's Partito Nazionale Fascista in 1922, he became its federal secretary in Novara, before joining its national directorate and being appointed to the one-party parliament. Volunteering for the wars in both Ethiopia and Spain, under the German occupation he became Prefetto – chief representative of the Salò interior ministry – in Genoa. Along with Milan and Turin, this north-western port city was one of the main centres of labour strikes during the antifascist Resistance. Faced with partisan attacks on soldiers and policemen, Basile called three Special Tribunals, which handed down eleven death sentences against antifascists. But he also worked to suppress strikes through indiscriminate collective punishment. On 1 March 1944, prefect

Basile had a poster put up around Genoa which threatened that in the event of further strikes, 'a certain number of you, drawn by lot, will immediately, within a few hours, be sent to Germany'. In June the occupation forces carried out this threat, with some 1,400 deportees. Basile faced a series of trials after the war, even being sentenced to death by one court. Yet, ultimately, he escaped punishment: his direct role in commanding the deportations remained unproven, while MSI allies even claimed that he had intervened to protect the workers. The retired Basile remained an outspoken MSI member.[27]

The judiciary's light-touch interpretation of the Togliatti amnesty – for instance, in rulings which acquitted those deemed 'not particularly cruel torturers' – pointed to continuities in the Italian state, which was not deeply purged after 1945.[28] The division was made between 'those truly responsible for Fascist rule and the great mass drawn along in their wake',[29] and the ranks of police chiefs, army officers and intelligence agents remained dominated by regime-era appointees.[30] Into the 1950s there were multiple cases of regime-era personnel orchestrating the deadly repression of worker and peasant organising.[31] Yet the Resistance had changed Italy's political culture in important ways. Not only had antifascist leaders authored a republican Constitution which proclaimed far-reaching freedoms and social rights, but there was a deeper democratisation, with the rise of mass parties organising millions of members that pressured officials into respecting the new charter. The MSI respected a different kind of code: its cadres defended their role in Salò, insisting that they had kept their oath to Mussolini, stood by the Nazi German ally and defended Italy's territory even when faced with overwhelming Allied force.[32] Some claimed that Mussolini had in fact saved the Jews, or that it was the Resistance that had provoked the Germans into reprisals.[33] Former hierarchs like Basile insisted that antifascist hegemony was preparing the ground for a Communist takeover. Yet the claim that the Salò Republic had represented a new dawn of social harmony had little hearing in broader Italian society. The men of the MSI were able to organise politically but in a country that massively rejected them.

The MSI would often bemoan its 'marginalisation' by what it called the 'partyocracy'. Yet, its real problem was its profound unpopularity, placing it far behind even other parties hostile to the new Republic, such as the Monarchists and the self-styled 'anti-political' Fronte dell'Uomo Qualunque. In the April 1948 general election, the MSI scored 2 per cent, enough to elect six parliamentarians. Did this demand that other legislators should respect its democratic legitimacy? Or should a liberal democracy perhaps 'arm itself' against a fascist party, with specific legislation to suppress regurgitations of fascist organisation?[34] For the major parties, this was also a matter of dealing with the regime's residue in a pragmatic or even opportunistic way. All parties integrated former fascist personnel, and given the postwar amnesties it was difficult to set absolute limits on what level of past complicity ought to be a bar to democratic participation. The Constitution only set a five-year ban on 'the leaders responsible for the Fascist regime' standing for election. One answer came from the 1952 Scelba law, so named after the Christian Democratic interior minister who authored it; it enacted one of the Constitution's transitional dispositions by banning the 'reconstitution of the Fascist party'.[35] Given the MSI's small size and attachment to a failed past, it did not appear as a serious electoral challenger to Christian Democracy; indeed, its existence as a minoritarian force may have helped the Resistance parties to show their continued antifascism. Yet, as the election of Rome's mayor had immediately shown, as soon as the MSI was tolerated, representing fascists who could not be silenced entirely, its numbers became part of the Republic's political arithmetic.

The MSI's hopes of gaining influence relied especially on the hardening Cold War divide, which tended to replace the Republic's foundational antifascism with anticommunism. Since the Allied liberation of Rome, a series of CLN governments had united Christian Democrats with Communists, Socialists, the liberal-socialist Actionists and other smaller forces. Yet, in May 1947, Christian Democratic premier Alcide de Gasperi threw the left-wing parties out of his coalition and ran in the April 1948 general election on a strongly anticommunist ticket, faced with a Socialist-Communist alliance. His party scored 48 per cent and a majority in both houses of parliament. There were also smaller anticommunist forces, notably L'Uomo Qualunque, ever promiscuous in its dealings with other parties. It placed second in Rome's first local elections in 1946, it elected 30 members to the Constituent Assembly that summer and it also had a strong base in the south.[36] These regions had been less affected by occupation and the Resistance and the labour movement there was also much weaker than in Milan or Turin. L'Uomo Qualunque, a leading contender to reorganise former regime personnel in an 'anti-antifascist' (but mainly anticommunist) party, expressed the cynical spirit of *aridatece er puzzone* – Roman dialect for 'bring back the old scumbag', or less literally, 'it was better in the bad old days'. Yet it proved ephemeral, and in 1948 almost all its vote folded into the Christian Democrats, whose rallying cry against the left was especially successful in an election held just weeks after the Communist takeover in Czechoslovakia. In June 1948, a young former *qualunquista* even tried to assassinate Communist leader Togliatti: his shooting was a dangerous moment for the young democracy, though Togliatti's party defused its militants' more radical impulses, and he eventually pulled through.

In January 1950, the MSI Congress elected a new leader, De Marsanich, a Salò veteran, regime-era business chief and union official. Where Almirante spoke of a new social order to replace both international capitalism and communism, the 'Nation State of Labour', the 'national conservative' Marsanich moved onto a less radical terrain, a Christian-inflected denunciation of 'materialism'. This posed an essential question of MSI politics: should a party that claimed the legacy of Salò uphold it as a model for the future, insisting that it had shown what a more social, even more totalitarian, fascism could have been? Did such radicalism not contradict the militants' insistence that where the Resistance had fought for one 'Faction', Salò fought for 'the Nation'?[37] And what were the parameters of national independence in the postwar world? For De Marsanich, the MSI needed to prove its credentials as an anti-communist ally for Christian Democracy, even if this meant taking decisions in conflict with the ones taken during Salò. Attitudes regarding Washington were decisive. Mussolini had declared war on the United States in December 1941, and many MSI cadres had fought US troops on Italian soil; however, most of its poten-tial electorate had not, especially in the southern regions where it had the best chances of mobilising support. While, upon NATO's creation in 1949, Almirante damned Italy's subordination to Wash-ington, in December 1951 De Marsanich endorsed the alliance in the interest of the global anticommunist struggle. This reflected the tension between cadres' identitarian bind to the past and elec-toral opportunism. While the Salò Republic had emerged from a direct conflict with the monarchy, De Marsanich's party allied with monarchists in the 1951 and 1952 local elections.

The MSI thus echoed the historical contradictions of fascism but on a smaller scale. A party to the right of Christian Democracy could seek potential bases of support among generally southern, conservative, more devout Italians; yet many militants, particularly Salò veterans in northern regions, insisted that the MSI had to compete with the antifascist left for working-class support. One was Giorgio Pini, a Mussolini biographer and junior minister at the Salò Republic's Interior Ministry: at the 1952 MSI congress, he insisted that it 'must choose the natural, dynamic, revolutionary function, reserved for an ardent, oppositional minority … [as against] the great error of letting itself be trapped in its function as a satellite and secular wing of static conservative forces'.[38] He soon split away to launch a separate 'regroupment' among left-fascists, soon establishing a collaboration with *Il Pensiero Nazionale*'s Stanis Ruinas. Another self-styled 'anti-bourgeois' fascist was Pino Rauti. An adept of esoteric theorist Julius Evola, Rauti upheld a 'spiritualist racism', the vision of the elite warrior caste whose action could create a new and higher civilisation. Rauti formed a current within the MSI called the Centro Studi Ordine Nuovo, and after the 1956 congress it split away to form a de facto separate party. It would remain a powerful influence on the MSI throughout its history, whether within its ranks or as an external faction. In the MSI's early period, Almirante upheld the idea of a 'National State of Labour', which defined it as a continuation of Salò's social programme. Unlike Rauti, he remained within the MSI even when pushed into a minority by De Marsanich's 'national conservative' wing.[39]

De Marsanich announced a 'strategy of insertion', which would also be pursued from 1954 by his successor Arturo Michelini. The aim was to build up the MSI's position within the Republic's institutions, in which spirit it backed various Christian Democratic-led local administrations and even some prime ministers in confidence votes. This did not just mean a pacified acceptance of the dominant order, for the MSI also mobilised militants around the conflicts which tormented the postwar Republic. One important example was the nation's borders. The Paris Peace Conference in February 1947 had forced Italy to cede Istria, Zara and Fiume to Yugoslavia and made Trieste part of a 'Free Territory'. This was itself subdivided into a northern Zone A, under US-UK command, and the southern Zone B controlled by the Yugoslavs.[40] The MSI strongly rejected all concessions and fought to restore the pre-war borders. The city's Christian Democratic mayor, Gianni Bartoli, founded a Committee to Defend the Italianness of Trieste and Istria, including MSI representatives.[41] In 1953, Belgrade suggested that it planned to annex Zone B, to the south of Trieste, and the new Italian prime minister, Giuseppe Pella, responded by threatening to send in troops. Faced with these rival claims, the Western Allies turned towards splitting the Free Territory,[42] but many Italians in Trieste – led by Bartoli and egged on by the MSI – protested angrily. Where in November 1918, Italian troops had first landed in Trieste by boat, on the 35th anniversary MSI members arrived by car or on foot, despite border guards' attempts to stop them. For four days violent protests against the Allies, backed by a student strike, shook Trieste: six people were killed. In 1954, a new treaty signed in London handed Zone A to Italy and transferred Zone B to permanent Yugoslav control.

The MSI was not a likely party of government, but nor did the ruling Christian Democrats ostracise it entirely. In March 1953, this big-tent Catholic party changed the electoral law to give extra seats to the majority coalition, but in June's contest its lists fell just short of this threshold, compelling it to seek allies. Calls for the party to reach a form of 'coexistence' with the MSI, even pushed from within the Vatican, remained hypothetical.[43] But, rising from 6 to 29 seats in the Chamber of Deputies, the MSI found ways to exert pressure on the Christian Democrats, and its agitation around Benito Mussolini's corpse was illustrative of this. In 1945, Mussolini had been buried in secret to avoid his tomb becoming a site of pilgrimage, but its location was revealed, and on the night of 22–3 April 1946 the leaders of a small Partito Democratico Fascista stole the body. This was embarrassing for the government, and while the graverobbers were soon arrested, the corpse emerged only three months later, passing via two Milan priests and then a monastery in Pavia. Yet, pressured by a MSI press campaign as well as Mussolini's widow Rachele, in 1957 the Christian Democratic government entrusted the body to the family. It resettled him in a crypt in his Predappio hometown on 30 August that year. With practical assistance offered by the Forlì MSI federation, each of the following Sundays saw thousands of admirers converge on Predappio, sporting regime-era uniforms and staging collective Roman salutes. Interior minister Fernando Tambroni ordered local police that no one should be allowed to enter the crypt 'in a black shirt',[44] whereas left-wing parties and local Christian Democrats opposed 'pilgrimages' in general. Faced with ongoing MSI efforts to organise collective visits, Tambroni tried to pressure bus companies to refuse bookings.[45]

As historian Sergio Luzzatto suggests, this was an early sign of the political importance of commemoration in postwar Italy, and it also posed the question of what role this party could have in a supposedly antifascist republic. Partisan veterans' groups demanded that Tambroni suppress the rallies in the name of upholding the Constitution, but the MSI press replied that this was reopening old wounds 'in the name of a buried and putrefied antifascism'.[46] This also heralded a dispute which more directly questioned the MSI's legitimacy. In the May 1958 general election, the MSI slipped back to 24 seats, but it also became the fourth largest force in parliament. This was an important position in a Cold War context in which the second biggest party – the Italian Communists – were effectively excluded from office; the third-largest party – the Socialists – retained close relations with the Communists; and there were no other mass parties on the right. The Christian Democrats formed two governments in the next two years, each of which relied on a smattering of smaller parties; the MSI voted confidence in the second of these administrations. In March 1960, however, Tambroni himself was called on to form a government. In the confidence vote in the Chamber of Deputies on 4 April it turned out that he only had a three-vote majority, and that it decisively relied on MSI MPs. Tambroni had formed a single-party cabinet, which did not integrate MSI members. Yet, for the first time since its foundation, the MSI could bear decisive pressure on the fate of a national government. Three Christian Democratic ministers immediately resigned in protest.

Such a situation appeared as a triumph for Michelini's 'strategy of insertion'. Only 15 years since the overthrow and execution of Mussolini, a democratic government was dependent on the neofascist party's support. Yet its entry into the republican mainstream was not complete. Faced with ministers quitting, Tambroni tendered his resignation on 12 April: the MSI then pulled its support for local Christian Democrat administrations. Yet the president of the Republic, Giovanni Gronchi, insisted that Tambroni test his majority in the Senate, and here he again secured a narrow mandate dependent on the MSI. Tambroni was on the centre-left of the Christian Democrats and minded to future openings towards the Socialists. Yet he had gained a poor image among partisan groups during the affair surrounding Mussolini's corpse in 1957, and the opposition to his government intensified in May when the MSI announced plans to hold its national congress in Genoa. Entitled 'Insertion for Renovation', it was explicitly intended to celebrate Michelini's success in deghettoising the party.[47] Yet this choice of host city was itself deeply controversial: because of Genoa's Resistance heritage, because rumours spread that Salò-era prefect Basile was due to address it[48] and above all because the existence of this government showed that the MSI was neither marginal nor just a circle of 'nostalgics'. The Genoa congress was widely portrayed in left-wing newspapers as a deliberate provocation; though this also jarred with the 'strategy of insertion', and it may even have been used by the more identitarian wing of the party to disrupt the alliance with elements of Christian Democracy.[49]

The Communist press bluntly denounced what it called the 'fascists' government'. Both this party and wider layers of the workers' movement began to mobilise, starting in Genoa. In early June, the left-wing parties, trade unions and partisans' groups in the city called a series of rallies against the planned congress; MSI leaders warned Tambroni of mounting public disorder in the port city. Tensions grew on 24 June when police banned a union rally in Genoa, claiming that it had failed to secure proper authorisation. This fuelled mobilisation over subsequent days, as protests called by left-wing parties and dockworkers' unions rallied tens of thousands of marchers, filling the streets with antifascist banners and anthems. On 27 June, the MSI handed Tambroni a report in which leader Michelini suggested that it would be better for his government to call off the congress rather than allow the antifascist parties to continue using it as a rallying point.[50] The situation then escalated dramatically on the afternoon of 30 June, during a strike called by the CGIL trade union. A procession of 100,000 people marched through Genoa, only to come up against the police forces massed in the Piazza de Ferrari. Police attempted to disperse the

crowd with water cannons but were soon overwhelmed. Some protestors took things further, torching police cars and fighting with
officers pulled from the police lines. Tambroni, gripped by panic,
poured fuel on the fire: he issued a directive authorising police
to use live rounds in 'emergency' situations.[51] The MSI called off
the Genoa congress, but the movement against the government
continued.

Tambroni's decision had immediate and lethal consequences.
On 5 July, the police opened fire on a protest in Licata, in the
Sicilian province of Agrigento, killing one person and wounded
24. In the capital, Resistance veterans' groups had called a rally for
the Porta San Paolo for 6 July, but the night before police banned
it on public order grounds. The organisers made an alternative
plan for MPs to solemnly lay a wreath in the square, which in September 1943 had been the site of the most important resistance to
the German invasion. Yet *carabinieri* had occupied the piazza in
advance, and as soon as the demonstration began it was broken up
by officers on horseback, who continued to baton protestors late
into the evening. On 7 July, police suppressed a rally in Reggio
Emilia, killing five workers, all Communist Party members. When
the following day the CGIL called a general strike accompanied by
rallies around Italy, the police opened fire on the crowd in Palermo,
killing four. In Catania, they beat to death the 20-year-old Salvatore Novembre. There were eleven dead in all: three of whom were
former partisans. Indignation continued to grow. In Reggio Emilia,
where most of the killings occurred, a demonstration on 9 July
rallied some 100,000 people. The CGIL promised further strikes.
Faced with the rising movement – a rallying point unknown since
the 1948 assassination attempt on Togliatti – the Christian Democrats could no longer tolerate Tambroni's leadership. Sixty-one
Catholic intellectuals signed an appeal condemning his conduct,
and on 19 July he finally resigned.

This display of state violence and the backlash against it was more
than the end of another short-lived cabinet, for Tambroni's failure
would put up a much stronger *cordon sanitaire* against the MSI

than had previously existed. In the short term, Amintore Fanfani formed a new Christian Democratic cabinet, this time supported by smaller centrist forces. But the strength of mobilisation against a government even passively reliant on MSI support galvanised opposition even within the Christian Democrats, who could no longer consider the MSI even a potential junior ally. While in local and regional government the main parties had each joined admin- istrations that were reliant on MSI support,[52] Tambroni's downfall ended even these arrangements. For historian Roberto Chiarini, this marked a total defeat for the MSI's 'strategy of insertion': the events of spring–summer 1960 'wiped away, in a few months, the positions of strength built up since the early 1950s'.[53] During the crisis the Communist daily *l'Unità* repeatedly called for the MSI to be dissolved, without succeeding in really questioning its legal standing.[54] But in political terms, the MSI was pushed into a seriously compromised position: a self-proclaimed 'party of order' that could not come close to power without dragging Italy into turmoil. Among the Christian Democrats, the effect of ecclesia- stical-conservative opposition to a pact with the Socialists was gravely weakened,[55] and under Aldo Moro's leadership the party began to turn to the prospect of a 'centre-left' alliance.

ANTICOMMUNIST FRONTS

The 1960s thus began with an intense struggle over the boundar- ies of the Republic's antifascism. This surprised many on the left who believed that the legacy of the Resistance had become stale institutional rhetoric rather than an urge to action in the present.[56] It also pointed towards a new situation in which the Christian Democrats, while still a bulwark against the Communists, sought reformist compromises. This was, then, a successful antifascist mobilisation. Yet it did not just continue the unfinished business of 1945. Especially notable was the involvement of young Italians and its importance even in regions without a strong partisan tradition, for instance Sicily, where it was also a rebellion against the police violence that continued to weigh on the island. This was just one of the new trends which put up barriers to the MSI's authoritarian project. Italy had emerged from Fascism not just war-torn but austere and mostly rural: average living standards under Mussolini had been closer to Stalin's Soviet Union than to France or Britain. Yet, on the wave of postwar reconstruction fuelled by Marshall Aid dollars, the 1950s and 1960s were times of rapid industrialisation, an 'economic miracle' comparable to West Germany and Japan. Regional inequalities persisted, but millions of southerners moved to the growing industrial centres, and Italy became more interconnected, less devout and more influenced by Hollywood. These processes did not happen overnight or uniformly. But parties like the Socialists and even parts of Christian Democracy could appeal to broad swathes of Italians with the hope of prosperity, social mobility and greater individual freedoms, as against the repressive traditionalism upheld by the MSI. It harshly damned the new 'centre-left' arrangements as a 'Trojan Horse for communism'.

The modernising and even secularising impulses in Italian society in this era are often spoken of in terms of 'the post-1968 years'. This most literally refers to political events: May '68 in Paris, the Vietnam War, strikes and factory occupations in Italy and the feminist battles that won rights such as divorce and abortion. Yet these collective movements also energised a more diffuse, less strictly political liberalisation of mores. The MSI took this as a threat rather than an impulse it could hope to channel. When Italians voted on whether to rescind the new divorce law in 1974, Almirante sought to use this ballot as a referendum on communism, insisting that Italians must not vote 'with the Communists, like the Communists, for the Communists', or 'as the Brigate Rosse would like you to', saying that the vote to keep the right to divorce would be 'above all their victory'.[57] Fifty-nine per cent of Italians did so regardless. The MSI also recruited members who were not old men of Salò, and even leading youth cadres like Marco Tarchi called for a greater openness to new cultural trends.[58] Some militants looked to non-Mussolinian inspiration for the challenges of their time. Especially important was Julius Evola, with his denunciation of individualist decadence in *Revolt against the Modern World* and *Ride the Tiger*.[59] Another – explicitly calling for a move beyond fascism – was the French Nouvelle Droite and its theorisation, inspired by both Antonio Gramsci and interwar 'conservative revolutionaries',[60] of culture as the premise of political action. This left lasting traces. Even in 2017, Fratelli d'Italia's *Trieste Theses* proposed that 'regenerating the value of the Patria' meant undoing the 'legacy of the post-'68 years', deemed – citing modern-day ideologue Éric Zemmour – the 'history of an absolute dispossession, an unprecedented disintegration, a dissolution in the "icy waters" of individualism and self-hatred'.[61]

Upon Michelini's death in June 1969, Almirante returned to the MSI leadership. Following the failed bid for collaboration with the Christian Democrats, this was widely seen as a reassertion of the MSI's neofascist identitarianism, and it immediately reintegrated Pino Rauti and most members of his Centro Studi Ordine Nuovo. Yet the MSI's shifting strategy responded to not only the failure of the strategy of insertion but also the mounting class and social conflicts of the post-'68 period. While reform-minded elements of Christian Democracy formed governments together with the Socialists, making important concessions to organised labour such as the employment protections in the 1970 'Workers' Statute', the MSI sought to directly confront both the political 'new left' and rising labour militancy.[62] It was in this vein that the 1970 MSI congress proclaimed the creation of a 'combined anticommunist front'. As well as reintegrating Rauti, who was co-opted onto the party leadership, this project sought to build a '*piazza di destra*': right-wing street protests which could also split off parts of the Christian Democrats' base. Not only did the MSI make a specific appeal to small-business owners, but it also gained sporadic funding from employers' federation Confindustria, as Almirante extended his contacts with top industrialists like the Agnelli family. The anticommunist front also integrated explicitly conservative forces. In 1972, the MSI integrated the royalist Partito Nazionale Monarchico to form the MSI-Destra Nazionale ('National Right'). While it had little prospect of entering the national government, this period also brought the MSI to its historic electoral highs, scoring 9 per cent in the May 1972 election.

Almirante's 'anticommunist front' focused on counter-mobilising against the left. Yet there were also more or less 'anti-systemic' mobilisations, whether directed against the government or else rallying conservative layers in defence of public order. An initial test came in Reggio Calabria, where in the summer of 1970 the MSI swung behind violent protests over the selection of the new regional capital; their main leader was a right-wing trade unionist, Ciccio Franco, who took up the old fascist slogan *'boia chi molla'*, and soon became an MSI senator. But also important, after the shop-floor movements that had surged in 1969, was the movement for 'public order'. The MSI especially sought a role in the 'Silent Majority' demonstrations, first held in Turin and then Milan in March 1971. Started by monarchist lawyer Adamo Degli Occhi, the *Maggioranza Silenziosa* was outwardly 'non-political'. Yet its rallies, with national flags rather than party banners, allowed MSI activists to join a broader space alongside Christian Democrats and Liberals, and they were fundamental to continuing its spread.[63] The protests echoed President Richard Nixon's appeal for mobilisation by Americans who did not share the values of leftist street protestors, but also Charles de Gaulle's rallying of his own supporters in tricolore-draped marches in response to the May '68 movement in France. This movement was indicative in two other ways. First, because Degli Occhi had been a monarchist partisan, and thus symbolised the MSI's reconciliation with figures who had fought against the Salò Republic rather than for it. In 1972, he would become one of the independent candidates on its lists. Yet for all the talk of the silent majority, Degli Occhi was also part of more determined plans to resist communism, in the military plots of this period designed to subvert Italian democracy. This was the second great lesson of this movement: the importance of the international anticommunist cause to allying otherwise diverse forces.

The starting gun for this approach had been fired in 1961 with an article in *l'Italiano*, the periodical founded by Pino Romualdi's son Adriano. In it, Mario Tedeschi – a veteran of the Salò-era Xᵃ Flottiglia MAS militia, later an MSI senator – spoke of a drastic threat, claiming that the Communists planned to seize power through a guerrilla strategy akin to Algeria's National Liberation Front. In 1963, leading Ordine Nuovo member Clemente Graziani published a pamphlet on revolutionary war that adopted this same colonial imagery,[64] arguing for a fight on 'the same terrain'.[65] While Ordine Nuovo called itself a 'study centre', it was in truth a party with some thousands of militants,[66] and Graziani called for the formation of an 'elite of professionals in revolutionary war',[67] citing the model of CIA agents.[68] This fascist-inspired anticommunism combined two kinds of radicalism. It evoked the militarised commitment of the 'political soldier', a mythology of self-sacrifice and redemptive violence inspired by Evola's rejection of modernity and its decadent values. Yet it also offered a militant auxiliary to state actors: what it called the 'Extended High Commands'.[69] This also produced an at least formal organisational divide: while in July 1969 founder Pino Rauti rejoined the MSI, and was immediately co-opted onto the party leadership, Graziani declared a continuity Movimento Politico Ordine Nuovo that was outside the MSI yet closely bound to prominent figures within it. This was not the limit of Ordine Nuovo's web of associates, for it also had support and protection from state figures, including within the Italian and NATO military command. For historian Franco Ferraresi, '[t]he same ideas (possibly pruned of some, although by far not all, Evolian overtones) were entertained by important and "respectable" sectors of the Italian ruling groups, including a number of the highest state authorities, sections of the army, of the judiciary, of the business and financial community'.[70]

The connection between neofascist violence and such military and intelligence figures was well illustrated by the conference on 'revolutionary war' held at Rome's Hotel Parco dei Principi in May 1965. This illustrated their ideological and even organisational overlaps with a wider anticommunist and colonialist cause. Speakers included right-wing journalists like Enrico de Boccard, an agent of military intelligence service Sifar; the Salò veteran Giorgio Pisanò, later an MSI senator, who spoke on the Resistance as an example of Communist 'revolutionary war'; the former MSI member and *Il Borghese* contributor Giano Accame, who spoke on the 'Counter-revolution by the Greek officers'; and Rauti, a figure with close contacts in Greece and the other Mediterranean dictatorships, who addressed '[t]he tactic of Communist penetration in Italy'. Attendees also included Stefano delle Chiaie, founder of terrorist group Avanguardia Nazionale, and Ordine Nuovo's Carlo Maria Maggi. Key to relations with the military high command was another right-wing journalist and secret services agent, Eggardo Beltrametti. He had a special fascination with the Organisation de l'Armée Secrète (OAS),[71] an underground network of military officers who had tried to prevent the French exit from Algeria in 1961–2. They mounted terrorist attacks in both France and the colony, even attacking French troops in the attempt to show that the Algerians had not laid down arms and thus sabotage the peace agreement. Defeated in 1962, many OAS leaders recycled themselves in anticommunist networks abroad and later in Jean-Marie Le Pen's Front National. De Boccard's speech at the Hotel Parco dei Principi explicitly cited the OAS as an example of 'anticommunist' revolutionary war.[72] Hysterical claims about the planned Communist uprising in Italy, filtered through the language of anti-colonial revolt and counterinsurgency, were cited as justification for pre-emptive measures.

This did not only mean plans to resist a hypothetical Communist takeover. For the OAS example already pointed to the idea of fabricating evidence for a left-wing terror campaign which it purported to suppress. On 12 December 1969, members of Graziani's Ordine Nuovo planted explosives at Milan's Banca Nazionale dell'Agricoltura, in what became known as the Piazza Fontana bombing. The blast killed 16 people instantly, injuring 88, with a further victim dying a year later. Apart from the innocents murdered by the bomb, there was also an eighteenth victim: the anarchist railworker Giuseppe Pinelli. One of dozens of suspects arrested in the hours following the bombing, he was officially reported to have fallen from a window from a Milan police station. Unaware of the neo-fascist group that had planned and executed the bombing, Italian media outlets uncritically reproduced police claims that the revolutionary left was responsible for the atrocity. On 16 December, Bruno Vespa announced on live TV that police had found 'the guilty man', the anarchist Pietro Valpreda. The suspect was widely vilified: for MSI's *Secolo d'Italia* he was 'an obscene and repugnant beast, penetrated to the marrow by communist syphilis'; for *Il Messaggero*, he was 'a human beast masquerading as a cheap extra'. Also scathing was the Communist *l'Unità*: it labelled Valpreda the 'monster of Piazza Fontana', hinting at a conspiracy – perhaps he was 'manoeuvred by someone else at will'.[73] Luigi Calabresi, a policeman implicated in Pinelli's death, was assassinated by members of far-left Lotta Continua in May 1972; Valpreda himself was only released from jail in December 1972, and he would not be fully cleared of charges until 1987.

This was an early realisation of what *Observer* journalist Leslie Finer termed 'the strategy of tension',[74] designed to fuel polarisation and thus the demand for authoritarian intervention. It was not the first such plot: there had been an attempted bombing at a Slovenian-language primary school in Trieste in October 1969, but it had failed for technical reasons. Indirectly linked to Piazza Fontana was the attack on the Milan police HQ on the first anniversary of officer Calabresi's death in which four people were killed. Ferdinando Pincioni, a magistrate who investigated this case, later summarised its moving parts: 'an anarchist as the ostensible culprit, Ordine Nuovo as the organiser, other groups linked to the armed forces and the secret services both instigating terrorist attacks and obstructing the course of justice, and a coup d'état or the formation of an authoritarian government as the final aim'.[75] It is worth emphasising that the MSI as a party did not orchestrate this strategy or the specific attacks. But through its political propaganda, MSI made its own contribution to the strategy of tension, as it used these supposed examples of 'red violence' to call for an authoritarian and anticommunist reordering of the state. This call for a new order took various forms: demands for the creation of a 'state of siege' and the introduction of military courts and the death penalty sat alongside the wider cause of forming what Almirante termed a 'qualitative democracy', based not on the equality of all voters but the representation of group interests in a corporatist state order, and headed by a strong presidency.[76]

There were not always neat separations between the MSI, the apostles of 'revolutionary war' and coup plotters. When, in a 1984 interview for *La Repubblica*, Almirante distanced himself from the terrorist Stefano delle Chiaie, the latter wrote a letter to the paper relating his meetings with Almirante when he was hiding from justice in 1971–2, and reported that Almirante had told MSI youth activists that the MSI and Avanguardia Nazionale fought 'the same battle in different trenches'.[77] In this same period, the MSI leader also publicly referred to the need for MSI activists to be able to physically 'defend themselves against communists'. One remarkable place where militants spanning different movements overlapped was the neofascist hangout which developed in Milan's Piazza San Babila. The MSI youth had its offices nearby, through which militants of many different organisations passed; but more important was the square itself and the bars around it. This territory was prowled by militants from Ordine Nuovo, Avanguardia Nazionale, the Squadre d'Azione Mussolini or those whose allegiances weren't quite so clear: *sanbabilini* more than members of parties. One, Nico Azzi, accidentally revealed the existence of a 'strategy of tension' on 7 April 1973 when he triggered the device he intended to plant on a commuter train; he had on him not just explosives but a decoy copy of Lotta Continua's newspaper. Police suppressed all protests, including a planned MSI rally against 'red violence' organised for 12 April, headed by local MSI leader Franco Servello and Ciccio Franco, the main leader of the Reggio Calabria revolt. But *sanbabilino* militants rioted and laid siege to the police headquarters: hand grenades were thrown and a young policeman was killed. In the effort to determine criminal responsibility, dozens of militants were arrested. The MSI insisted it had nothing to do with the implicated *sanbabilini* Maurizio Murelli, Vittorio Loi and Azzi: it turned out that Murelli held an MSI membership card for 1972 but considered himself part of the local scene rather than the party.

The MSI publicly distanced itself from such attacks and even offered financial compensation to the policeman's family. Yet if it did not, as a party, pursue a terrorist strategy, the MSI of the Years of Lead openly defended the use of undemocratic means to stop communism and its supposed forebears, in which spirit it openly supported military regimes in the Mediterranean and Latin America. The Italy of this period was far more prosperous than Greece, Spain or Portugal; it had a much more dynamic culture, a free press and markedly less state killings of civilians. Yet the MSI strongly pleaded in defence of these regimes, even calling for them to be allowed to join the European Economic Community.[78] Some neofascists took such regimes' inspiration even more seriously, such as the naval commander Junio Valerio Borghese, head of the Nazi collaborationist Xa Flottiglia MAS paramilitary unit during the Salò Republic. He was honorary MSI president from 1951–3, and in 1967 he formed his own Fronte Nazionale together with other military officers and began preparations for a coup on the Greek model. The plot involved both Salò veterans and younger terrorists from Della Chiaie's Avanguardia Nazionale, and also members of the P2 masonic lodge and a wider array of 'men of order'.[79] The takeover of state agencies planned for 7–8 December 1970 was, however, called off at the last minute, and once the plan was exposed the plotters were forced to seek the embrace of the brother regimes abroad. Borghese headed to Franco's Spain, as did Della Chiaie, and the latter would spend almost two decades on the run, even working for the secret services of military regimes in Chile and Bolivia.

The MSI's political response to the events in Chile starkly illustrated its weak democratic mores. Salvador Allende had narrowly won that country's September 1970 presidential election at the head of a Popular Unity coalition uniting Socialists and Communists. This was widely recognised as the world's 'first elected Marxist government', but it immediately faced massive destabilisation. Nixon ordered the CIA to 'make its economy scream' and domestic business elites were also determined to thwart Allende's programme of agrarian reform and nationalisations. Capital flight and blockades by haulage firms soon brought soaring inflation and shrunk Allende's base of support: with coup threats mounting, he introduced army officers into his government, only for the generals to seize power on 11 September 1973. Faced with the tanks approaching the presidential palace, Allende committed suicide, and the new regime then proceeded to slaughter thousands of his supporters and other left wingers. Chile had a long democratic tradition: the coup was especially a shock to public opinion in Italy, a country whose main opposition was Communist and in which the future formation of a Communist-Socialist government hardly seemed implausible. For Communist leader Enrico Berlinguer, writing a series of articles for party journal *Rinascita*,[80] the Chilean disaster showed the risks of the left arriving in power with a narrow electoral mandate against the resistance of existing state institutions and conservative interests; his response was to try to draw the party into a pact with the Christian Democrats, as a junior partner, to soften the opposition against it. This 'Historic Compromise' between Italy's two main parties was precisely what the MSI sought to avoid.

MSI leaders drew explicit parallels with their strategy in Italy, boasting that they were a bulwark against a Chilean-style turn to the left. Writing for *Secolo d'Italia* in October 1972, before the coup, Cesare Rivelli explained that the turbulence in Chile was a 'foretaste' of 'what might already have happened [in Italy]' if not for strong local election results for the MSI, which warned the Christian Democrats off integrating the Communists into government.[81] As historian Gregorio Sorgonà explains, while the party sought to burnish the democratic credentials of such regimes as Franco's geriatric dictatorship in Spain,[82] it had no such indulgence for left-wing governments that did obey constitutional means. In a period in which the Christian Democrats had repeatedly made alliances with the Socialists, known as the 'centre-left', one piece in the MSI's paper insisted that Allende's example in Chile showed that 'the centre-left is the natural antechamber of a communist regime tout court'.[83] If the MSI was not itself preparing for the violent overthrow of democracy in Italy, it was willing to grant that this could be necessary in the right circumstances. The MSI paper's front-page headline, in response to the news from Santiago on 11 September 1973, openly supported the coup, proclaiming: 'For freedom in Chile, the officers depose Allende.'[84] Almirante emphasised that what happened in Chile 'would happen elsewhere, if the Communists pushed things'.[85] His defence of 'constitutionality' had nothing to do with the defence of the real Italian Constitution that had emerged from the Resistance; rather, it was an insistence that the military intervention was necessary to prevent a Communist takeover.[86]

PACIFICATION

Chapter 1 spoke of a postfascist approach to Italian history which honours victims in the name of national pacification. This framing is often applied by postfascist leaders to the Years of Lead, referring to its history not in terms of what the MSI did or said but in terms of the 'criminalisation' and violence it suffered.[87] The party began developing this language during the 1970s, speaking of neofascist terrorism suspects as victims of antifascist ideology who were 'arrested for their opinions' and 'anti-communist prisoners'.[88] Yet today, this framing is instead used to refer to MSI activists killed by left wingers in the Years of Lead: Meloni has explicitly compared such cases to the Italians who died in the *foibe* – as victims of ideologically inspired violence who should today be honoured by all political sides.[89] Such claims are able to draw on several evocative examples of futile reprisals and even unprovoked attacks.[90] The most important single case is that of Sergio Ramelli, a member of the MSI youth front who was ambushed by members of far-left group Avanguardia Operaia as he returned home from college on 13 March 1975. As the 18-year-old got off his scooter, his attackers beat him over the head with metal tools: Ramelli slipped into a coma and died 47 days later. Ramelli was a teenager, had no important political role and was not attacked in response to violence by him. Upon his death on 29 April 1975, Giorgio Almirante honoured him as a victim of the 'political hatred' against his party: 'the MSI-DN know[s] that for Sergio Ramelli there will be no city-wide mourning, no protest strikes, no marches spreading threats'.[91] It would, he promised, continue both dignified and fearless in its cause: 'loyal to a political commitment to civilisation against barbarism, [our party] does not speak words of revenge or incitement to hatred, but in the name of his martyrdom, it renews its call to courageously fight for justice, for freedom, for order, for security, for pacification among all citizens without discrimination'.[92]

In fact, there was a broad recognition of the brutality of the crime: leaders of the main left-wing parties immediately condemned the killing, including the Socialist mayor of Milan, Aldo Aniasi, and the Communist leader Enrico Berlinguer, who wrote to the murdered teenager's family to extend his sympathies. A plaque put up by MSI members outside Ramelli's home, signed 'your *camerati*', wrote that he 'fell for Italy'. Since the 1980s, a series of streets and parks have been renamed in his honour, often with tributes that speak the language of pacification. For instance, in the Lombardy region, Como has a 'passeggiata Sergio Ramelli' that simply calls the teenager a 'victim of political violence'; Monza's Giardini Sergio Ramelli honours him 'in the name of national pacification that brings together, in shared piety, all our country's innocent victims', wording which also appears in a more recent tribute in Lodi.[93] The homages to him each 29 April span most of the political spectrum but take wildly different forms: both the centre-left mayor of Milan, Beppe Sala, who lays flowers at his house, and hundreds of neofascist militants who gather to shout 'presente' with arms outstretched.[94] On one recent anniversary, Walter Veltroni wrote for *Corriere della Sera* on what he termed the 'polarised extremisms' of this period and the innocent lives they claimed. Veltroni, a former Communist youth leader, refused to draw distinctions between political sides: even if Ramelli was an MSI member, he should be seen as neither left nor right wing but a long-haired youth whose brief existence ended in tragedy.[95] Yet the force of Almirante's response, for those who uphold the legacy of the MSI, lies in the fact that it was not only about this teenager but about antifascist 'hatred'.[96] It expresses not only Ramelli's innocence, but also the party's own, as a victim of ideological terror. Still today, it refuses to accept that such major atrocities as the Bologna Centrale bombing were indeed 'of fascist origin'.[97]

The postfascist retelling of the MSI as a victim rather than a perpetrator of political violence is deeply self-indulgent, seeking to confer on the party a democratic pedigree which it did not earn at the time. From the early 1970s, Almirante tried to define the MSI as a party of order, uniting neofascists but also allying with *afascista* (nonfascist) conservatives. But while the party reached out to other forces calling for solemn peaceful marches in defence of 'order' from 'communism', it also sought to exert its authority within a neofascist subculture ridden with violent and terroristic groups. The spaces in which the MSI organised, and even its own local sections, were often also hangouts for members of terrorist groups and the partisans of violent reprisals and escalation. Yet the attempt to make the party into the spearhead of a broad anticommunist front, able to integrate even liberal elements of right-wing opinion, suffered from the MSI's own evident porousness to terrorists and overlaps with armed militant groups. The killing of a policeman in Milan on 12 April 1973 clearly illustrated this. This problem in fact intensified after the official repression of Ordine Nuovo, and then Avanguardia Nazionale, on charges of 'reconstituting the Fascist Party': these judicial measures created conflicting internal pressures within the MSI both to solidarise with the 'persecuted' militants and to make public displays of its own opposition to political violence. Yet, as Davide Conti writes, even the stances it did take were not enough to save it: for instance, when, in 1974, Almirante warned the anti-terrorism inspectorate of the possible attack on the Italicus train, which then did take place, the effect was not to 'the MSI's favour, by distancing it from extremist groups; it ended up confirming the existence of ambiguous relations between the space of terrorist criminality and the MSI leadership'.[98]

This relates to the wider problem of the MSI's usefulness as an ally for other anticommunist forces, given that a party of such clear fascist identity was sure to inspire militant opposition. It even made contact with US Republicans, offering to help mobilise Italian-Americans in Richard Nixon's 1968 election campaign, pointing to its self-conception as a junior partner in an American-led anticommunist alliance.[99] But while it could at times rally other hard-right forces around itself, neither the Christian Democrats nor Washington needed what the MSI was offering. Its membership base had limited value to coup plotters, and for the Christian Democrats who sought to pacify and integrate the workers' parties, the MSI's role was purely inflammatory. To have included it in the 'area of government' could only have pushed Italy deeper into civil strife, indeed at a point when the various forces of the left were much stronger than at the time of the Tambroni cabinet. In this sense, the contemporary decline of the far-right dictatorships the MSI admired as anticommunist bulwarks,[100] in Greece, Portugal and Spain, is telling. Between 1973 and 1976, all three embarked on democratisation processes, each involving a contest between revolutionary drives from below and state authorities seeking to contain them. If these upheavals appeared to revive Western European communism, both local conservatives and Gerald Ford's Republican administration relied on a much more intricate game of reforms and pressure rather than simply reimpose authoritarian rule. In Italy itself, in 1976, a Christian Democratic government ruled for the first time thanks to the Communists' external collaboration, again demonstrating this party's firm commitment to the Republic's institutions.

The MSI's inability to block this also had effects on its alliances in Italy. In July 1976, a group of MPs split away in an attempt to form a 'national conservative' outfit called Democrazia Nazionale. The hope was that this would be better able to ally with the Christian Democrats and other small centre-right parties like the Liberals. This was clearly the product of the strategic impasse which Almirante had headed into, with the MSI trapped between its inability to form coalitions with the main big-tent Catholic party and its failure to rein in or even distance itself effectively from terrorism. Headed by MSI parliamentary leader Ernesto De Marzio, the split sought to create a conservative party without neofascist connections, realising the project of a 'constituent process of the right'. Most sitting MSI parliamentarians joined the split. Yet its services were also unwanted: Christian Democracy was unwilling to abandon its arrangement with the Communist Party at a time of widespread social tension and mounting economic crisis, and Democrazia Nazionale soon became a parliamentary rump, with minimal following among MSI activists. Almirante's 'anti-systemic' positions and commitment to party identity had the support of most of the base, including its voters, and when snap elections were called in 1979 the split group was crushed. The MSI kept most of its score from the 1976 election, with 5 per cent and 30 MPs, whereas Democrazia Nazionale lost all its seats. This episode nonetheless pointed to the future: one of De Marzio's protégés, like him a son of Puglia, was Pinuccio Tatarella, one of the main architects of the postfascist Alleanza Nazionale in the 1990s.[101]

Such integration into the mainstream right remained a distant prospect for the party. Almirante's response to the killing of Ramelli would instead be the first of a series of cases where the MSI leader called for 'pacification', while insisting that the party itself was foreign to the extremist circles who perpetrated the attacks. While, in the late 1970s, the Italian state would surely adopt authoritarian means in clamping down on militant groups, including new powers of arrest and the detention of thousands of Italians not involved in violence, Almirante's party called for much harsher measures, in an attempt to demonstrate its distance even from neofascist terrorists. Faced with atrocities like the killing of Aldo Moro, Almirante often called for the use of the death penalty, and launching a petition for its restoration in 1981 he insisted it should be for 'red terrorists' but also those who may have 'passed through the MSI and grown disgruntled'.[102] The MSI leader thus called for capital punishment to be used even for the perpetrators of the Bologna Centrale bombing, which killed 85 people on 2 August 1980. The judicial investigations would eventually lead to the conviction of militants from the Nuclei Armati Rivoluzionari (NAR), who were indeed former MSI members. Yet such investigations were not only a sign of the effectiveness of the Italian state in crushing terrorist groups; they also pointed to the complex and often opaque webs of connivances behind atrocities, even pointing to parts of the state who had a hand in orchestrating terrorism. In many cases, justice was not done to the victims, in the sense of identifying the material perpetrators, but 'collaborators of justice' who provided information in exchange for reduced punishment did help dismantle terrorist organisations.

Especially explosive were the revelations resulting from judge Felice Casson's inquiries into the car bomb that killed three *carabinieri* in Peteano, Friuli in 1972. In this 1984 investigation, Ordine Nuovo man Vincenzo Vinciguerra admitted that he had planted the bomb in Peteano. Yet he also set this attack within the wider operation known as Gladio: the NATO and Italian secret services structure that planned armed resistance against an eventual Communist takeover, with the bomb in this case coming from a Gladio arms stock. Vinciguerra's revelations thus provided many insights into the subordinate role of neofascist militants within wider networks of power, which he now rejected. But there was also a more specific revelation regarding Almirante himself.

The second author of the attack was Carlo Cicuttini, a local MSI leader in the Friuli region, who made the anonymous phone call which attracted the *carabinieri* officers over to the car bomb, and had fled to Franco's Spain in the wake of the attack. Vinciguerra alleged that Almirante had sent Cicuttini money, via lawyer Eno Pascoli, to have his vocal chords surgically altered, and thus prevent his voice being identified in recordings of the phone call. In 1986, the money transfer alleged by Vinciguerra was found to have taken place, and Pascoli was then convicted of 'favouring terrorism'. However, Almirante used his parliamentary immunity to protect himself from prosecution, and in 1987 he benefited from an amnesty on account of his age.[103]

While unable to rally the right around itself, the MSI benefited more indirectly from the weakening of ideological tensions in the early 1980s, as the main parties sought to suppress political violence. This was well illustrated in April 1983 by president Pertini's visit to the hospital where Paolo di Nella, a 19-year-old MSI member, lay comatose after a street attack. Pertini would not get to see di Nella alive, but this was the first time the head of the antifascist Republic – himself a former partisan – had paid such recognition to an MSI man. There were also symbolic gestures from elsewhere in the Socialist Party, notably from Bettino Craxi, who had been appointed to form a government after the 1983 election. For the first time, Craxi formally invited the MSI into consultations on cabinet formation. The party was not seriously considered for inclusion in the new five-party administration; Craxi's move was apparently designed to push back against the legitimation recently gained by the Communists. Yet there was a certain cooling of hostilities even between these parties. Especially notable in this sense was Almirante's appearance at Enrico Berlinguer's funeral in June 1984, at which he visited the Communist leader lying in state: what he termed a gesture of recognition to an 'honest opponent'. Giancarlo Pajetta, the Communist, took Almirante by the hand to see Berlinguer's *camera ardente*, and in turn attended the MSI leader's own funeral in 1988. The exchange

of signs of respect is today widely cited as symbolic of a pacification of tensions. Yet this also provides a means of ennobling
Almirante himself: in 2020, Fratelli d'Italia representatives in Ter-
racina, south of Rome, even proposed a 'Piazza Giorgio Almirante
e Enrico Berlinguer' – in everyday use this would more likely to be
reduced to 'Piazza Almirante'.[104]

Even insofar as the MSI managed to break 'out of the ghetto'
in the early 1980s, this did not depend on it renouncing fascism.
Indeed, it did not do this, as illustrated by one of the first opportunities for dialogue it received from a political opponent, the Partito
Radicale's Marco Pannella. This was a libertarian party, well known
for its pro-civil liberties stance and legal assistance to even its
adversaries, and in February 1982, Pannella accepted Almirante's
invitation to the MSI party congress. Before arriving, Pannella had
told newspapers that the real fascism lay not in this party but the
ever dominant Christian Democrats. Yet in his opening remarks,
Almirante pre-empted the idea that the association with 'fascism'
was shaming. 'You have perhaps come to tell us that fascism is not
here. Well, dear Pannella, I reject that, because fascism is here!'
After protracted applause, he continued: 'Before you are men
and women, almost all younger than me, who represent fascism
as freedom. Not fascism-regime, but fascism-movement, a *social*
tradition, the values of state, labour, nation.' This was the tradition of 'fascism as opposition, the only anti-systemic opposition',
which unlike the Radicals would 'never cosy up to the parties of
the regime, of power'.[105] The MSI had, Almirante said, 'always
had the highest respect' for the antifascism that existed 'when
fascism was a regime' – but now it was a purely moribund, destruc-
tive force, which directed hatred against the militants of the MSI.
Pacification meant that 'free men and women' had every right to
defend their own political camp, even if it was a fascist one. This
same congress announced a programme of events to celebrate the
centenary of Benito Mussolini's birth in 1983. Its title crowned Il
Duce 'a man of the people'.[106]

3

A Party of Good Government

On the night of 30 April 1993, the crowd outside Rome's Hotel Raphael was shouting slogans – but also waving banknotes. The former prime minister Bettino Craxi slept at the Raphael while on business in the capital, and an unusual mix of Romans came to pay him a visit. When Craxi emerged from the front door, the chanting turned into a deafening whistle; as he was bundled into a waiting car, helmeted riot police crushed the crowd back against the wall opposite the entrance. As his minders raced him away, protestors threw coins, shouting 'do you want these, too, Bettino?' The Chamber of Deputies had just voted to protect the former premier and long-time Socialist leader Craxi from four of the six charges he faced in the corruption scandal known as Tangentopoli – 'Bribesville'. The protest outside the Hotel Raphael was partly stirred up by right-wing parties; the MSI MP Teodoro Buontempo had, one of his *camerati* claimed, come up with the idea of coin-throwing.[1] Yet there were also many others, from students to people arriving from a nearby rally for Achille Occhetto, whose Party of the Democratic Left had just announced it was withdrawing its support for the Socialist-led government. Not only right wingers were outraged at the vote to protect Craxi: Eugenio Scalfari, editor of centre-left paper *La Repubblica*, called it 'the gravest day in our republican history since the kidnapping and murder of Aldo Moro'.[2]

Craxi's Socialist Party still headed the government, in alliance with the Christian Democrats, but both parties had been mired in chaos for months. The scandal had begun in February 1992, when Socialist Mario Chiesa was exposed taking bribes for cleaning contracts at a Milan nursing home. After a tip-off to magistrate Antonio Di Pietro, police burst into Chiesa's office, whereupon he tried in vain to hide bundles of illicit cash in the toilet. Confronted about this on the TG3 news programme, Craxi tried to dismiss Chiesa as a 'rogue' element in an 'honest' party. Yet this proved to be the first in a torrent of corruption cases which swept through Italy's main parties and also engulfed Craxi personally. In these 'Clean Hands' investigations, prosecutors launched inquiries into most sitting parliamentarians, with many famous faces hauled before televised interrogations. Only a minority of the indicted politicians were ever convicted; yet the reputations of the Socialist and Christian Democratic parties were fatally wounded, and by the end of 1994 both had ceased to exist entirely. For their oldest opponents, the crumbling of these historic pillars of the postwar Republic was a moment of liberation. At a rally on 25 April 1992, the official holiday celebrating the Resistance against Nazi-Fascism, veteran MSI MP Franco Servello proclaimed victory: after a 'long and lonely struggle' the party could look forward to 'the end of the Republic born of the Resistance and the advent of the new Republic which we dreamt of and fought for, for so many years' – a strong 'presidentialist' order to replace the exhausted parties.[3]

In this moment of declining faith in the old parties, the MSI boasted of its outsider status; its membership cards proclaimed it to be the 'party of the honest', unlike the 'partyocracy' at the centre of webs of corrupt influence trading. But it also made a specific appeal to parts of the now orphaned Christian Democratic base, as it emphasised its law-and-order credentials. The MSI especially vaunted its zeal in the fight against organised crime, including in the wake of the so-called *maxiprocesso*, a trial against the Sicilian Mafia that had begun in Palermo in 1986. The so-called Antimafia Pool brought some 475 alleged mafiosi to trial, with 338 convictions, including Totò Riina, head of the Corleonesi clan, sentenced to two life sentences in absentia. When his conviction was upheld by the Cassation Court in early 1992, he ordered the murders of the investigating judges, Giovanni Falcone and Paolo

Borsellino, as well as Salvatore Lima, a Christian Democratic politician. Lima, seemingly deemed a turncoat by former Mafia allies, was executed on 12 March; Falcone, his wife Francesca Morvillo and three policemen were then killed in a motorway bombing on 23 May; and Borsellino was murdered along with five escort agents on 19 July. The MSI claimed Borsellino in particular as a martyr figure. A man of the right if not a party member, Borsellino had in the 1950s been part of the MSI student organisation, and in May 1992 it nominated him to succeed Cossiga as president. Fini called for military courts to try the murderers.

Even before the Bribesville scandal, the MSI had gained a certain institutional recognition thanks to its relations with Francesco Cossiga, president of the Republic from 1985 to 1992. Formerly a hard-line interior minister and in 1979–80 prime minister, after becoming president Cossiga began to burn his bridges with the Christian Democratic party. Italian presidents are elected by legislators rather than the public, and generally serve as non-partisan guarantors of the Constitution rather than intervening in day-to-day politics. Yet Cossiga made increasingly sharp attacks on the 'partyocracy' and Christian Democratic 'cronyism' in terms which echoed longstanding MSI rhetoric. While journalists often remarked on Cossiga's caustic *picconate* – 'pickaxe blows' – this also helped the MSI's criticisms of the main parties seem less unusual. Cossiga also had sympathetic words for MSI leaders. After the 1980 bombing of Bologna Centrale station, then Prime Minister Cossiga had condemned an attack 'of clear origins', blaming 'terrorist techniques of fascist origin'.[4] Yet, in a 15 March 1991 meeting with the parliamentary secret services commission, Cossiga apologised to MSI representative Giuseppe 'Pinuccio' Tatarella, admitting that such a judgement had smeared not just the perpetrators but his whole 'political camp'.[5] In homage to Cossiga, in the April 1992 general election the MSI used the slogan 'every vote is another pickaxe blow'.[6] Tatarella even called for president Cossiga to lead a new right-wing bloc against 'the parties', in what he called a 'neo-Gaullist' role.[7]

This bloc soon became a reality, though under a different leading man. Postwar Italian elections had long been held under a proportional voting system, reflecting the assumption that democracy was built on mass parties who chose their own candidates. With the collapse of the old parties, in 1993 this began to change, and the Republic held direct mayoral elections for the first time. The MSI won many smaller towns but also placed second in the first-round ballots in both Rome and Naples. The runoffs would test its ability to attract switchers from other parties. Fini was the MSI candidate in the capital, where he faced a runoff against the Green Francesco Rutelli. Soon before the 5 December second round he received a remarkable endorsement from Berlusconi, who said that given the chance he would back the MSI over the left. Fini fell short but took some 47 per cent of the vote; in the runoff in Naples, Alessandra Mussolini scored 44 per cent. The MSI had lost but shown its ability to rally votes far outside its base. Then, in January 1994, Berlusconi announced that he was entering the electoral field, with a new party as well as a new coalition.[8] His declared enemy was the Party of the Democratic Left, led by former Communists. While this party had seen part of its left wing split away, the demise of its historic Christian Democratic and Socialist rivals seemed to open its path to high office. Calling for a counter-mobilisation, Berlusconi was willing to cast a wide net: he not only formed his own party but also welcomed the MSI into his coalition.

We saw in Chapter 2 that Almirante's MSI repeatedly sought to rally parts of the Christian Democratic base and other right-wing forces in an anticommunist front. With this party's demise, the effort to tap into its electorate was also aided by changes in the MSI itself. Becoming leader in 1987, 35-year-old Fini promised to combine modernisation with continuity, proclaiming himself a 'fascist for 2000'. But his first spell as *segretario* proved short-lived, and, after weak European election results in 1989, the January 1990 party congress elected Ordine Nuovo founder Pino Rauti as MSI leader in his place. This signalled a sharp change of political direction: Rauti promised to tap into the left-wing electorate by reviving the 'revolutionary' and 'anti-bourgeois' spirit of the fascist tradition. But Rauti was soon laid low by medical complaints, and poor results in the 1991 Sicilian regional elections prompted a fresh leadership contest, restoring Fini to the secretary role. For political scientist Piero Ignazi, this brief period under Rauti paradoxically aided Fini's own project of modernising the MSI: while the 'fascist left' had spent 40 years preaching the virtues of a turn away from the right, its belated and unsuccessful moment of control served to inoculate the party against this line.[9] Instead, the rest of the decade saw Fini's MSI redefine itself a force of the 'European right', a broad-tent right-wing party which could fit within Berlusconi's coalition and even claim to create an Italian equivalent of the US Republicans.

The end of the Cold War had shaken the internal balance of the party system, with the corruption scandal dealing the final blow. Journalists labelled the years between 1992 and 1994 the shift from a 'First' to a 'Second Republic', laying to rest the Catholic- and Marxist-influenced mass parties which had shaped postwar Italy. One key development was the rise of anticorruption and probity as defining issues of political identity: a star of the trials, magistrate Di Pietro, entered the electoral arena. Yet the destruction of the old parties also enabled an influx of figures with power bases outside the electoral arena: the new Republic especially centred on Silvio Berlusconi, the Milanese tycoon who built his base not through a mass party but rather through the private TV stations he controlled. This was surely a paradoxical outcome of the downfall of the old system: Berlusconi was a longstanding ally of the now-reviled Craxi, and his TV empire had been able to go national in the 1980s thanks to the Socialist premier's deregulation of the broadcast market. Other small parties who had never entered government were also well placed to seize the moment: Umberto Bossi's northern-regionalist Lega and the free market, socially liberal Radicali both used the anti-political mood to denounce an overmighty central state – what Bossi's party coarsely termed 'thieving Rome'. The MSI proclaimed itself to be the party of 'la gente', ordinary folks, not 'tangente', the bribe. The moral authority of the old ruling parties lay in ruins, and Italy entered a new era, in which the MSI was no longer reduced to the margins.

ALLEANZA NAZIONALE

'In 1994 we decided to enter the field with the Right, that is, with the Lega and with the fascists.'[10] Speaking a quarter-century after he formed his first government, Berlusconi boasted that he had 'invented the centre-right' – a combination of forces which had never previously ruled postwar Italy. The 'five parties who governed Italy since the beginning of the Republic kept the Lega and Fascism out of the so-called constitutional arch: they never let them enter the government'. But 'in '94 we brought them in: it was us who legitimised them, us who constitutionalised them!'[11] That the octogenarian tycoon called his allies 'fascists' was not the most diplomatic of approaches: even in December 1993, before the 'centre-right' alliance was sealed, MSI leader Fini had insisted that 'like all Italians, we are not neofascists but postfascists'.[12] In Chapter 1, we saw Ignazio La Russa claim that it was not Berlusconi who legitimised the MSI but rather history itself, as the fall of the Berlin Wall vindicated this anticommunist party. In reality, the process was double-sided: the MSI had long sought a place for itself within the 'area of government' and used this moment to emphasise its credentials as part of a broader right; yet it also benefited from the fact that other forces within this camp, and Berlusconi in particular, were willing to normalise the old neofascist party. The mainstreaming of the MSI was thus not a one-sided process of it choosing to abandon its identity or change its positions; rather, it was able to find a different place for itself, in a context marked by the collapse of the previous party system.

What was especially remarkable about the MSI's breakthrough was the polarisation of the 1994 campaign around the historic political identities in the main coalitions, with the right-wing parties organised as an anticommunist front against the Democratic Left. The Cold War was over: the Soviet Union was gone, the continent was headed towards monetary union and former Communist leaders declared their allegiance to balanced budgets and free market reforms.[13] Yet with the old party of the left distancing itself from its own record, Berlusconi's electoral campaign was more obsessively anticommunist than the Christian Democrats had been since at least the 1960s. The tycoon set the tone with his 26 January 1994 televised speech declaring his candidacy, an address delivered to millions of Italians' living rooms from his own desk. He announced that he was running to stop the former Communists, 'men double bound to a failed past'. He insisted that 'our leftists claim to have changed. They say they have become liberal democrats. But they haven't. Their people are still the same, their mentality, their culture, their deepest convictions, their behaviours have remained the same.' To this he counterposed a gospel of free enterprise and individual freedom, calling for what he termed a union of all 'moderates' to save Italy from the left. It would be 'liberal in social policy, free-market in economic policy'.[14] Where Berlusconi refused to believe that the ex-Communists had changed their 'deepest convictions', his approach was rather more indulgent towards Fini's MSI: it could 'no longer be considered a far-right party'.[15]

The 1994 election campaign, fought in alliance with Berlusconi, thus crowned the MSI's entrance into a broader right-wing camp. With the effective disappearance of the major parties rooted in the World War II-era Resistance, Berlusconi forged a 'centre-right' coalition which, he promised, would be made up of 'totally new men' – or at least ones who had not previously governed Italy. To this end, ahead of the election held on 27–8 March 1994, he created his own party, Forza Italia – many of its candidates drawn from his own business empire – and also formed alliances with the northern-regionalist Lega Nord and Fini's MSI. This legitimisation clearly had its limits, for the Lega was both jealous of its strongholds and unwilling to make a direct pact with neofascists. In the single-member constituencies in southern-central regions, Forza Italia and the MSI ran together as the 'Pole of Good Governance', while in the north a separate 'Pole of Freedoms' united the Lega and Forza Italia, without the MSI. Despite this unwieldy arrangement, the parties romped to victory, with a campaign promising sweeping tax cuts. The MSI took 110 seats in the Chamber of Deputies (up from 45 in 1992), leaving it just one seat behind Forza Italia, while the Lega's more geographically concentrated vote brought it 118 seats. This provided the right-wing bloc with a large majority in the Chamber, though it fell just short in the Senate. The MSI had taken over five million votes, and headed into national government for the first time.

In Berlusconi's first cabinet, the MSI had a mostly junior role, premised on its gradual insertion into governmental responsibility. The MSI's Tatarella became one of two deputy premiers, but while the Lega's Roberto Maroni combined this job with his responsibilities as interior minister, Tatarella was charged with post and telecoms. Fini's party did not control major offices of state or any of the big-spending departments, instead taking over the ministries for transport, agriculture, culture and the environment. The main force for instability was, instead, Bossi's northern-regionalist Lega, which would ultimately topple the coalition in December. In these months, Fini sought to confirm the MSI as a reliable governmental partner, though he emphasised that this did not mean denying its roots. In an interview for *La Stampa* on 1 April 1994, four days after the election victory, he was asked how his party had been able to reach government without breaking from the past in the manner of the Communists. He replied that judgements on fascism and antifascism now 'belonged to history', allowing his party to 'look forward without being trapped in the contradictions of the past'. Yet he also made a comment sure to please party militants, adding that Il Duce remained Italy's 'greatest twentieth-century statesman'.[16] Such comments from the height of government were traumatic for antifascists; Liberation Day on 25 April brought a million-strong march in Milan, with demonstrators angrily resisting Bossi's attempt to join it. In Rome, the

MSI held a 'Mass for national reconciliation' with Salò veterans and a handful of former partisans.[17]

The MSI's first entry into government also prompted a certain alarm in other Western capitals, with protests abroad over the party's normalisation in turn gaining extensive media coverage in Italy itself. Some European figures refused to engage with the members of what was widely called a 'neofascist' party, an impression only hardened by Fini's post-election comments on Mussolini.[18] Upon the first meeting of European ministers following the March 1994 election, Belgium's deputy prime minister, Elio Di Rupo, refused to shake hands with his Italian counterpart Tatarella, even though the latter could broadly be considered something of a moderate in MSI ranks.[19] In Chapter 1, we mentioned Fini's boat journey into the Adriatic in November 1992 to assert Italian territorial claims in war-torn Yugoslavia; and right after the new government formed there was also alarm in the international press when MSI heavyweight Mirko Tremaglia repeated his claim that Italy's 1975 border treaty with Yugoslavia should be 'ripped up'.[20] Fini soon put a stop to his *camerati* pursuing a 'parallel foreign policy'[21] and Berlusconi's party itself stepped in to quell alarmism: the *Washington Post* cited the Forza Italia foreign minister, Antonio Martino, who insisted that Socialists in Europe were whipping up controversy because 'they are struggling to find their own identity now, and it seems they can only do so in terms of reviving the old struggle against fascism'.[22] Yet it also remained unclear what exactly the identity of Fini's party now was, and whether it could indeed become a 'mainstream conservative movement'.[23]

Now that the MSI had become a party of government, many commentators spoke of the prospect of an 'ideological Bad Godesberg'. The name came from a spa town near the West German capital Bonn, where that country's Social Democrats (SPD) had held their congress in 1959. In the late nineteenth century, the SPD had been something of a model for other socialist parties in Europe, producing a popularised version of Marxist theory and committing itself to a revolution that would usher in a socialist society. Yet even at the turn of the century it was observed from various sides that its practical focus on gradual improvements stood in tension with its proclaimed end goal. Its support for Germany's war effort in 1914, and then, after the overthrow of the Kaiser, its defence of the Weimar Republic against both revolutionary and reactionary threats, showed that it sought a reformist role within a liberal democracy rather than to replace it. Since the Nazi seizure of power in 1933, the SPD had been banished from all government roles, including after 1945, but at Bad Godesberg in 1959 it set out a programme which offered a more realistic summation of its present-day goals. Having always rejected Soviet socialism and supported the Western camp in the Cold War, in the meeting at the spa town the SPD formally abandoned its Marxist heritage in favour of a 'liberal socialism' which sought to reorient a market economy to social ends. The idea of a 'Bad Godesberg moment' then gained currency in the Italian left, first among anticommunist social democrats but then within certain minority sectors of the Communist Party, who turned towards more openly reformist positions throughout the 1970s.[24]

The idea of a 'Bad Godesberg of the right' was raised by those who called on the MSI to abandon its ties to historical fascism, and the metaphor became especially entrenched when the party met for its congress at another spa town, Fiuggi, south of Rome, in January 1995.[25] Ever since Fini's return to the leadership and the collapse of the First Republic, figures both in and outside the MSI had proposed a redefinition of the party, as the barriers to governmental participation began to fall away. First was the Catholic intellectual Domenico Fisichella, who had been a contributor to journals in the orbit of the MSI, like *Intervento*, since the 1970s.[26] Writing for *Il Tempo* on 19 September 1992, he called for a new formation on the right. To bring 'order' amid the 'chaos' of the Italian political system, it was necessary for 'those who have had enough of the joys of progressivism to form a National Alliance'. This meant overcoming old taboos: such a process would entail 'different moments of political commitment in and among the parties: changes of leadership, mergers, separations and cultural revisions'.[27] If the left was changing its spots to seek broader appeal, the right had to respond in kind. This theme, and the 'Alleanza Nazionale' name which Fisichella had proposed, were then taken up by MSI figures.[28] One such leader was the party spokesman, Francesco Storace, in an article published in *Secolo d'Italia*. He called for a 'step forward with respect to our tradition' in order to build a 'new right' together with other forces. With the end of the 'partyocracy' born of the Resistance, the MSI had to turn Italy into a 'presidentialist republic' where the executive would rule rather than parliament and its parties.[29]

Storace warned against merely 'gripping to the party banner' through 'another 40 years of opposition': the MSI had to seize its opportunity. Yet he drew criticism from many leaders reluctant to put out the long-guarded flame. Many especially rejected the analogy with the Italian Communist Party changing its colours after the fall of the Berlin Wall. For Assunta Almirante, there could be 'no question' of dropping the MSI's identity. She especially opposed the idea that her husband could be cited as a precursor for the turn. For Franco Franchi, for three decades an MSI MP, 'the only parties which dissolve are ones that have nothing left to say'.[30] For Alessandra Mussolini, it was 'totally unimaginable that anyone thinking of self-dissolution ... could find a following in the party'; she promised to 'resolutely defend [its] real political and ideal roots'.[31] In response, Storace made clear that he sought a 'confederation' built around the MSI rather than a dissolution of the party.[32] Fini insisted that the aim was not to renounce what had gone before but to continue it. From its approaches to Christian Democracy to the Destra Nazionale of the 1970s, the MSI had repeatedly sought to become the cutting edge of a wider alliance of the right, and the dissolution of the old Catholic-centrist party demanded that it step up to the historical moment. This was, Fini insisted, not a dissolution of the MSI but its continuation in more favourable conditions: the Alleanza Nazionale was not 'a party but a strategy, to call together all those who did not want a communist Italy and do not want a left-wing Italy'.[33]

At a 12 December 1993 central committee meeting, Fini used an old slogan to emphasise the continuity with the postwar tradition: 'no one can ask us to renege on fascism, when we clearly declare that we do not want to restore it'.[34] Yet he proclaimed the need for a 'clear and irreversible shift': the right should no longer be defined by the old antifascist–fascist binary, but seize the opportunity to join together in shaping the Second Republic. During its years of marginalisation the MSI's internal battles had often revolved around opposed visions of a future society: a 'National State of Labour', a 'traditionalist revolution' or schemes to replace an elected parliament with a representation of social 'categories'.[35] Yet, the opportunity to become part of a large coalition and even take up roles in government turned it towards a more tactical approach.[36] Even a series of short-term decisions could redefine the party in a manner that its militants had never really deliberated or agreed upon, given that the process of reforming the party was itself open-ended. Fini insisted that the party could remain true to its own traditions while also 'realising, together with other Italians who were never in the MSI, the dream of creating a better, fairer, cleaner, more respected Italy'.[37] This did not mean dissolution but evolution. It was on this basis that he called for the MSI to finally enter a 'third phase of its development' by becoming a broader front. Even more doubtful militants could swallow the idea that this was above all a marketing operation governed by electoral opportunism, not a real change of political identity.[38]

In 1994, the words 'Alleanza Nazionale' had already appeared in the MSI's electoral title. In the congress held at Fiuggi in January 1995, it formally dissolved itself into the Alleanza Nazionale. To mark the change it proclaimed a set of theses, 'Let's Think about Italy', which spelled out its commitment to liberal-democratic values. In the preamble Fini paid tribute to 'the people of the MSI ... which sacrificed itself for an ideal cause', continuing even through its decades of 'isolation and criminalisation'.[39] But this history was diluted within a much longer tradition that was not limited to neofascism: the 'right that had lived before, during and after the 1920s'.[40] Throughout the whole period from 1948, the MSI had always insisted that it did not seek to 'restore' the Mussolini regime: yet here Fini proclaimed the embrace of democratic competition. The generation who had made their careers in the Republic, and had now seen the collapse of the main antifascist parties, proclaimed their acceptance of the Constitution. The formal dissolution of the MSI was a traumatic moment for its old standard-bearers, and indeed was not accepted by all: Pino Rauti's wing split away to create a new force called MSI-Fiamma Tricolore. The departure of this old devotee of Julius Evola – and a figure heavily involved in the judicial affairs surrounding 1970s neofascist terrorism – itself provided a kind of ratification to the MSI's Fiuggi turn. It had as yet attracted few figures from outside the neofascist tradition:[41] in 1994, it elected fewer non-party independents on its lists than Almirante's 'MSI-Destra Nazionale' had in 1972.[42]

The document combined a celebration of the MSI tradition with the call for its 'evolution', in language echoing the 'end of History'. It proclaimed that 'the century of ideologies is ending, and burying the totalitarianisms that marked it'. This also had the function of separating a negative judgement on the dictatorial element of Mussolinian Fascism from any similar repudiation of the exalted tradition of 'the glorious MSI sections', the party of 'Almirante, De Marsanich, Romualdi and Michelini'.[43] In this sense, there was little real critical reckoning with the MSI's tradition, but rather a proclamation that questions of fascism and antifascism no longer mattered to present-day politics. A section entitled 'dissolve all the *fasci*' recognised that, while antifascism had been necessary in 1945 to restore democracy, this experience must also be 'consigned to history'. Hence, 'if the Right is correctly asked to unreservedly state' that at a certain point antifascism was 'the historically essential moment for the return of those democratic values that fascism had trampled upon, it is equally ... right to demand all should recognise that antifascism is not a foundational value unto itself'.[44] Rather, antifascism's 'promotion from a contingent historical moment to an ideology was used by Communist countries and the [Italian Communists] to legitimise themselves throughout the postwar period'.[45] Antifascism had survived fascism for 50 years for 'international and domestic reasons which no longer apply', and it was now time for it 'to go together with fascism, so that both face the judgement of history'.[46] If 'some in Italy and Europe conjure[d] up ghosts', there was to be no 'black opera on the Italian political scene at the turn of the millennium'; what was instead called for was a 'great, peaceful, libertarian, "conservative revolution"'.[47]

Fiuggi gestured to a culture of pluralism, including elements from the fascist tradition, but also the 'conservative revolution' promoted by antidemocratic reactionaries in the 1920s. It insisted that the 'political Right is not the daughter of Fascism', and 'the Italian right' had its roots in Italian national culture in general. To this end, it rhetorically namechecked a mishmash of ideological reference points – such as Joseph de Maistre, Carl Schmitt, Giovanni Gentile, Julius Evola and Gabriele d'Annunzio – and also Catholic social teaching and – as part of an 'inherence ... woven with national culture' – Dante, Machiavelli and 'even Antonio Gramsci'. Yet many turns of phrase revealed the ways in which the party remained steeped in fascist ideas: it counterposed the 'productive bourgeoisie' with the 'parasitic bourgeoisie' and called for the 'reconstruction of the national community'. The nation was itself defined in ethnic terms, such that a recognition of 'diversity' also had to include the preservation of Italian homogeneity. Hence the proclaimed 'absolute aversion toward racism' – which the theses deemed a 'totalitarian' ideology – sat alongside the claim that declining birth rates would lead Italy to become 'ethnically and culturally distorted and impoverished'.[48] Even old reference points appeared in updated language: the *foibe* were described in terms of 'ethnic cleansing', a term which had recently entered common use due to the Balkan Wars. The document dismissed the 1975 border treaty with Yugoslavia and called for future Slovene and Croatian EU membership to be conditional on the restitution of Italians' property expropriated after World War II, including their 'right to return' and 'rebuild their ethnic, social, linguistic, cultural fabric'.[49]

ELEPHANT IN THE ROOM

Fini's talk of 'pacification' between fascism and antifascism had already stirred doubts in his party prior to the Fiuggi congress. In December 1993, Fini had visited the Fosse Ardeatine, which had in 1944 been site of the bloodiest single anti-partisan reprisal in German-occupied Rome. Following a Communist partisan attack on the SS Bozen military police unit on the Via Rasella on 23 March 1944, killing 32, the occupiers drew up a list of 335 political prisoners and Jews. They then transported them to the Fosse Ardeatine caves, where they murdered them the following afternoon. Fini's visit was a symbol of contrition, but Alessandra Mussolini insisted that pacification meant an agreement among equals: 'to make peace, it is necessary to shake hands between sides. If not, it's a capitulation, which I do not agree with. And so far there's been no handshake, so the time isn't ripe.'[50] The conflict within the party over Fini's line returned to the news in May 1994, when one of the Nazis who had drawn up the list of victims, SS man Erich Priebke, was tracked down in Argentina by *ABC News*. His discovery was a sensation, making the front pages of almost all the national dailies. Party leader Fini agreed that Priebke should be prosecuted,[51] but the SS man also enjoyed much indulgence and calls to let the past stay in the past. In June 1994, when Rome city hall voted on a motion to become a party to the case, the MSI group was divided:[52] most councillors followed Fini's line and voted in favour, but Sergio Rampelli – future head of the Fratelli d'Italia parliamentary group – abstained, as did Buontempo; Antonio Augello voted against what he called an 'instrumental' document 'based in neo-antifascism'.[53]

Despite the rhetoric of 'consigning fascism to the past', Fini's public statements during the party's first spell in government had to be sure not to offend his militants. This was also visible during the Priebke affair, in the pointed distinction he drew between Italian fascism and Nazism. Another interview for *La Stampa*, on the 50th anniversary of the Allied landings at Normandy, was telling in this regard.[54] When he was told it was alarming that he needed to intervene to force his councillors to vote for the motion condemning Priebke, Fini insisted that he backed the prosecution and that those who considered the MSI to be a philo-Nazi party only showed their 'misunderstanding of who we are and what we have done'.[55] Moreover, separating a judgement on wartime Fascism from the motivations of postwar neofascists, Fini insisted that he had 'discovered the values of freedom and democracy in the MSI' because it had stood for these principles in an age when communism spread across Europe. Even in postwar Italy, he insisted, they had defended democracy against an overbearing antifascism: the 'Roman salutes and references to the Duce were, for us, the demonstration of an identity which others wanted to violently repress'.[56] In this sense, 'pacification' in fact required that others should respect the MSI's own identity, including its references to fascism. Also clearly visible in Fini's comments was the attempt to rescue the Mussolinian past by separating it from his embrace of Adolf Hitler: 'Up till 1938, a minute before the signing of the Racial Laws, I think it would be very difficult to pass a negative overall judgement on fascism.' He insisted that while he had identified with fascism, he had 'never defended the concentration camps'.[57]

Indicative of the challenges to antifascism, Priebke's defence – first with his acquittal in August 1996 and then a retrial in summer 1997 – drew indulgent judgements from many across the right wing of Italian politics. Venerable conservative journalist Indro Montanelli made one of the most striking interventions, citing his correspondence with Priebke: for the *Il Giornale* founder, the SS man had no choice but to 'follow orders' or else he would have had to 'commit suicide'.[58] Priebke's initial acquittal, on the grounds that he had obeyed the German military code, drew outrage from victims' groups, but right-wing pundit Vittorio Sgarbi denounced the atmosphere of recrimination. Having met the defendant at Regina Coeli jail, Sgarbi claimed that while Priebke had long been a free man, he was now being prosecuted only 'after he did an interview [with ABC] where he confirmed his anticommunism'.[59] Sgarbi agreed that the SS man's actions made him 'morally reprehensible', yet he was 'innocent in penal terms'.[60] For MSI veteran Teodoro Buontempo, the antifascists behind the initial attack were 'guiltier' than Priebke, and also to blame for the reprisal at the Fosse Ardeatine;[61] judge Maurizio Pacioni even launched an investigation into the authors of the partisan action. Priebke's first retrial in July 1997 handed down a long jail sentence, and he spent the rest of his days under house arrest in Rome. This, too, stirred up objections. The Lega leader Bossi used the Alleanza Nazionale's response to the case to highlight this party's 'fascism'.[62] One of his own MPs, Antonio Serena – a former MSI youth activist – more indulgently termed Priebke the victim of a 'hate-spewing Jewish lobby'.[63]

As Bossi's comments indicated, this was a period of conflict on the right: in December 1994, the Lega Nord pulled out of Berlusconi's government, and then made a pact with the centre-left to support a technocratic cabinet. This also helped Fini to position his party as a more reliable partner for Forza Italia, and indeed the Fiuggi document in January 1995 strongly criticised this party's agenda for regional autonomy. Divisions over what was called the 'national question' hardened, as the northern-regionalist Lega Nord began to call for the independence of the area it called Padania, even holding a mock election for a 'Padanian parliament'.[64] The postfascist party, traditionally more rooted in southern-central Italy, staunchly defended the centralisation of the Italian state. In the April 1996 general election, Forza Italia and Alleanza Nazionale ran jointly with small Christian democratic forces but separately from the Lega Nord. In this contest, won by the centre-left, Fini's party again picked up voters: Alleanza Nazionale hit a historic high 15.7 per cent, though it fell to 93 seats in the lower house, whereas Bossi's Lega Nord lost half its MPs, falling to 59, despite surpassing 10 per cent for the first time. While Forza Italia was still the main right-wing party, on 20.6 per cent, this result also put Fini's party closer than ever to challenging it, and he also sought to undercut his ally-rivals by appealing to their base. The April 1998 Verona congress, which drew up Alleanza Nazionale's new programme, was telling: building on the agenda set out at Fiuggi, the document was rich in rhetoric about the centrality of the market, albeit combining this with references to the state's role in shielding citizens from the effects of globalisation. Yet much had not changed. Polling conference attendees, political scientist Piero Ignazi found that only 3 per cent considered Mussolini's regime the 'best possible', but 61 per cent found it 'a good regime despite some dubious choices' and another 18 per cent saw it as the 'inevitable response to the communist threat'.[65]

In this spell of opposition, Fini sought not just an alliance with Berlusconi, but to claim the leading role in the wider right-wing camp. Since 1994, there had been proposals to fuse Forza Italia and the Alleanza Nazionale into a single party; yet this also raised problems given both the neofascist competition from Rauti's MSI-Fiamma Tricolore and the question of how to merge a party of politicised cadres with Berlusconi's personal vehicle, which lacked local branches or structures for collective decision making.[66] Ahead of the June 1999 European elections,[67] Fini sought to out-manoeuvre Forza Italia by forming a separate coalition with the former Christian Democrats grouped around Mario Segni and Pierferdinando Casini. Together they formed the 'Elefantino' list, so nicknamed with reference to the US Republicans' logo. *La Stampa* wrote that this promised 'the birth of a liberal-democratic party that would cut the Alleanza Nazionale's last postfascist roots and be strong enough to offer itself as the real moderate party of the centre-right'.[68] This was, moreover, conceived in the context of an electoral reform planned by Massimo d'Alema's centre-left government, which sought to harden the system's majoritarian logic and create something akin to a US-style two-party divide. Yet, the April 1999 referendum on the proposed change failed, and in June's EU elections the Fini–Segni pact took barely over 10 per cent, whereas Berlusconi's list scored 25 per cent. With the Lega Nord also performing dismally, on 4.5 per cent, Berlusconi's leadership of the right-wing camp remained impregnable.

The May 2001 general election brought the right-wing alliance back to national government, with Forza Italia easily the strongest force in a coalition including both Alleanza Nazionale and the Lega Nord. Bossi's party had put its separatist pretensions on ice, but again suffered heavy setbacks, becoming clearly the third most important force. At the start of Berlusconi's second cabinet, the Alleanza Nazionale again took over junior ministries, but there was a difference compared to 1994: Fini was himself the deputy premier, and later in this term he also became foreign minister. Together with Bossi, he wrote one of the parliament's most important pieces of legislation, on immigration. Building on a law passed by the previous centre-left administration, which established the terms of illegal and regularised migration, the Legge Bossi-Fini of 2002 significantly toughened the apparatus of migrant removal, with forced removals of undocumented migrants, the use of the navy to police Italy's maritime borders and harsher penalties for people-traffickers. The Alleanza Nazionale's Verona programme of 1998 had declared immigration to be 'necessary and probably inevitable', and at the 2001 Naples Congress it saw the influx of newcomers as 'inscribed in our future for at least two generations'.[69] Yet, while these conferences emphasised the link between immigration, problems of public order and Italy's changing demography, they, like the Legge Bossi-Fini, did not seek to stop all immigration but to use punitive measures to ensure a 'strong government' could regulate who was allowed into Italy.[70]

During Berlusconi's first brief stint as prime minister in 1994–5, the creation of the Alleanza Nazionale had already been decisive in reframing the old neofascist MSI as a 'postfascist' force, and

Fini would make a further move away from the fascist past during the second government led by the tycoon. Upon the right-wing coalition's election victory in May 2001, the Alleanza Nazionale leader had become deputy premier, and in this same capacity he made a highly publicised visit to Israel over 23–6 November 2003. This was an official visit arranged between the countries' respective embassies, and during his time there he met with both Israeli President Shimon Peres and Prime Minister Ariel Sharon. While the MSI had previously damned the Racial Laws of 1938 and made generic statements denying that it was an antisemitic party, Fini's comments upon his visit to the Yad Vashem in Jerusalem went further in denouncing Italian Fascism's role in the Holocaust. Just days before the trip, he suspended former Lega Nord MP Antonio Serena, who, having earlier claimed that Priebke was a victim of a 'Jewish lobby', circulated a video of Priebke's biography among MPs with a note terming this a 'document of supreme human value'.[71] With Serena on his way out of the party, Fini's visit to Israel was a moment to draw a line under the issue: he later claimed that his words there would 'finally take fascism off the Italian political horizon and consign it to the judgement of history'.[72]

Visiting the Yad Vashem, Fini condemned the 'shameful' Racial Laws of 1938 and their role in paving the way to the Shoah.[73] In a speech, he insisted that it was 'time to take responsibility', 'denounce the shameful pages in our past' and embrace 'the duty to pass on memory, and do everything possible to prevent the fate which the Nazis reserved for the entire Jewish people being reserved for even one human being in future'.[74] 'In the face of racism and antisemitism, no one can say I wasn't there, it's not up to me, it's up to others to do something', he added.[75] Yet, while this sounded like a condemnation of his own side, there was also an element of redemption based in the contradictions in its own history. While, he lamented, most Italians had failed to act to stop the crime in its tracks, Fini could celebrate the memory of one of the 'Righteous among the Nations' – Giorgio Perlasca. A former Fascist who had volunteered in the wars in both Spain and

Ethiopia, Perlasca had nonetheless spent the final years of World War II helping to save Hungarian Jews.[76] At a press conference following his visit, at which he was also photographed wearing a kippah as he lit a candle, Fini was asked whether fascism should be termed 'the absolute evil'. The Alleanza Nazionale leader replied that such a phrase would be appropriate as a description of Fascism's role in the extermination of the Jews.

While Fini had led his party for over a decade, his comments sparked strong protests even among many of its top leaders. News agencies had, inaccurately, reported a blunter statement – 'Fini: fascism is the absolute evil', proclaimed *La Repubblica*[77] – and cited responses to this harsher judgement.[78] Salò veteran Mirko Tremaglia, an MP for the MSI since 1972 and a close collaborator of Almirante, told the paper that Fini had gone too far in embracing antifascism: 'since 90 per cent of antifascists are communist, antifascism cannot be the foundation of this Republic. I don't need any certificates of my democratic standing.'[79] Upon his return to Rome, the Alleanza Nazionale was forced to calm tempers, with an intervention at a book presentation that was then reproduced in the party newspaper. Here – seemingly the only time the words 'absolute evil' passed his lips in public – he used them in a much more qualified sense that was less directly offensive to the heirs to the fascist tradition. For Fini, 'if the Holocaust represents absolute evil, this also applies to the acts of fascism that contributed to the Shoah. We know that there are also many other moments in fascism's complex history, but if we want them to be recognised by all Italians without triggering the conditioned reflex accusation of revisionism, we must uncompromisingly denounce its misdeeds and tragedies.'[80]

FACTIONALISM

'I think Mussolini was a good politician. He did what he did for Italy. There haven't been other politicians like him these last fifty years.'[81] Followed by French TV ahead of the 1996 general election, a 19-year-old Giorgia Meloni didn't seem keen to denounce fascism. The leader of Alleanza Nazionale's high-schooler wing Azione Studentesca, she became a local councillor in Rome in 1998. As Stéphanie Dechezelles writes, this was a time in which the culture of the neofascist youth was changing. There were still scraps with left wingers during late-night poster-ing sessions, and cadres able to boast of past battle scars enjoyed special authority among younger militants; yet this was no longer the marker of leadership qualities that it once had been.[82] Meloni often cites her young age as a reason not to consider her politi-cal activity within the framework of fascism and antifascism, as such labels were irrelevant to those who became politically active in the 1990s. Yet the MSI whose youth wing she joined in 1992 remained deeply shaped by its past, not least in the section she fre-quented, at Rome's Colle Oppio. Named after refugees from the Yugoslav borderlands of Istria and Dalmatia, and led by swimmer Fabio Rampelli, Colle Oppio was a historic centre of the more identitarian wing of the party, and its fascist attachment would not disappear just because Fini had proclaimed its allegiance to freedom and democracy. Rather, the years following the turn at Fiuggi showed the limits of its cultural change and the multiple different trends at work within the party.

With few exceptions, almost all the main leaders of Alleanza Nazionale were former MSI cadres. But they repeatedly reorga-nised into different internal factions, of which three in particular governed party life at the turn of the millennium. There were the elements closest to Fini, uniting the 'liberal' and 'pluralist' currents. Then there was Destra Protagonista, which was in the tradition of Pinuccio Tatarella and now led by Ignazio La Russa and Maurizio Gasparri; it generally had the warmest relations with Berlusconi. Then there was the Destra Sociale, led by Rauti's son-in-law Gianni Alemanno and Francesco Storace, which defended a 'communita-rian' economic model and was most explicitly hostile to neoliberal economics.[83] The differences between them had already been visible in the late 1990s, and the second Berlusconi government would heighten their conflicts. In this sense, the Jerusalem speech in November 2003 was a watershed moment: before Fini touched down in Rome again, Mussolini's granddaughter Alessandra had already announced that she was quitting the party. Speaking to leading talk show presenter Bruno Vespa, she insisted that 'Fini has betrayed – betrayed how we feel. I am tired of watching these blatant tactical moves and cynical politics, and I choose my heart, respect for feelings and dignity. Fini has not done that.'[84] Lazio regional president Storace held a thousands-strong rally, with Assunta Almirante as guest of honour, at which he promised to defend the MSI's legacy even if this meant a split with Fini.[85]

Leading figures in Destra Protagonista put their own spin on Fini's comments. At the faction's December 2003 conference in Arezzo, La Russa insisted that little had changed: 'There is no break [from what was done at] Fiuggi but a logical and consistent continuation of the theses that we agreed on voting for there – unless, that is, anyone was not sincere and had mental reservations.'[86] His comments markedly limited the critical scope of Fini's intervention and directly contradicted any idea that Fascism was an 'absolute evil', to be condemned en bloc. 'I thank Fini because he has made us freer in historical judgment today', *Corriere della Sera* quoted La Russa saying; '[o]nly having condemned – without ambiguity or mincing words – the negative pages of fascism which Fini has rightly included in the absolute evil that is racism, antisemitism and the Shoah' would it also be possible, like other democrats, also to speak of 'the no few positive pages in the Fascist period and the far from shameful and sometimes stirring aspects of the [Italian Social Republic]'.[87] This ability to condemn the Holocaust while also recognising fascism's merits, the MSI veteran insisted, was a sign of continuity in the party's tradition: far from being disoriented, Alleanza Nazionale was 'the modern, European and democratic right that we wanted', even while 'reaffirming the same identity we have always had, the values of the nation, of the social, of security'.[88]

In this factional context, the battle over the party's youth wing, which emerged at its Viterbo Congress in 2004, was also decisive.

The activists raised up by the youth section had produced important leaders of the MSI, including Fini himself, and it remained
an important battleground between the party's internal factions.[89]
One candidate was Giorgia Meloni, a 27-year-old local councillor from Rome. She was supported by Destra Protagonista, the
current within Alleanza Nazionale founded by Pinuccio Tatarella, which had generally enjoyed closer ties with Berlusconi, led
by Ignazio La Russa. Fini sought to stem this current's influence
within the party and thus supported rival candidate Carlo Fidanza,
who was supported by Alemanno's Destra Sociale and closer to the
more 'rebellious' youth. Francesco Boezi suggests that the Destra
Sociale representatives' hostile reactions to Fini's visit to Israel put
'more moderate' figures off voting for Fidanza. Meloni's memoir
would speak of 'bitter, argumentative clashes between the supporters of the two candidates – by a handful of votes difference, I was
elected president'.[90] Yet, Fidanza later recalled, this congress was
also important to raising a future generation of leaders: 'Viterbo
left its mark on an entire generation ... it was above all the moment
where we really grew up, forging a leadership class that is today the
spine of Fratelli d'Italia.'[91]

Beyond disputes regarding the party's postfascist identity, there
were also notable conflicts over civil rights questions. In the 1980s,
partly under the influence of Pino Rauti, the MSI had already
begun taking greater interest in a broader array of social issues.[92]
Several revolved around the idea of new forms of alienation and
social breakdown brought about by the decline of traditional community, which the party labelled the 'challenges of modernity
and globalisation'.[93] This was also visible in the work of Azione
Giovani, including during Meloni's leadership, with its campaigns
against drugs and the contraceptive pill. Yet the role of Catholic
teaching and of the Church as an institution became especially
controversial in the party as its leader Fini increasingly embraced
more liberal positions without the support of most of his activists.
Indicative in this sense was his position in favour of a June 2005
referendum on assisted procreation; leading Church groups called

for a boycott in a successful attempt to make the vote invalid. Fini's stance was rejected by the leaders of both the Destra Protagonista and Destra Sociale, and Alemanno resigned as vice-president of the party in protest. Youth leader Meloni also opposed Fini's position.[94] The Alleanza Nazionale congress in July sought to heal the divides: it passed Fini's report, promising to 'reaffirm, ten years since the party's birth, its national, Catholic, social, liberal identity'.[95]

POPOLO DELLA LIBERTÀ

Often in this chapter I have spoken of decisions taken and prompted by Fini personally. The Alleanza Nazionale was, without doubt, a party heavily centred on its leader, and from November 2004 it was also emboldened by his status as the Italian foreign minister. Yet there were also intense factional battles over candidates and positions, which were formalised in the existence of a 'triumvirate' in which each wing of the party was represented. Berlusconi had again relaunched the prospect of a 'centre-right constituent process', which was meant to create a single party; yet even within Alleanza Nazionale, the factional leaders (called its 'colonels') were unwilling to let Fini raise himself above its internal structures. On the first weekend of July 2005, the leader's congress report promised to 'overcome the competition among [different] currents',[96] and he promised that he would 'govern the party without recognising [their] existence'.[97] Just two weeks later, the conflict came to a head: the Rome daily *Il Tempo* reported a conversation overheard in a bar close to the Chamber of Deputies, in which environment minister, Altero Matteoli, and the two main leaders of Destra Protagonista[98] – Ignazio La Russa and Mauro Gasparri – were overheard openly discussing whether Fini could go on as leader. The conversation turned on Fini's ill health and 'trembling hands', with the party vice-presidents speculating that he must not be allowed to lead the party into the 'constituent process' for the new party, or indeed the next general election.

While the revelations brought grovelling apologies, Fini's response was swift: he sacked the entire leadership layer, making it clear that he alone was party president.[99]

Fini had tried to integrate the MSI into a broader tent, and to this end he tried to consign both fascism and antifascism to history in the name of 'pacification'. This was a contentious process which encountered major resistance in the party ranks. This was possible because of a wider reordering of the political terrain that was also closely connected to the implosion of the old party system. While Ignazio La Russa insists that 'history itself' freed the MSI tradition from its condition of illegitimacy and marginalisation, the fact that other forces on the right chose to interpret the fall of the Berlin Wall in this particular way was also decisive. Silvio Berlusconi's right seized on 1989 as a condemnation of the overweening state – or even the public sector – and, for the purposes of mobilising the largest possible flank against the left, even welcomed longstanding fascists into his coalition. In the 2006 election, the 'centre-right' House of Freedoms coalition included openly neofascist groups, including Roberto Fiore's Forza Nuova, Luca Romagnoli's Fiamma Tricolore and Alessandra Mussolini's Azione Sociale. These were small forces, and Berlusconi put some conditions on the alliance, refusing the candidacy of Avanguardia Nazionale founder Adriano Tilgher. But the billionaire's ambitions were also broader, seeking to integrate the old Alleanza Nazionale within a party under his own leadership. This merger was briefly realised in 2009, but it did not last, and its fallout would lead to a series of splinters; in 2012 it resulted in the creation of a new postfascist party, Fratelli d'Italia.

The April 2006 general election was the Alleanza Nazionale's last. Neither of the smaller neofascist parties elected MPs, and while they secured nearly 500,000 votes, this did not stop Alleanza Nazionale from slightly increasing its own vote to 4.7 million, albeit with a loss of seats from 99 to 71. The overall result was a narrow defeat for the right: the centre-left Unione took a one-seat majority in the Senate and won by fewer than 25,000 votes in the contest for the lower house. Berlusconi challenged the result in court, without success; but Romano Prodi's new cabinet, which was reliant on various liberal and pro-Europeanist forces as well as Rifondazione Comunista, was highly unstable. In this context, Berlusconi revived the project of forming a single centre-right party that would unite his supporters with Alleanza Nazionale, and in May 2006 again called for a 'Partito della Libertà'. This was reciprocated by Fini, who attended an Alleanza Nazionale executive meeting on 18 July with a document entitled 'Rethinking the Center-Right in a European Perspective'. Here, he called on the old party to 'go beyond Fiuggi' and join the European People's Party – since 1976 the EU's main Christian Democratic bloc – in time for the 2009 European elections. This agenda was accepted by the party congress in October 2006, but it faced internal opposition. In July 2007, Francesco Storace, who had been health minister in the last Berlusconi cabinet, proclaimed a new party called La Destra, which claimed to uphold the abandoned tradition of the MSI. He was joined by Sicilian postfascist leader Nello Musumeci, businesswoman Daniela Santanchè and Teodoro Buontempo, who in the 1970s had been the leader of the MSI's youth wing Fronte della Gioventù.

In January 2008, the Prodi government lost its Senate majority, and snap elections were soon called for April. This time, Alleanza Nazionale and Berlusconi's party ran one fused list, named Il Popolo della Libertà, with the Lega Nord and small Christian Democratic forces as allies. The build-up to the merger came with some conflict: Berlusconi's clear efforts to assert his leadership prompted accusations from within the postfascist camp that he had fomented the La Destra split himself in order to weaken his main ally-competitor. Fini opposed La Destra's inclusion in the centre-right coalition, and it instead ran in a separate list together with another small neofascist party, Fiamma Tricolore. There had already been conflict, upon La Destra's creation, when it adopted the MSI youth's historic torch logo, leading Azione Giovani leader Meloni to accuse him of illegitimately appropriating it, and the split group's lead candidate Santanchè hammered home its identitarian spirit in a war of words with Alessandra Mussolini. Santanchè had previously been Alleanza Nazionale's equalities spokesperson, and issued an 'appeal to Italian women' claiming that Berlusconi only ever wanted women 'on their backs'; Mussolini coarsely retorted that Santanchè was 'the perfect incarnation of a politically "horizontal" woman'. La Destra's candidate insisted that Il Duce would 'turn in his grave' to see her 'as Fini's assistant'.[100]

Berlusconi's coalition again romped to a majority in the April 2008 general election. The former Alleanza Nazionale was represented in his new cabinet, with La Russa responsible for defence, Meloni for youth and Andrea Ronchi for European affairs, while Fini became president of the Chamber of Deputies. Upon taking up this institutional role – supposedly above party politics – Fini stepped aside as Alleanza Nazionale president, announcing that the work of Fiuggi would now be completed with the fusion into Popolo della Libertà. La Russa was to take over in a caretaker capacity. Yet there were also signs that the full embrace of Berlusconi did not mean a final break with the neofascist tradition. On 8 September 2008, La Russa joined president Napolitano at an event to mark the 65th anniversary of the German invasion. The commemoration was held at Rome's Porta San Paolo, where demobilised troops and civilians had resisted the initial Wehrmacht onslaught. Where Napolitano, a former member of the Communist Party, paid tribute to the soldiers who refused to join the Salò army, La Russa added that this side were not the only patriots. He observed that 'he would be betraying his conscience' if he did not recognise that soldiers who fought for the Salò Republic, 'subjectively, from their point of view, fought believing in the defence of the Patria, opposing the Anglo-American landings'. Hence, 'even recognising different positions, they deserve the respect of all those who look objectively at Italy's history'.[101] La Russa made these comments the day after Rome's mayor, Gianni Alemanno, had passed a similarly ambiguous judgement, terming Fascism a 'project to which many people adhered in good faith'.[102]

The controversy demanded that Fini respond. That same weekend he was billed to speak at Atreju, an Azione Giovani gathering named after the lead character in *The NeverEnding Story*. Fini told activists that while some had surely joined Salò 'in good faith', it was wrong to equate the two sides: 'the men of the Resistance were on the right side, those of Salò on the wrong one'.[103] He pushed further than before, arguing that his party had not just surpassed fascism, in the sense of confining it to the past, but *was* antifascist: he claimed that 'the Italian right and especially the young must unambiguously say loud and clear that they identify with the values of our Constitution', indeed 'fully identify with antifascist values'.[104] Members of Azione Giovani were shocked and angrily heckled Fini.[105] Storace stuck the needle in, accusing Fini of 'irresponsibly stirring up hatred and making a far-left target of those who do not resign themselves to the truth of people who for decades denied even the *foibe* tragedy'.[106] Centre-left critics pointed out that while Fini 'personally' distanced himself from fascism, Alemanno and La Russa had surely meant what they said. Youth minister Meloni sought to ease tensions with an open letter. Her carefully calibrated statement returned to Fini's earlier rhetoric of pacification, as she declared 'enough about fascism and antifascism'.[107] She insisted her generation ought to be able to get over the past:

> I appeal to everyone, in and outside Azione Giovani ... across Italian politics. Please! We were born on the heels of the 1980s–90s, we are all turned soul, heart and head toward the new millennium. We must all reject this attempt to lock the wonderful youth, who held Italy's largest youth rally a few hours ago, into the cramped space of almost a hundred years ago.[108]

OUT OF THE PARTY

Fini had become the leader of the MSI youth, then the party itself with Almirante's personal blessing, but increasingly became a liberal 'moderniser' in conflict with his party. With the end of the Cold War and the Italian political system based upon it, he led the veterans of the MSI over a series of hurdles, in the attempt to form a broader party which could mould the Second Republic. Some Christian Democrats congratulated him on the bid to form a 'normal' right. Each time, there was a progressive distancing of his party from an identity focused on neofascist assumptions and a growing separation between judgements on the MSI tradition and the historical regime. This required several stages, from the first project for the Alleanza Nazionale, to the formal dissolution of the MSI, to the condemnation of the 'absolute evil' and, finally, to Fini's own 'identif[ication] with antifascist values'. Each such statement came with multiple qualifications and contradictions; often the tone of the intervention and the backlash against it, notably in the case of the 2003 visit to Israel, had a broader effect on public perception than the literal content of what was said. But through all this we see that the political normalisation of a post-fascist party was not just an artefact of its obedience to antifascist speech codes, but rather a by-product of its involvement in government. Berlusconi was often less bound to pay even formal or conditional respect to antifascism than Fini, making many statements that trivialised Mussolini's rule and the 'holidays' on which he sent opponents. Only on 25 April 2009, four weeks after the two parties fused, would Berlusconi mark Liberation Day for the first time, 15 years after he first became prime minister.

What Berlusconi in 2019 called the 'legitimisation' and 'constitutionalisation' of 'the Lega and the fascists' also had a contradiction in the norm erosion in which he was himself involved. While corruption had already become a highly visible political issue in Mani Pulite, the governments which Berlusconi led – allied to his own personal involvement in multiple criminal cases – intensified a strong politicisation of the justice system and its decisions, which in turn embroiled his allies. His party raised to high office figures steeped in organised crime and the P2 masonic lodge, and passed *ad personam* legislation designed to protect his business interests;

and he was banned from public office in 2013 after his definitive conviction for tax fraud. Many current Fratelli d'Italia leaders who joined the MSI in the early 1990s, including Meloni, claim that they first entered politics in response to the murder of antimafia prosecutor Paolo Borsellino; the party claimed to be 'clean' and 'honest' unlike the 'partyocracy'. They would later vote to protect associates such as Marcello dell'Utri – later jailed for his historic role as a mediator between Berlusconi and Cosa Nostra mafiosi – from prosecution, and indeed to back up Berlusconi's story that he had pressured Milan police to release the teenage prostitute Karima El Marough, alias 'Ruby Rubacuori', from custody on the grounds that he believed she was the niece of Egyptian dictator Hosni Mubarak.[109] The political 'legitimisation' often demanded a dubious attitude towards legality.

As president of the Chamber of Deputies, marginalised from a direct political function, Fini grew impatient with Berlusconi's use of his office to evade charges – a problem connected to his overbearing control of the fused party and the former MSI leader's own related loss of influence. One point of tension owed to Fini's public support for granting voting rights to immigrants in the name of integration, which was rejected by the large majority in the party. After a heated exchange where Fini threatened to form a separate parliamentary group,[110] on 22 April 2010, at a national leadership meeting of the fused party at the Auditorium della Concilazione, Berlusconi publicly berated Fini from the stage, accusing him of deliberately undermining it and challenging him to resign from his institutional post. Fini stood up and shouted back: 'What are you doing, kicking me out?' Soon Berlusconi did just that. Fini and a smattering of allies formed a new grouping called Futuro e Libertà, which allied with some of the same liberal and Christian Democratic forces included in the Elefantino coalition back in 1999. While Fini insisted that his new party would not be a 'small Alleanza Nazionale but a bigger Popolo della Libertà', from the outset his project lacked resources and activists. His supporters were in the minority of the board of the Fondazione AN, the party foundation, and Fini was soon distanced from the party which he had led for two decades.[111] He would later insist that the reason he had been expelled from Popolo della Libertà was not about economic or integration policies, but rather that he had refused Berlusconi's request to press the parliamentary Justice Commission to shorten the statute of limitations barring convicts from public office.[112]

Fini's critics within the postfascist camp often accused him of being the 'kind of Right that wants to please its opponents', and in December 2010 he joined with the parties of the centre-left in launching a no-confidence motion against Berlusconi. It failed by a narrow three votes. Yet the mounting financial crisis was undermining the bases of the tycoon's fourth government. On 5 August 2011, European Central Bank chiefs Jean-Claude Trichet and Mario Draghi sent it an ultimatum: unless it mounted wide-scale privatisations and labour reforms, the European Central Bank (ECB) would no longer guarantee its credit supply. The open letter looked like a whole programme for government – a suspicion confirmed when president Napolitano appointed former European Commissioner Mario Monti to the Senate. Amid mounting market pressure, and EU leaders' signals that they would not step in to help the government, Monti was levered into the prime minister's office. For some in Popolo della Libertà, this was outrageous interference. Long-time Berlusconian MP Guido Crosetto damned the party's failure to stand up for itself, and voted against the budget-tightening European Fiscal Compact.[113] Faced with a fait accompli, Berlusconi ordered his MPs to support Monti's cabinet of technocrats, alongside the centre-left Democrats and Fini's allies. Crosetto was not the only leading figure in to bristle at this, and figures from Gianni Alemanno to youth wing Giovane Italia began pushing former youth minister Giorgia Meloni as a candidate in a party primary. Berlusconi moved to cancel the contest; on 30 November 2012, Meloni told *La Repubblica* that any idea of splitting back into Forza Italia and Alleanza Nazionale would be 'nostalgic folly'. Four weeks later, Meloni and Crosetto announced that they were creating a new party: Fratelli d'Italia.

4

In-Laws, Outlaws

'[We had to] break out of the ghetto, without going "moderate".'[1] Half a century since the foundation of the MSI's youth wing, former leader Gianni Alemanno told right-wing daily *Libero* about the attitude its cadres had brought into the institutions. Alemanno still upholds the MSI's traditions: he even wears a Celtic cross necklace belonging to his friend Paolo di Nella, the fellow MSI member murdered in 1983. On one recent anniversary, Alemanno observed that while di Nella is evoked as a symbol of pacification, he was an 'intransigent', symbolising 'the purity of the Struggle "on the field of Honour"'.[2] In 1982, he had bonded with di Nella in Rome's Rebibbia jail, when they were investigated for a Molotov cocktail attack on the Soviet trade mission. They were eventually acquitted, but this wasn't the last time Alemanno saw the inside of a cell. In 1989, as MSI youth leader, he was arrested at a protest against George H. W. Bush's visit to the Allied war graves at Nettuno. This was only the start of Alemanno's journey through the Republic's institutions, and in this same Facebook post commemorating di Nella he defended the path taken: his party had to overcome the 'logic of opposed extremisms and blood feuds to be able to serve our People and National Community'. It could not hope to gain national leadership if it remained a party of street fighters. Yet it was 'even more necessary not to betray the deeper values of Tradition and Identity and the people still rooted in them'.[3] The political protégé of Pino Rauti, in 1992 he became his son-in-law, marrying his daughter Isabella.[4] Yet, after the dissolution of the MSI, he moved in a different direction, joining Berlusconi's coalition. From 2001, he was the minister of agriculture and forests, and was then elected mayor of Rome for Popolo della Libertà in 2008.

While Alemanno took to more institutional environments, some of his supporters surely hadn't 'gone moderate'; they greeted his election as mayor with Roman salutes and flares outside city hall.[5] Yet, with Italian and international media relaying these scenes, the new first citizen made a series of interventions aimed at presenting a less contentious tone. The week after his election, he visited the Fosse Ardeatine, as Fini had in 1993. Even during the campaign, Alemanno had emphasised his support for Israel and condemnation of antisemitism,[6] and upon his election he announced plans to build a Holocaust museum. Some doubted the need to spend more on such memorials: councillor and La Destra leader Francesco Storace said it was only right to commemorate the Holocaust, but decried more 'public money being wasted' to please 'the same-old [Riccardo] Pacifici', head of Rome's Jewish Community.[7] Yet Alemanno's gestures also had other audiences in mind. He accompanied hundreds of Roman school children not just to Auschwitz but also to *foibe* sites;[8] even his intervention at the Fosse Ardeatine moved its story away from a specifically anti-fascist account. For Alemanno, the Resistance's 'values of freedom, against the [German] occupiers' were surely 'above dispute'; but in the interests of 'mending splits in the nation' it was important to 'shed light on the element of hatred and civil war, and condemn abuses on all sides'.[9] In September, Alemanno headed to Israel, again seemingly treading the same path as Fini. But, ahead of his departure, he publicly insisted that Fascism, apart from the Racial Laws, could hardly be considered the 'absolute evil' when many people had joined it 'in good faith'.[10]

Historical revisionism by local mayors has often been divisive, even testing in testing the limits of legality. In Affile, east of Rome, in 2012 Mayor Ercole Viri unveiled a mausoleum honouring Salò defence minister Rodolfo Graziani. He termed the general, who spent his final years in Affile, an 'example to young people' who was honoured 'as a local citizen',[11] while the council website praised

Graziani for 'directing his entire action to the good of the Patria through his inflexible moral rigour and soldierly duty'.[12] Others pointed to Graziani's record as a war criminal: as well as having 100,000 Libyans interned in concentration camps in 1930–1, he ordered the use of mustard gas during the invasion of Ethiopia in 1935–6, and in the Salò Republic decreed the death penalty for those resisting the draft. In 1948, he was convicted of collaborationism, with specific reference to his role in Salò, but he served only four months of his 19-year sentence and then became the MSI's honorary president in 1953. The official opening of the mausoleum drew such major postfascists as Francesco Lollobrigida – Meloni's brother-in-law and from 2018 head of the party's parliamentary group – but also prompted a criminal case against council leaders for 'fascist apologism'. Mayor Viri, of this same party, was convicted in a first trial in 2017, but the verdict was overturned by the Cassation Court in 2020 on the grounds that 'commemoration' – in this case, a shrine emblazoned FATHERLAND / HONOUR, with a bust of Graziani's head – is not 'exaltation'.[13] Graziani's home village of Filettino also boasts a children's park named after him, and Fratelli d'Italia mayors elsewhere have honoured figures like Fascist aviator Italo Balbo, a colonial governor of Libya, and Fascist education minister Giuseppe Bottai, who excluded Jews from Italy's classrooms.

Much as US white supremacists at the turn of the twentieth century built monuments to the Confederate Lost Cause, Italian postfascists vaunt their power through symbolism, which proclaims that even top regime leaders can be honoured for reasons other than their fascism. Yet the fascists they bring into the public realm do not only take the form of statues or street signs. They also sometimes appear among the personnel they bring with them, or the militant groups their administrations allow to gain influence. This was visible during Alemanno's spell as mayor of Rome, which soon earned his administration the names 'Parentopoli' ('Relativesville') or even 'Fascistopoli' on account of the former *camerati* who rose to prominent roles. One notable case was former 'Naziskin[head]' Stefano Andrini. After a spell in jail for attempted murder, in the 1990s he produced a magazine together with Avanguardia Nazionale founder Stefano delle Chiaie, but then took up a more mainstream role with Alleanza Nazionale minister Mirko Tremaglia. In 2009, Alemanno appointed him as CEO of the Italian capital's waste management business AMA.[14] At the end of Alemanno's time as mayor, a scandal broke called Mafia Capitale, centring on the distribution of public tenders among criminal gangs. At its centre was Massimo Carminati, who, since the 1970s, had been a leading figure in the terrorist group NAR and the Banda della Magliana, a Mafioso organisation implicated in political murders during the Years of Lead. Carminati, together with his less political criminal associates, including Salvatore Buzzi, the head of a web of cooperatives, were able to take control of municipal services contracts, which allowed them to embezzle tens of millions of euros. Both men were handed lengthy prison sentences in 2017. However, Alemanno's precise role in Mafia Capitale, and in this sense the case's properly political aspect, remains unclear: the latest hearing in January 2022 handed him a jail sentence for illegal financing and influence trafficking, but he is yet to exhaust his appeals.

While Carminati used public contracts for criminal financial ends, this is hardly the only sense in which neofascists try to gain a foothold within the Republic's institutions. They do so through their presence in public politics, mainstream TV debates and even electoral alliances with more established right-wing parties. Much as La Russa spoke of Almirante's success in bringing unwanted 'stepchildren' into democracy, this permeability of Italian democracy to neofascist representatives is justified even by mainstream pundits on the grounds that all opinions should be able to be 'constitutionalised', separating them from political violence.[15] Is it not true that killings declined steeply in the 1980s? That the appointment of even far-right ministers has not produced dramatic social conflicts akin to the Years of Lead? Even amid protracted social and economic crisis, the level of political violence in today's Italy is much lower than half a century ago. Yet the relation of cause and effect here is dubious. First, because neofascists are able to run in elections does not mean there has been a straightforward pacification of these militants, some of whom have murdered, beaten and harassed ethnic minorities and left-wing activists in recent years, motivated by the same conspiracy theories which appear in their campaign materials. Moreover, it is not the case that their ability to participate in democratic forums has broken their tie to fascism. Rather, as this chapter shows, they bring fascist ideas into mainstream platforms and even institutional settings. As we shall see, this has also raised questions over the meaning of constitutionality and the legislation governing fascist expression, and in 2017 prompted a far-reaching public debate.

Until Fratelli d'Italia's recent advance, journalistic accounts of Italy had often paid more attention to the spectacle of extra-parliamentary groups than to the postfascist tradition. There are important distinctions to be drawn between their political creeds and their forms of activism, as they are often at loggerheads with one another. The neofascist milieu has many disparate elements, and the historical reference points that they have in common do not define them as a single tendency.[16] We see this even in the rival groups that claim the tradition of Rauti, including CasaPound, which is famed in the international media for its postmodern aesthetic, relatively youthful base and much-publicised provision of food aid to what it calls 'Italian families'. But there are also older parties, like Forza Nuova, which is a mobilising force in anti-LGBT and anti-abortion movements and was an important actor in street protests against lockdowns and vaccine-based restrictions during the Covid-19 pandemic. Alongside these we also find organisations like the Milan-based Lealtà Azione, which first emerged in skinhead and football hooligan circles, and the Veneto Fronte Skinheads, a product of the neo-Nazi music scene of the 1980s. A closer examination of the cases of Rome, Milan and Verona shows that these forces each have eclectic ideological references, strategic outlooks and forms of activity, not to mention local particularities.

Given such variety, we might doubt that the individual militant is drawn to one or the other by their treatises so much as by the webs of family and friends that structure their recruitment. Yet, certain basic assumptions bind them together, and the circulation of both ideas and personnel allow them to join common political mobilisations, even when they are not electoral allies.

THE MARCH FROM ROME: CASAPOUND

Pierre Milza asks whether modern neofascism is 'the resurgence, in modern guise, of the currents that ran through the twentieth century' or an 'absolutely new phenomenon, related to the post-modern and post-industrial era'.[17] He argues that it 'adapts its arguments to a social demand that has evidently changed since a century ago, having to take into account in its electoral calculations the adherence to democratic principles of a majority of Europeans'; yet he concludes that it 'has remained fundamentally what it was', even through its development.[18] This means not only rebranding but adapting to changes which have remoulded the whole political spectrum. This is partly because of the changes of the post-1968 years – through the liberalisation of social mores, the softening of hierarchies and a long decline in political parties' ability to direct or even discipline their social bases – and partly because of the diversification of media. But we should properly speak of two distinct moments, in which the social movements of 1977 represented a distinct cultural shift. Made up of myriad local experiences and demands, it was not aimed at building the 'party of insurrection', or still less electoral politics, but challenged institutional power of all kinds, from parties and media to universities and psychiatric wards. In 1960, the youth revolt joined forces with the official workers' movement, and after 1968 it integrated much of its energy into major reforms as well as wage rises. In 1977, this did not happen. This was the time of the 'historic compromise', with external Communist support for the Christian Democratic government. Created amid economic crisis and soon implementing austerity measures, this pact bound the Communists to the government and forced the opposition into extra-institutional channels. But this was also a time when factory mobilisation had started to ebb, as had the small Leninist parties that arose in the '68 period proper.

This also gave rise to different ways of doing politics. In the '77 movement this meant an emphasis on 'being together' and everyday life outside of the Republic's institutions. State crackdowns following the Red Brigades' kidnapping and murder of Aldo Moro in 1978 hit social movements hard, striking not only at armed groups but also thousands of activists in far-left organisations who were not involved in violence. Following this repression, social centres developed in the 1980s and 1990s as spaces mostly used by activists outside of institutional parties. More than just activist hangouts or the home of DIY music scenes, social centres provided a base for outreach through mutual aid, cultural events and street mobilisation. In many cases they secured a more formalised existence that was recognised by municipal councils. This phenomenon mostly developed to the left of the Communist Party or even railed against it. Yet the kind of cultural change it represented also had distant echoes in neofascist movements, notably in the youth groups on the fringes of the MSI. First was the world of magazines and cultural reviews that emerged in the 1970s, for instance youth member Marco Tarchi's satirical *La Voce della Fogna*, and the three Camp Hobbit festivals where neofascists put on alternative rock concerts, plays and political discussions.[19] Such innovations earned some suspicion from MSI leaders, but also pointed in the direction of a more cultural approach to political action – even meaning its fusion with escapism and fantasy, at a time when other militants were sinking into terrorism. Yet the alternative rock scene developed more broadly in the subsequent decade, including in groups which had open neo-Nazi affiliations or held the 'Third Position' against capitalism and communism.

In 1995, after earning his political spurs in various small neofascist groups, Gianluca Iannone co-founded Rupe Tarpea

Produzioni, a record label that served as producers for neo-Nazi rock group Hobbit. One of its other acts is ska band Zetazeroalfa, of which Iannone is lead singer. It debuted in 1997 at the Cutty Sark, a pub a few hundred metres from the old MSI section at the Colle Oppio. While Zetazeroalfa lyrics often allude to historical fascism, it has always promoted a rebellious and irreverent image: what neofascists call 'non-conformism'. One song on its title album ironically declares its 'ska dedicated to the Italian Republic / ska dedicated to officers, freemasons and sons of bitches!'[20] Iannone and his bandmates later formed the initial nucleus of social centre CasaPound, whose website credits the group's role in its creation: Zetazeroalfa 'began to set the lucid madness of the Cutty Sark crew to music. The group acts as a thickener of souls, the clan grows larger and becomes cemented.'[21] Telling of the kind of camaraderie this produced, one of the group's songs is called 'Cinghiamattanza', giving its name to a ritual where shirtless, male audience members beat each other with their belts: a bare-chested 'dance among *camerati*'. As the lyrics put it: 'One: I take off my belt; two: the dance begins / Three: I take good aim; four … the leather in the air gives form to the dance / Only the warrior caste practices cinghiamattanza.'[22] The beatings are, however, not only consensual: in 2008, Iannone received a ten-month prison sentence for his role in a brawl with left-wing activists at a concert in the Abruzzo region, and the following year he got another conviction for punching a plainclothes policeman in Mussolini's hometown of Predappio, which he visited upon the anniversary of Il Duce's death.

At the turn of the millennium, Iannone's associates entered more public political activity. The 1990s had already seen attempts to create neofascist social centres, and in 2002 several groups occupied a property to the north of Rome which they labelled CasaMontag. It was named after Guy Montag, the hero of the dystopian novel *Fahrenheit 451*, who rebels against a conformist order where he is made to burn books. This occupation represented what one participant called the attempt 'to show by example that we, too, can do what the Left has done for decades'.[23] Even before Alemanno became mayor, various neofascist groups were able to occupy buildings in the capital, such as Casa d'Italia and Cerchio e Croce. In December 2003, Iannone and his *camerati* occupied a six-storey building on Via Napoleone III, in the capital's Esquilino district, which took the name of the philo-Nazi poet Ezra Pound. While from its foundation the word CASAPOVND was spelled out in two-foot-high stone lettering, the two Chinese-run shops in its lower floor also pointed to this neighbourhood's multicultural population. It may seem odd that city hall, even under centre-left administrations, would allow a property worth millions of euros to be illegally occupied by a neofascist group, and remain so for two decades. Yet CasaPound has enjoyed remarkable official indulgence, which reached its height under Alemanno's administration. The Rome council removed CasaPound from the official list of 'abusive occupations', attempted to buy the building on its behalf and even granted a charitable foundation run by CasaPound control of other properties.[24]

CasaPound defined itself as a 'rebellious' movement that stood outside the left–right divide: what Iannone termed a movement of the 'extreme upper centre'.[25] It declared itself not only a 'non-conformist occupation', a space available for militant use, but one 'meant for inhabitation'. Terza Posizione founder Gabriele Adinolfi, an ideologue for the group, emphasises this difference, distinguishing it as 'a niche culture' 'with positive value' but which risked a 'subcultural, ghettoising' approach – 'the comfortable wish to barricade ourselves in' – as against 'going on the offensive', 'daring and entering the fray'.[26] CasaPound is well known for outreach, including its direct distribution of food outside of supermarkets, whose success is also owed to its knack for stunts, reported by duly prepared press releases and then projected back into Italy by international reporters struck by its 'hipster fascist' aesthetic.[27] This is also visible, for instance, in its claim to fill in for absent law enforcement and even conduct border patrols at sea[28] and to promote conspiracy theories which command mass media attention, such as a 2019 scandal about alleged child abduction by social services in Bibbiano, Emilia-Romagna.[29] However, advice bureau and food bank efforts are also promoted by social centres closer to the institutional right, such as Casaggì, a self-managed 'identitarian space' created by the Alleanza Nazionale youth in Florence in 2005.[30] It refers to many of the same thinkers as Casa-Pound: the poet from which the Roman social centre took its name as well as Tolkien, Evola, D'Annunzio, the French fascist Robert Brasillach and Ernst Jünger, a theorist of 'conservative revolution' who rejected the Nazis. Casaggì has openly claimed that its story derives 'from Fascism and its immense heritage of ideas' – its 'timeless and eternal values'. It is today attached to Fratelli d'Italia, claiming local groups around Tuscany.[31]

Compared to Casaggì, CasaPound has historically been more independent in its alliances, but formed a national party organisation at the end of the 2000s.[32] From its inception, it was attached to another small extraparliamentary party, the Movimento Sociale Fiamma Tricolore. While this had begun life in 1995 as Pino Rauti's vehicle, he was expelled by a new leadership under Luca Romagnoli and Giulio Castellino, and in 2004 it integrated other neofascist leaders such as Piero Puschiavo of Veneto Fronte Skinheads. In that June's European elections, Romagnoli was elected to the European Parliament. In 2005, it joined a wider regroupment, including Alessandra Mussolini, Forza Nuova and former Avanguardia Nazionale militant Adriano Tilgher's Fronte Sociale Nazionale, which then ran in the 2006 general election as a minor partner in Berlusconi's 'centre-right' bloc.[33] Iannone was also a candidate, but the alliance of small neofascist parties did not win any seats and the pact soon fell apart.[34] In the April 2008 general election, a separate alliance of Fiamma Tricolore and Francesco Storace's La Destra again failed to win seats, scoring 2 per cent nationally. Two weeks later, Alemanno was elected mayor of Rome with Popolo della Libertà. This caused a split in Casa-Pound, and Castellino created a grouping seeking closer ties with Alemanno,[35] seemingly aimed at providing a base for the mayor within the movementist 'social right'.[36] Later in 2008, CasaPound declared itself to be a national party, forming sections in other cities while also racking up a few dozen local councillors. In some early cases these were elected on Popolo della Libertà lists, even at a time when this was the largest party of government nationally and controlled Rome city council.[37]

CasaPound has often claimed to have many thousands of activists. Membership demands a much higher degree of engagement than registering as a supporter of an electoral party; this means not just ideological sympathy but also volunteer commitment and participation in the activist community. CasaPound does, nonetheless, also devote real effort to public debates and the written word. Placing itself in the broadly 'social' fascist tradition, it has distanced itself from certain parts of the regime's heritage: for instance, Iannone has claimed that his movement rejected the Racial Laws of 1938, because Jews had contributed to the 'Fascist Revolution'.[38] In 2005, CasaPound founded the bookshop Testa di Ferro, and it also boasts publisher Altaforte, run by Francesco Polacchi, and a summer school of debates called Direzione Rivoluzione. These forums also seek to integrate figures from outside the neofascist tradition: in this sense, its online magazine *Il Primato Nazionale* is especially indicative. Founded in 2013, and becoming a print monthly in 2017, it frequently features figures such as Diego Fusaro, a student of Marxist philosopher Costanzo Preve and today one of Italy's most in-view public intellectuals. Calling himself a scholar of Antonio Gramsci, Fusaro adopts fragments of Marxist terminology and integrates them into a nativist frame, with his characteristic denunciation of 'turbo-capitalism' and 'hyper-globalisation', which he accuses of promoting the 'Third-Worldisation' of Italy. CasaPound also often hosts book presentations on the neofascist tradition that include historians who do not belong to its own circles.

While CasaPound cites fascism as a source of ideological inspiration, it shows ideological novelties with respect to Rauti's wing of the MSI. Notable in this regard is its eclectic array of reference points. These include Salò-era fascism, as well as left-wing anti-imperialists such as Irish Republican Army hunger striker Bobby Sands, and – more unusually for a neofascist group – the betrayed promise of the Italian Constitution written in 1946–7 by the main Resistance parties. A January 2018 *Primato Nazionale* editorial celebrated the Constitution's invocation of the protection of labour and the need for the state to intervene where private property and market competition contrast with society's well-being.[39] Guest contributor Fusaro has also emphasised this theme. In one 2018 piece for *Il Primato Nazionale*,[40] he cited former Bank of Italy Governor Guido Carli's claim that the Constitution is 'the point of intersection between the Catholic and the Marxist conceptions of the relations between society and state'; Fusaro argued that this is what the 'global-elitist', 'postdemocratic', 'no border', 'free market' elite now seeks to destroy.[41] He accuses these same 'elites' of a war against the cultural fabric of Italy, with the 'gender totalitarianism' of 'forcing children to write gay love letters', or the bid to 'Third-World-ize' Europe through mass immigration.[42] CasaPound's belated appropriation of the document, as a generic banner of Italian nationhood, includes the claim that the document is not antifascist in spirit,[43] an argument only falsely used by antifascists to determine the boundaries of the 'constitutional arch'.[44]

CasaPound's website boasts of its 'militants, supporters and friends working in institutional politics, cultural posts and associations decisive to the nation's social life'.[45] It denies that it is an 'extra-parliamentary force' or 'violent': it 'is not interested in showing its muscles', 'rebellious extremism' or 'hooliganism'.[46] This comes with a caveat: it 'cannot allow anyone to challenge its legitimacy to act and exist' and will not 'refuse confrontation when it is forced upon us and necessary for our political and physical survival'.[47] It places a premium on physical preparedness, with many of its local sections' activities devoted to combat sports, wrestling, boxing and the martial arts. Yet the language of self-defence is also euphemistic and self-indulgent. A 2016 parliamentary report found that CasaPound members had been arrested 20 times in the previous five years, in response to 359 reports; from 2013 to 2018 the Osservatorio delle nuove destre reported 66 attacks.[48] This is also a party which has alleged a 'totalitarian' and 'immigrationist' threat to Italian society and calls for a complete migration ban until all 'illegals' are repatriated.[49] In two cases, militants who were either in CasaPound or closely associated themselves with it have murdered West African immigrants. On 13 December 2011, Gianluca Casseri, a CasaPound activist in Pistoia, launched a shooting spree against Senegalese traders in Florence, murdering Samb Modou and Diop Mor and injuring three other men. In Fermo, in the Marche region, on 5 July 2016, Amedeo Mancini beat to death the Nigerian Emmanuel Chidi Nnamdi, whom he called a 'monkey'. After the killing, several photos circulated of Mancini taking part in various CasaPound initiatives; antifascist activists reported seeing him steward a Salvini rally in this province in May 2015.[50]

This was a period in which the Lega extended its relationship with CasaPound, as new leader Salvini created a nationwide, nationalist party. In the 2014 European elections, Mario Borghezio MEP – a veteran of both Jean Thiriart's 'national-revolutionary' Jeune Europe movement and Ordine Nuovo – ran in central Italy, with CasaPound activists mobilising for his successful campaign. Then, as the Lega leader launched a personal vehicle called 'Us with Salvini' intent on mobilising in central-southern regions, CasaPound's vice-president, Simone di Stefano, announced an allied 'political subject' called Sovranità. It was included in Lega's rally against Democratic Prime Minister Matteo Renzi on 28 February 2015, with di Stefano among the speakers. The Casa-Pound representative told reporters that while other neofascists might prefer to 'remain marginal', he was interested in 'winning',[51] and during his intervention proclaimed that CasaPound agreed with 'every single word of Matteo Salvini's programme',[52] citing its support for Italy leaving the eurozone, stopping immigration and putting 'Italians first'. Di Stefano was followed on stage by

Meloni, likewise speaking against the backdrop of waved Russian flags, at a lectern whose branding invited the audience to join the Lega. This intervention prompted internal criticism for her subordination to Salvini,[53] and when another rally was held at Rome's Brancaccio theatre on 11 May, she was absent; instead, di Stefano boasted that Sovranità was winning over Fratelli d'Italia councillors.[54] In the 31 May 2015 local and regional elections, CasaPound ran Sovranità candidates on Lega lists as well as independently.

While this national-level collaboration did not last, the cooperation with Salvini surely drew considerable focus to di Stefano. After the Piazza del Popolo rally he was invited onto TV station La7,[55] on which he debated Democratic MP Emanuele Fiano, the son of a Holocaust survivor. When Fiano commented that he 'didn't make a habit of discussing with fascists' and began to speak of fascism's guilt in the Holocaust,[56] Di Stefano interrupted to insist that whereas this happened 'years ago', today's problem is an intolerant antifascism. He repeatedly pushed the centrist Fiano to defend a slogan popularised among far-left militants during the Years of Lead: 'killing a fascist is no crime'. When Fiano replied that 'it is a crime to kill anyone', di Stefano continued to bark the same question. Later that same year, Fiano authored a bill aimed at strengthening legislation against fascist propaganda.[57] The postwar Scelba law banning fascist apologism has often been used to suppress violent neofascist groups but is not consistently applied to fascist propaganda; its constitutionality was also challenged by MSI members, citing their right to freedom of association. Two Constitutional Court rulings in 1957 and 1958 ruled that eulogising fascism was a crime only if liable to promote the 'reconstitution of the fascist party', opening it up to highly subjective interpretations, with many contrasting rulings on the admissibility of, for example, collective fascist saluting.[58] The 1993 Mancino law strengthened the code's antiracist dimension, but Fiano's bill more specifically defined the forms of banned fascist propaganda: it aimed to criminalise the 'propagation of images or content proper to the Fascist Party or the German National Socialist Party or the related ideologies' as well as 'publicly recalling the symbolism or gestures' of these parties 'or the related ideologies'.[59]

Fiano's bill reached the floor of the Chamber of Deputies in July 2017. The first discussion came the same week as a furore around a beachfront owner in Chioggia, Veneto[60] who had created a seaside display with photos of Mussolini and quotes from both the dictator and Ezra Pound, with text insisting 'in my place, the regime is still in charge'.[61] The owner received a police visit, but Salvini then also came to the beach to pose in front of the offending materials. The Lega leader cited the incident as grounds to abandon existing laws against 'fascist apologism'; he told his followers that it is 'crazy to put ideas on trial'.[62] Many right wingers came to the concession owner's defence; Fratelli d'Italia senator Daniela Santanchè said that she had a 'beautiful wooden bust of Il Duce on [her] nightstand', but insisted this gift was not a 'tribute to fascism'.[63] Most interventions regarding the Fiano bill focused on symbolism: *Libero* editor Alessandro Sallusti damned it as 'illiberal' since 'being a fascist is not and should not be a crime' if it did not mean 'propaganda to reconstitute the Fascist Party'.[64] Giampaolo Pansa called the legislation 'pointless', because there is no 'fascist threat',[65] and emphasised the triviality of criminalising the wearing of 'a pendant with Mussolini's face'. CasaPound mounted their own shorefront patrol in Ostia to drive away immigrants illegally selling wares on the beach.[66] Meloni ridiculed the Democrats for ignoring real crimes while imposing 'three years [in jail] for having a cigarette lighter with Il Duce'.[67] In the parliamentary debate, her party colleague, La Russa, insisted the law prohibited not only 'speaking, saying, writing, thinking, depicting, drawing, painting, sculpting things that this political regime does not like. But it also ... tells you how you have to move your body.' Adding, 'be careful about raising your hand over your shoulder', the veteran MSI man raised his arm in a mock Roman salute.[68]

MILAN'S BLACK BARON

La Russa has often joked that being called a fascist is a 'compliment'. At the start of the 1970s, he was already a well-known MSI cadre in Milan, a city whose neofascist movement both used this party's sections as hangouts and came together outside of them. This was most famously illustrated by the Piazza San Babila. Maurizio Murelli, the neofascist jailed for throwing two hand grenades on 'Black Thursday' in 1973, would later describe the square as 'a sort of little D'Annunzian Fiume, the only "unconquered" part of the Milan of the time'.[69] Others remembered it a little differently: for Mario Capanna, one of the leaders of the left-wing student movement in those years, it 'was [the far-right's] meeting place and permanent base for provocations and punitive expeditions ... you only needed to cross the square with an eskimo coat or a beard ... or even just [the wrong] newspaper, to be beaten or even stabbed'.[70] To challenge neofascists could be a death sentence. At 10.30 pm on 25 May 1975, five militants saw Alberto Brasili and Lucia Corna walking through the square and stripping off an MSI election poster.[71] Neither of the young couple were known as activists, but the way they dressed might have suggested they were generically left wing. The neofascists caught up with them, then repeatedly stabbed them both – in Brasili's case, fatally.

Piazza San Babila is no longer associated with neofascists. The bars overshadowed by its vast regime-era *palazzi* became yuppie hangouts in the 1980s, and the square ultimately became a reference for journalists for different reasons. It was here that Silvio Berlusconi gave an impromptu speech from the running board of his car in 2007, announcing the creation of a united right-wing party, which became Popolo della Libertà. Even when neofascists do meet in the piazza, we see a different scene to the Years of Lead, albeit with some of the same names. Indicative in this regard were the events held for La Destra and Fiamma Tricolore's joint 2008 election campaign, running as a separate alliance outside of the Berlusconian coalition. Their first rally in the city was on March 5, with billed speakers including leaders of these small parties but also Murelli and two members of a neofascist group called Cuore Nero. Another rally on 30 March convened at the Teatro Nuovo, on the west side of the square, addressed by lead candidate Daniela Santanchè. She told militants that she would not 'betray [the party's] memory' but was also 'forward-looking': some may call her fascist, but she was 'proud to identify as fascist, if fascist means being against the cultural hegemony of the Left, if it means kicking illegals and irregulars out on their arses, if fascist means the Patria must belong to those who love it'.[72] The part of this statement qualifying it with 'if fascist means ... ' was almost drowned out by cheering and shouts of 'Duce, Duce'.

Some of the audience members who greeted Santanchè's words with Roman salutes held a banner proclaiming 'Cuore Nero'('Black Heart'), with a tricolore marked by a black skull-and-crossbones. This association was founded in 2007 by Alessandro Todisco – a member of 'Bonehead' skinhead circles and an ultra at football club Inter – and Roberto Jonghi Lavarini, who calls himself 'the Black Baron'.[73] He claims an aristocratic lineage, combined with what he calls a 'spiritual and traditional (chivalrous, aristocratic and imperial) conception of the world, of life and of my political engagement'.[74] Cuore Nero's first effort to create a base in April 2007 was thwarted by a firebomb attack on their building, but in September 2008 it opened a centre near to the city's Maggiore cemetery. Cuore Nero has used the symbol of a bundle of sticks bound with an axe; in one online video, leading activist Francesco 'Doppiomalto' is shown citing reading material from Nietzsche, D'Annunzio, Hegel, Mussolini, Evola and Gentile,[75] but insists that the *fasces* symbol is not inherently fascist: it is 'used in cities around Italy, though sadly that does not mean fascism exists in those cities'.[76] In one 2008 interview – standing in front of a banner with the words Cuore Nero written in black gothic font in a white strip surrounded by red – Todisco claimed it is a 'cultural' association that planned to distribute food to locals.[77] Jonghi Lavarini, a former MSI militant who used to run tour groups to Mussolini's home town, speaks of his 'well-known historical judgement on fascism, overall a quite positive one'.[78]

Jonghi Lavarini, a supporter of the Augusto Pinochet Foundation and Russian theorist Alexander Dugin,[79] noted in this same interview that despite his 'historical' observations, he was welcome in Popolo della Libertà. He had already advertised his attendance at a November 2010 rally in Milan, three months after Fini's expulsion. The rally, held at the Teatro Nuovo, billed Santanchè as a speaker alongside Ignazio La Russa and the city's mayor Letizia Moratti, elected with Berlusconi's support.[80] Writing of the union of 'the right' with Popolo della Libertà, Jonghi Lavarini emphasised the symbolism of the venue, including in a blog post adorned with a photo of him together with Defence Minister La Russa.[81] Noting the 'betrayals of others' – an apparent reference to Fini – he wrote that 'in the name of loyalty to its common ideal roots, the *missina* [MSI] right rediscovers and renews its political unity and action in the symbolic Piazza San Babila, at the PdL [Popolo della Libertà] demonstration in support of Silvio Berlusconi's government'.[82] Jonghi Lavarini also spoke as a Popolo della Libertà representative at other party meetings in the city, for instance in an event at a branch of the right-wing party which still bore the name of Gabriele d'Annunzio.[83] In 2011, he stood for Popolo della Libertà in the Milan local elections but was not elected. Of course, the politics of a local council candidate from ten years ago – and even his boasts of closeness to institutional figures – may not seem particularly significant. Yet Jonghi Lavarini's record also shows the porousness of the boundaries between neofascists and the institutional right.

This has included collaboration with Fratelli d'Italia leaders, most notably Carlo Fidanza. As Chapter 5 explains, when *Fanpage* produced a documentary exploring this connection in 2021, Meloni expressed amazement that Fidanza, the party's leader in the European Parliament, had associated with him.[84] This suggested a poor grip on party affairs, not least given that Jonghi Lavarini was a Fratelli d'Italia candidate for the 2018 general election.

During the campaign he presented a book damning 'radical chic' together with Santanchè in an upscale Milan nightspot,[85] making an intervention that suggested his candidacy in the 'centre-right' coalition had done little to moderate his worldview. Calling for a right-wing front that would be 'clearly politically incorrect, like Daniela Santanchè', he said it should 'go into the institutions head held high' to 'uphold our idea – a nigger is a nigger, a white is a white'.[86] Insisting 'our battle is a racial one', he denounced the left, 'who wouldn't let their poodle mate with a non-poodle', worrying about the 'extinction of pandas and penguins but not our race'.[87] To laughter, he claimed 'they want us all to be faggots and half-castes', denouncing a 'multisexual' ideology that would 'blend society like a smoothie' rather than respect harmony among 'differences'.[88] Jonghi Lavarini knew that some might call him a 'conspiracy theorist', but 'there are global political groups who want to ethnically substitute our people, by [us] no longer having children, and financing immigration'.[89] Denouncing an 'anti-national' Italian left that serves 'international finance capital',[90] he expressed his hopes for 'a truly centre-right government'.[91]

Jonghi Lavarini has also referred to brokering ties between right-wing parties and a Milan social centre called Lealtà Azione. This is not an electoral party but has at least several hundred, if not over a thousand, activists in the Lombardy region who are sometimes involved in electoral campaigning for others. In 2021, *Fanpage* recorded Jonghi Lavarini saying: 'They [Lega, Fratelli d'Italia] have institutional parties, the brand, and the others [movements like Lealtà Azione] have an activist base like no other party in Milan. And in exchange, since they can't give them institutional jobs, they [the extraparliamentary groups] say "I'll elect you but you put my guy in … " In the regional offices they're all Nazis.'[92] Jonghi Lavarini surely overstated the scale of this phenomenon and even its ideological profile. While it began life in the 2000s as the local referent of the Hammerskins, a US-based neo-Nazi music scene, and still today hosts concerts with such bands, Lealtà Azione has expanded wider. It has no public political programme, calling itself a 'social association'; in this vein it carries out similar activities to CasaPound, such as the distribution of food among needy households and offering a walk-in advice bureau. In September 2021, when Lealtà Azione opened a new meeting place in Gaggiano, south Milan, one leader spoke of antifascist opposition to its opening as 'pointless, stupid polemics aiming to restrict our association within the ideological bounds of a hundred years ago'.[93] One of the associations it runs, called Bran-Co, publicises its distribution of food and prominent involvement in 'calcio alla pedofilia',[94] a day of sport designed to send a message against child sex abuse.

Representatives of institutional parties have praised the group for its volunteer spirit and accepted invitations to appear at its events. In July 2018, the month after the Lega joined the national government, Igor Iezzi was one party MP to speak at a Lealtà Azione meet-up in Milan. 'I think it's the third time I've come', he told reporters. 'We have a dialogue with them. We work with them on – they are very rooted on the ground. I've often collaborated with them, not only – as you might think – on immigration.' Asked if it was antidemocratic, he replied that the police authorities had never decided to shut it down. It is, he insisted, not a political ally but a 'cultural association with various ramifications from sport to animal-rights issues'. Asked if he was seeking their votes, he replied that he thought he 'had them already and isn't ashamed of it'. Iezzi moreover positively compared Lealtà Azione's respect for the law to left-wing demonstrations that 'smash up cities'.[95] Another speaker at this same event was the Milan Fratelli d'Italia leader Fidanza, who rebutted criticism for associating with this group. He said he was there to talk about 'autonomy, federalism and sovereignty', issues central to 'the country's political agenda and dear to Fratelli d'Italia', and would discuss them with anyone 'who invites us, naturally in respect of the law and civil existence'. He would even agree to speak at a left-wing social centre Leoncavallo if it invited him, 'but there's much more openness on the right than on the extreme left'.[96]

This focus on legality – that any political collaboration is above criticism, if legal, and that extremism belongs only to the other political side – is common in the institutional right. For Forza Italia's Giulio Gallera, it was legitimate to debate 'within the limits of the Constitution and the laws'.[97] Yet while Lealtà Azione claims to stand above the ideological divides of 'a hundred years ago', this claim seems more dubious when we look at its 'memorial association', Memento. It leads hikes to sites of World War I, but also Mussolini's hometown of Predappio, and organises activities such as maintaining the graves of soldiers from the Salò Republic and commemorating its martyrs. To this end, it cooperates closely with the memorial groups created by Salò veterans in the postwar decades. While few real veterans are still around, their activities are continued by hundreds of young activists who adopt military-style formations and collective Roman saluting, albeit often in T-shirts and hoodies. Lealtà Azione can be said to have a certain dynamic of competition with CasaPound, as each group expands from its own initial city of reference. Yet these memorial events bring activists together, even including elected officials from Fratelli d'Italia. The unofficial commemorations held on 29 April each year to mark the death of Sergio Ramelli, the 18-year-old MSI activist murdered in 1975, are indicative of this. Hundreds of uniformed militants gather to collectively Roman salute and shout 'Presente!' Such anniversaries, often held at night such that the Celtic cross banners are illuminated by flames, unite Ramelli with other 'fallen *camerati*' from 29 April 1945 – men of the Salò Republic killed the day after Mussolini. They are held up as examples of the beginning of postwar antifascist terror; victims of the creed that 'killing a fascist is not a crime'.[98]

VERONA'S RIGHT-WING FAMILY

In November 1943, with the creation of the Salò Republic, the reconstituted Partito Fascista Repubblicano held its congress in Verona. It issued a new programme, declaring the "'Jewish race" foreigners and enemies in wartime', and promising to 'socialise' industry and 'abolish the "internal capitalist system"'. While public antisemitism was often diluted in the postwar MSI, especially by those who wished to distance this experience from Nazi Germany, the Verona Congress's 'anti-bourgeois' tones were commonplace in 'social' currents of fascism. Yet, this wartime reference is not the only reason why this part of north-eastern Italy has a deep association with this end of the political spectrum. In the 1970s, the Veneto region in which it lies was a centre of Ordine Nuovo, Franco Freda's Fronte Nazionale and other terrorist groups; judges identified the 'Padua–Verona nexus' between which militants moved. In 1973, the MSI had been forced to remove its leadership in Padua and put its 250 members under special measures due to militants' connections to violent and criminal groups.[99] In more recent decades, Verona has been identified as a laboratory[100] for a new kind of politics: one in which neofascists benefit from the protection and even career opportunities provided by right-wing parties in city hall. From the election of the Lega's Flavio Tosi as mayor in 2007 through his replacement in 2017 by his former deputy Federico Sboarina, Verona was widely labelled one of the main centres of the international far right, through the collaboration of right-wing institutional parties and neofascists, and a mix of ethnonationalism and religious conservatism.

Verona's recent history illustrates the Lega's specific role in opening up space for neofascists, even before Salvini made his alliance with CasaPound. Such an alliance may seem to belie the party's origins: at the February 1994 party congress, Umberto Bossi claimed the mantle of historical antifascism, insisting that the Lega Nord 'continued the partisan liberation struggle, betrayed by the partyocracy' and would 'never, never' 'ally with the fascists, never with their grandchildren, never!' It only took two months before the Lega Nord joined Berlusconi's first government alongside Fini's party, but, after breaking off this pact in December 1994, Bossi repeatedly denounced the Alleanza Nazionale as 'fascists'. Yet, while in this limited sense responding to northerners' 'antifascist' expectations, this party was also ethnonationalist. Party posters claimed that immigration was 'leading to fascism',[101] and in 2000 Bossi defended Austrian far-right leader Jörg Haider on the grounds that while 'Hitler exterminated the Jews, the Communist masons want to exterminate all European peoples with immigration. They're the real Nazis – red Nazis.'[102] Especially after 9/11, this political focus was expressed in Islamophobia: the Lega Nord mobilised to ban kebab shops from town centres (as was put into practice in the Lombardy region). It also issued electoral propaganda combining Osama Bin Laden's face with the words 'No Mosques' and, playing on stereotypes about both northerners' and Muslims' diets, made posters proclaiming 'yes to polenta, no to cous cous'.[103] Bossi-era posters also warned that northern Italians risked being deprived of their homeland 'like [American] Indians' who failed to restrict incomers.

But why is the Lega so strong in Veneto, especially among blue-collar voters?[104] While the Lega is often seen as the beneficiary of disgruntled workers abandoning the left, blue-collar votes were far from necessarily 'red' even when Italy had mass Communist and Socialist parties. Unlike industrial heartlands like Turin or historic centres of the labour movement like Emilia-Romagna, Veneto never had a strongly class-polarised vote, and throughout the postwar period its politics were dominated by Christian Democracy. As well as religious devotion, this owed much to its late industrialisation: while there were some pockets of rapid growth (notably the Porto Marghera petrochemicals hub), what dominated was a much broader mass of small manufacturers, where workers were socially closer to their employers and voted along similar lines. Yet the economic processes that began in the same period as the Lega's emergence in the 1980s – outsourcing, deindustrialisation and the cost pressures placed on exporters through Italy's entry into the European monetary system – destabilised this balance, even before the Mani Pulite investigations exploded the old Christian Democratic party. This also encouraged mobilisation around regional identity and opposition to both the perceived wastefulness of the central Italian state and spending on southern regions. In this sense, the Lega premised its electoral offer to blue-collar Venetians not on welfare or workplace rights so much as economic and 'cultural' protection against the effects of globalisation. Illustrative in this regard is its fusion of tax cuts to keep exporters competitive and opposition to migrant labour. This also feeds into a broader nativist politics, repurposing the anti-immigration slogans which workers from Veneto had confronted when they emigrated to Switzerland and Germany.[105]

This often takes the form of the call for the strong state: in 2001, councillor Tosi ran a campaign calling on residents to 'sign up to immediately clear out the gypsies', for which he received a criminal conviction.[106] Tosi's victorious mayoral campaign in 2007 emphasised a public order agenda of expelling street hawkers and installing anti-homeless benches; he soon moved to shut down the left-wing social centre La Chimica. Yet the new administration was good news for a certain militant group not obviously associated with legality: Veneto Fronte Skinheads. This group began life in 1986 as part of the RAC (Rock Against Communism), White Noise and Blood & Honour music scenes, and for over three decades has held a 'Return to Camelot' festival, hosting Zetazeroalfa as well as internationally famous bands like Skrewdriver. Veneto Fronte Skinheads members have repeatedly confronted Gay Pride rallies, disrupted antiracist meetings and been involved in brawls in public spaces. In 1995, several leaders were handed criminal convictions for incitement to race hate, which were later overturned on the grounds that the relevant Mancino law was enacted after the incidents concerned. In 2004, founder Puschiavo joined Fiamma Tricolore, whose leader Luca Romagnoli was a member of the European Parliament, and which joined Berlusconi's coalition in the 2006 general election. While it did not win any seats in that contest, in 2007 another historic Veneto Fronte Skinheads figure, Andrea Miglioranzi, was elected to Verona council. The incoming mayor picked him as one of two city hall representatives on the board of the local Resistance history institute, before then retreating faced with a backlash; however, he still appointed him to the boards of various municipal enterprises. In 2012, he stepped back as a councillor but became president of the city's waste management firm Amia. Described by a local paper as 'known for dressing like a nineteenth-century count',[107] Miglioranzi is the bassist for rock group Gesta Bellica, in which Alessandro Castorina, another historic Veneto Fronte Skinheads leader, is guitarist. Its tracks include 'Foibe', 'Red Scum', its cover version of Bunker 84's 'Victime des Démocracies' and 'Il Capitano', a 2001 tribute to SS man Erich Priebke.

Castorina runs a football merchandise shop called Camelot, which suffered an anonymous bomb attack in 2005. The incident prompted a parliamentary question by Antonio Serena, the ex-MSI youth, ex-Lega member and ex-Alleanza Nazionale senator suspended from that party for defending Priebke. In a 2006 query addressed to the interior minister, he complained that while 'right-wingers' in Verona had been persecuted for 'crimes of opinion', antifascist attacks went unresolved. What were these criminal opinions? One, *La Stampa* reported, was that Castorina had called a former comrade a 'nigger lover'.[108] The 1995 trial also found that Veneto Fronte Skinheads members had held a celebratory dinner to mark the centenary of Adolf Hitler's birth.[109] A 1997 police investigation into 47 members found Nazi memorabilia and firearms. But later, in 2008, there came a crime that wasn't an opinion: five local neofascists killed 29-year-old graphic designer Nicola Tommasoli in a street ambush. The attack had no apparent relation to Tommasoli's political opinions, but perhaps it was because he looked 'different'.[110] Many local neofascists damned this futile aggression: one involved in CasaPound's Radio Bandiera Nera was reported as commenting, 'he wondered if they'd beat up a communist', but '[t]hey did something like a thug, not a fascist. I'm a fascist. Fascism is socialisation, progress.'[111] *La Stampa* cited Veneto Fronte Skinheads president Giordano Caracino as 'distancing himself from what happened' but adding: 'Fights are part of youthful headiness. We're not for the Christian ethic of turning the other cheek. There's only so much talk of this because in Verona we're all right wing.' This same paper also reported that Miglioranzi had commented that the killers 'weren't guys who should be crucified'.[112]

While not all of Verona is right wing, members of Gesta Bellica are not the only ones to have influenced the city's politics, including in close connection with the Lega and Fratelli d'Italia. Another scene in the city revolves around Luca Castellini, a long-time leader among football ultras at Hellas Verona, a club known for racist chants and even displays of fascist and Nazi flags. He faced media scrutiny in November 2019 after some of the home team's fans directed monkey noises against Brescia forward Mario Balotelli, born in Palermo to Ghanian parents. When interviewed about this incident, Castellini claimed that Balotelli will never be 'completely Italian' but specified that his club was not racist: 'we, too, have a nigger in the team – he scored yesterday and all of Verona applauded'.[113] These comments earned him a ten-year ban from home games. He was also interviewed at a march for Armed Forces Day. Castellini explained that his position was to defend Italy's differentness, as against 'ethnic substitution and multiracial society'. He claimed that, as opposed to 'peoples, territories, spiritual belonging', 'multiethnic society is nothing but an uprooting of people's roots to create a bastard [people] that can be controlled by the markets ... so for us both abortion and multiethnic society, so, forced migration, is the principle of globalisation'.[114] Pressed on what abortion has to do with immigration policy, he added that 'abortion limits and controls birth. And alongside the lack of European births there are the new Europeans, who obviously aren't European, so Europe is being substituted. Europeans aren't being born and they are being substituted by foreigners, immigrants.'[115]

Such speech could be connected with Forza Nuova's extremism: Castellini had also praised Adolf Hitler at a 2017 ultras rally, at which he chanted 'our team is *fantastica*, it plays in the formation of a swastika'.[116] Such positive references to German Nazism are rare among institutional right-wing parties, and this group often criticises Fratelli d'Italia for its 'betrayals' and 'retreats'. Yet the ideological connection between the defence of the traditional family, the 'pro-life' cause and the threat from immigration is not so distinctive: it is, indeed, habitual among Lega and Fratelli d'Italia representatives. One notable example is Lorenzo Fontana, who became Tosi's deputy mayor in 2016 and the national minister of families in 2018. Speaking to the Lega's national congress in 2017, he proclaimed: 'we don't need immigrants to cope with Europe's demographic crisis, we need to help European peoples to have more European children ... We want a Europe where marriage is between a mother and a father, we don't want to hear the other disgusting crap even mentioned.'[117] In the last parliamentary business before the 2018 election, the right-wing parties, aided by abstentions from the centre-left and Five Star, managed to thwart a bill to introduce *ius soli*, which would have granted citizenship to the children of immigrants. Far beyond this city, Forza Nuova and Lega members have each mobilised, and likely cooperated, in 'whistle-blower' groups which monitor the activity of pro-refugee NGOs.[118] Reports on Castellini after the Hellas Verona racism scandal highlighted the connection: at a rally in 2015, Fontana had marched directly next to the Forza Nuova militant at the head of a 'Verona Family Pride' march, behind a banner proclaiming these words in the sculpted sans serif font beloved of ultras.[119]

Fontana is often labelled a 'traditionalist Catholic'. Yet in Verona, 'pro-family' politics also take a very modern form. They blend a civilisational politics rooted in the French Nouvelle Droite, the Christian fundamentalism typical of US conservative pro-life and anti-LGBT movements and the conspiracy theories beloved of neo and postfascists.[120] Mayor Sboarina declared Verona a 'pro-life city' and his council devoted funds to pro-life organisations.[121] The connection between local politics and Catholic fundamentalism was most clearly illustrated in March 2019 with the staging in Verona of the 'World Congress of Families'. Sponsored by Fontana's ministry, city hall and the regional government, the speakers included Salvini, Education Minister Marco Busetti,

Mayor Sboarina, Russian Orthodox figures and even a Mormon elder. Forza Nuova members are active in groups like ComitatoNO194, which aims to remove all abortion rights; the son of its leader Roberto Fiore is a spokesman for ProVita, to which it appears to have many practical connections, and which was one of the sponsors of the World Congress of Families.[122] One Forza Nuova member labelled the bishop of Verona, Giuseppe Zenti, a 'hostage to the homosexual lobby' after the cleric said the themes in question did not 'deserve the violent and ideological language of these days'.[123] Addressing the conference, Fratelli d'Italia leader Meloni encapsulated the participants' foundational rejection of 'gender ideology'. She explained that identity is being reduced to digital serialisation: 'I can't define myself as Italian, Christian, woman, mother, no. I must be citizen X, gender X, parent 1, parent 2, I must be a number. Because when I am only a number, when I no longer have an identity or roots, then I will be the perfect slave at the mercy of financial speculators.'[124]

Where, in pro-life groups, neofascists join a broader right-wing mobilisation, the relationship can work the other way around, more directly conferring institutional legitimisation on them. In September 2019, Verona hosted CasaPound's national meet-up Direzione Rivoluzione. It included representatives from both the Lega and Fratelli d'Italia, including members of both the city and regional governments, albeit in a personal capacity.[125] La Russa addressed the CasaPound event in the most ingratiating terms, telling the audience that 'it was important for me to be [here] because I want to help give cultural legitimacy to this movement'.[126] The garrulous La Russa repeated a favoured joke of his, that when people call him a fascist, he replies 'steady on the compliments!'[127] His intervention referred to the existence of a 'sovereigntist front' which should be 'united at the grassroots level', including CasaPound; this 'in the name of a slogan that unites us all, invented by Giorgio Almirante: "Italians first"'.[128] This did not mean being against Europe but against one 'that puts Italians last'.[129] If La Russa likely sought to win these militants around to his own party's electoral agenda,

CasaPound's vice-president, Simone di Stefano, insisted that each force had a different role to play.[130] While it had withdrawn from the electoral arena, 'CasaPound has not stopped doing politics: our ideas are an added value, they have been taken up by other parties and movements'. For him, an electoral victory of the Lega and Fratelli d'Italia could be taken for granted, 'but it is not that simple. We have to build something solid: it is not just a matter of winning elections, it has to be an overwhelming victory, it has to be able to make a clean sweep of a system.'[131]

Yet, even this electoral success was a victim of the competition between the two parties. In 2017, at the end of Tosi's second term, he had to stand down, and was replaced by his deputy Sboarina. Not only did the new mayor began to distance himself from the 'incompetence' of his predecessor, but the city also became the centre of the nationwide competition between the Lega and Fratelli d'Italia, In 2019, the Veneto Fronte Skinheads founder Miglioranzi signed up to Meloni's party, and in 2021 Sboarina became the leading Fratelli d'Italia mayor in Italy.[132] However, while the party had proudly welcomed Miglioranzi to its ranks, announcing it in a press conference, the connection soon became an embarrassment.[133] In June 2020, he was suspended by Meloni's party due to a judicial investigation into his management of public waste firm Amia, centred on Mafioso involvement; in November 2021, he was handed a 32-month prison sentence for corruption as part of the case. Tosi himself came under investigation but was cleared, before making the handling of this service part of his 2022 campaign to reclaim the mayoralty from his former deputy Sboarina.[134] The June 2022 contest did not, however, prove quite the foregone conclusion that might have been expected. In the first round the two far-right candidates achieved over 56 per cent of the vote combined, with another 3 per cent for a list combining 'pro-family' and no-vax groups. Yet Tosi then refused to support Sboarina in the runoff, and the centre-left candidate secured a narrow victory – ending, for now, the experiment in a city known as a laboratory of the far right.

5

A Modern Right

Clichés about Italy's idiosyncrasies often mask deeper realities. One is the observation that it has had 70 governments since World War II. This paints a colourful picture: of Italians rallying behind the latest demagogue who then disappears leaving only broken promises. But the appeal of the outsider is not eternal but postmodern: a result of the end of the mass parties of the twentieth century, which reached their height in the years after World War II. From 1947 to 1992, the dozens of cabinets revolved around one party, the Christian Democrats, whose large numbers provided the main pillar of all governments. Its pivotal position was owed to its structural competition with the second biggest party, the Communists. The big-tent Catholic party habitually relied on smaller allies to form a majority, from centre-left pacts with Socialists to centre-right alliances with Liberals. Yet, while in this period the Communist Party never joined a national government, it helped structure the Republic, as a transmission belt between its own base and the national institutions. It had as many as two million members, deep roots in trade unions, cooperatives and working-class communities, and up to a third of the electorate. These parties had different ideological inspirations but also represented different parts of society; their local implantation, including their thousands of local party sections, were shaped by factors such as the relative impact of Fascism and the Resistance, the varied levels of industrial development and the organising pull of the Church, cultural and associational life and the labour movement. The Communist base was strongest among blue-collar workers in northern cities but also in regions with a long history of 'red' peasant organising like Emilia-Romagna; it also organised artisans, the unemployed, small traders and much of the intellectual professions. Christian Democracy had its core base among the middle classes and business, but was broadly stronger in rural Italy, the south and areas such as Veneto, whose profile we mentioned in Chapter 4. Over the decades, Italians' allegiances evolved, through such diverse processes as secularisation, consumerism and the rise of white-collar employment. This brought a gradual recomposition of these parties and the rise of various new forces, without fundamentally challenging the main blocs.

While in the 1980s there was a weakening of these parties' grip on their bases, the end of the Cold War and the Bribesville scandal pushed them towards collapse. The bulk of the Communist Party pivoted to a new social-democratic or even liberal identity; the Christian Democratic party all but disappeared. At first, this was widely greeted as a turn towards modernity: pundits and politicians spoke of Italy's prospects of becoming a 'normal' country – more peaceful, more 'European' and no longer bound to the 'Catholic–Communist' binary or even fascism versus antifascism. It would do without the mass parties: in just three years the number of Italians who were members of a party collapsed from more than four million to less than one million. The suddenness of the old parties' replacement also gave the newly rising electoral forces a strikingly artificial character, which replaced the political cultures built up over the twentieth century with brands and slogans drawn from marketing agencies or icons abroad. Left wingers discussed foreign models such as Germany's SPD and increasingly Bill Clinton's Democrats and Tony Blair's New Labour; Berlusconi declared his personal vehicle to be 'European, Christian, free-market and liberal' and the now 'postfascist' Fini looked to examples like the US Republicans. These parties coalesced into broad coalitions called 'centre-left' and 'centre-right', with fragments of old parties, but also new assumptions which came to frame all government action. This did not mean a renewal of the postwar constitutional pact but rather the growing erosion of democratic choice by unchallengeable market forces.[1] The European single currency was widely assumed to be the quickest route to 'normality', or perhaps a panacea for other ills that would impose the external constraint necessary to force Italy to become 'competitive'.[2] What was missing was the structural reforms, and the investment in education and infrastructure, that could make this possible; and the call for sacrifices now for pay-off tomorrow became an ever more constant asset-stripping of the public realm. This also hurt democracy itself, as the parties became less able to meet voters' concrete demands or aspirations for the future. Italians are poorer today than in the late 1990s and have lower wages, and even working-age Italians are less likely to have jobs. Those who saw ever less benefits from the electoral process stopped taking part: while up to the 1980s turnout regularly topped 90 per cent, in 2022 it slumped to under 64 per cent.

This decline of Italians' attachment to political parties has not produced a return of the social conflict that had dissipated in the 1980s. Rather, the result has been an increasingly volatile electoral politics, through the rise of 'outsiders' who channel anger but also express lowered expectations of what kind of change is even possible. Recent decades have seen not only a series of technocratic cabinets but the normalisation of the idea that political decisions stand above democratic choice. Illustrative of this was the formation, in 2011, of a technocratic cabinet led by former European Commissioner Mario Monti, whose ministers implemented austerity measures in the name of stabilising Italy's debt crisis. Supported by the liberal-Europeanist Democrats and Berlusconi's Forza Italia, but entirely made up of unelected officials, his cabinet helped fuel the rise of a kind of photographic negative in the form of Beppe Grillo's Five Star Movement. Opposed to everyone within political power, it claimed to represent everyone without political power, a mood expressed in its 'Fuck Off Day' protests in 2007. It proposed a rehash of Mani Pulite, desecrating the hated 'parties' and what it called their inherent corruption. Former comedian Grillo, who stood atop a byzantine internal structure,[3] made repeated provocations against what he called the 'partyocracy'; making a nod to far-right voters, he promised to 'March on Rome' and staged a photo-op outside CasaPound.[4] Such nihilism surely offended many antifascists. Yet polls after its first general election run in February 2013, in which it took 25 per cent of the vote, showed that it rallied support from across the political spectrum, with strong scores among the young, southerners and public employees.[5] Yet it was also notable for its near total lack of social policies – it was not an anti-austerity party, or one that challenged neoliberalism, but one that boasted of its unideological character: Italians were invited not to mobilise in a party or to build a different kind of society but simply to vote to 'clear out' the whole party system. In this same election, the newly created Fratelli d'Italia scored just 2 per cent, below even the percentage that the neofascist alliance La Destra–Fiamma Tricolore had taken in the previous such contest. Whereas Five Star exuded novelty, Fratelli d'Italia appeared as a backward-looking rump of the old MSI rather than a force to be reckoned with.

Yet the volatility has continued to shake up the party system. In June 2018, Five Star formed its first government coalition, with Lega leader Salvini as interior minister. He rallied the right-wing electorate and parts of Five Star's base behind his anti-immigration agenda, and in summer 2019 resigned in an attempt to force early elections, capitalising on his success. This hope was disappointed, as Five Star instead made a pact with the Democrats and Matteo Renzi's centrist Italia Viva. This was the first of several setbacks for Salvini, and the momentum within the right-wing camp began to turn away from him. Although, since its creation, Fratelli d'Italia had enjoyed a steady rise (from 2 per cent in 2018 to 4 per cent in 2018 and 6 per cent in the 2019 European elections), this gained pace after the Lega leader left government, and in late 2019 it hit 10 per cent for the first time. The formation of Mario Draghi's 'national unity government' in February 2021, moreover, allowed Fratelli d'Italia to nearly monopolise the role of opposition. Though the Lega was back in office, Salvini was unable to impose a strong agenda on either Draghi or the other govern-ment parties, and by July 2021 Fratelli d'Italia had overtaken it in national polls, on around 20 per cent support. Meloni has claimed this was not just due to missteps by Salvini but her own party's hard work: she often insists that her party faced a higher hurdle in reaching 5 or 10 per cent and becoming a credible electoral force at all than to move from this level to major-party status. Yet the single main force behind its growth is the pre-existing right-wing electorate. Salvini's party had, in the mid-2010s, benefited from this dynamic, winning votes from the former Alleanza Nazionale as well as Berlusconi's tumbling Forza Italia.[6] Only in late 2020 did Fratelli d'Italia's poll scores surpass the historic highs reached by Fini's party, which peaked at 5.9 million votes (16 per cent) in the 1996 general election. From this perspective, the September 2022 election was not a sudden breakthrough for the far right, but the result of a process underway since the 1990s. Pollster SWG found that 50 per cent of Fratelli's d'Italia's electorate came from the other right-wing parties, 17 per cent from Five Star, a similar amount from 2018 abstentionists and 16 per cent from its previous voters.[7] Its absolute vote (7.2 million) quadrupled its 2018 levels, but the overall right-wing coalition only increased its votes by 150,000 compared to four years previously. Hence the main factors in its success were shifts within the right-wing coalition, together with the collapse of the Five Star Movement.

So, is Fratelli d'Italia's victory the latest example of a success-ful 'populist' outsider? Or is it the end of the 'populist' moment, as an ex-fascist party becomes mainstream and conservative, thus constituting a 'modern right'? This chapter argues that it repre-sents something else. Its radicalism corresponds to a division of the political space between the limited array of policies that an Italian government can today hope to influence and those where its action faces strong external constraints. This was illustrated by the 2022 electoral campaign, in which Meloni's strategy relied on two main axes. One was about 'reassuring': the insistence that her government would not challenge Italy's international position (*col-*

locazione) by seriously diverting from the Draghi-era plan for EU post-pandemic funds. She strongly and repeatedly affirmed her commitment to NATO, arms supplies to Ukraine and the euro, and even criticised the Lega for suggesting that Italy could exceed EU budget deficit limits. Yet this was directly combined with a search for heightened conflict on issues around identity and immigration. Illustrative of this was her decision to republish a video of a Guinean immigrant raping a Ukrainian woman, in order to assert an association between race and crime. Even after Facebook and Twitter removed the post, and even despite the victim's own complaints about the video being circulated, Meloni continued for more than a week to talk about the issue and how she had been 'censored' by an intolerant left. Certainly, there are *some* tensions between 'Atlanticism', acceptance of the European order and harsh identitarian talking points: during the campaign, Fratelli d'Italia was one of the few parties to vote against a motion in the European Parliament which condemned human rights abuses in Viktor Orbán's Hungary. Yet this also illustrated the agenda of making Italy more like the central European nationalist governments: unable to seriously change the balance of forces in the EU, yet proudly identitarian and reactionary in dealing with their domestic opponents.

A 'NATIONAL CENTRE-RIGHT'

Pino Rauti's funeral on 5 November 2012 was a great meeting of the dispersed children of the MSI tradition. There was Giorgia Meloni, Ignazio La Russa and Maurizio Gasparri from Popolo della Libertà, the largest party in parliament.[8] There was Assunta Almirante and Francesco Storace, Rauti's daughter Isabella and her husband, the mayor of Rome Alemanno. Hundreds of militants waved Rauti goodbye with fascist salutes. But it was the attendance of Gianfranco Fini that made the most headlines. As the president of the Chamber of Deputies arrived at Rome's Basilica di San Marco, dozens of mourners began to shout 'fuck off' and 'get lost'. While Rauti and Fini had been *camerati* in the MSI for some two decades, the Alleanza Nazionale founder had a dismal reputation among those who opposed his many concessions to antifascism. This was surely the reason why the shouting and spitting also included shouts of 'Badoglio', the ultimate insult for someone from this political tradition. The name refers to the marshal who fought in Mussolini's wars only then to break with him in July 1943, abandoning the Nazi ally and siding with the Anglo-Americans. Isabella Rauti, at the time a member of Popolo della Libertà, intervened to calm the crowd, suggesting that her father's funeral was not the best place to fight this battle.

When Fratelli d'Italia was created in December 2012, Meloni and her allies had to assert their particular claim to the MSI tradition, as an independent force within the broader 'centre-right'. There were, indeed, other contenders. In 2013, Storace and allies, including Fiamma Tricolore's Luca Romagnoli and Futuro e Libertà leader Roberto Menia, formed a Movimento per Alleanza Nazionale which mooted forming a rival party. In response, Meloni and La Russa passed a motion at an assembly of the Fondazione AN – the foundation inherited from Fini's old party – which granted Fratelli d'Italia the sole claim to the MSI's historic logo.[9] At first the party integrated 'Alleanza Nazionale' into its name as well, with posters in the 2013 general election identifying this as a party of the 'national centre-right'. While Meloni and La Russa had been ministers in the Berlusconi government, in its first few years the party leaned hard into its rejection of the Fini era. This was partly a response to their former leader's own comments: when the party held its first congress in March 2014, in Fiuggi, where the MSI had been dissolved almost two decades before, Fini ridiculed the 'spoiled children' and their 'farce' of 'aping history' by trying to recreate the Alleanza Nazionale in wholly changed conditions.[10] Meloni retorted that it was Fini who was the 'father' who had left 'his children abandoned'.[11] Fratelli d'Italia started out small and in a relatively weak position. In the 2013 election it had elected nine MPs – well down on the 71 that the Alleanza Nazionale had scored on its final outing in 2006 – and it scored 3.7 per cent in the 2014 EU elections, falling short of the threshold to enter parliament.

At a time when Salvini launched televised attacks on antifascism and focused his party on an obsessive anti-immigration message, there was something of an arms race in 'sovereigntist' rhetoric between Salvini and Meloni, which was also inspired by the ideas circulating on the international far right. Faced with rising numbers of refugees crossing the Mediterranean, both leaders embraced 'great replacement theory' and launched harsh attacks on pro-migrant NGOs. Ahead of the rally with CasaPound on 28 February 2015 there was another clash with Fini, who claimed Meloni had become a 'good luck charm' for Salvini; she retorted: 'I am no one's good luck charm, it's up to others if they want to be the charm for big finance, Freemasonry, the lobbies and powerful interests.'[12] The following week the Fratelli d'Italia parliamentary group fell from nine to eight, as Massimo Corsaro broke away, decrying its political subordination to Salvini. In a letter to leader Meloni and parliamentary chief Fabio Rampelli, he claimed it had 'grown distant from the reasons the movement was founded', namely to create a broad 'container' for all those on the right lacking a party. Corsaro claimed she looked like a mere 'consultant' for CasaPound. For him, Fratelli d'Italia was indulging the Lega's populist 'no euro' agenda when instead it ought to pursue a pro-business line on tax and labour reforms. It had echoed trade union attacks on the centrist government rather than pursue the 'more modern economic vision' that would be able to gather the 'orphans of the right' in a single party.[13]

Such language in many ways echoed the Alleanza Nazionale years and the idea of merging the party into a more 'liberal' force. There were surely contradictions in Corsaro's call for a 'Western-style' centre-right. His letter damned the old 'grievances' among the party's 'old colonels', suggesting that their obsessions risked alienating figures like businessman Guido Crosetto. From 2001, Crosetto was a Forza Italia MP, but under Monti's technocratic government he was a critic of the budget-cutting European Fiscal Compact, and in December 2012 he was one of few figures not from the MSI tradition to take part in founding Fratelli d'Italia. Yet Corsaro, himself a veteran of the Milan MSI, damned euro exit in a manner which bore traces of anti-systemic radicalism and even conspiracy theory: he insisted that since a return to the lira was impractical, this undermined 'a more serious challenge to the Europe of masons and bankers'.[14] The reference to masonic influences may have raised doubts over Corsaro's liberalism; and, having left the party, he again made headlines with a vehement attack on the Democrat Emanuele Fiano, who is Jewish. This came the day after the beginning of the 2017 debate over the centre-left MP's proposed bill on tightening legislation against fascist symbolism and propaganda. In a Facebook post, Corsaro alleged that Fiano's prominent eyebrows were meant 'to cover up the signs of circumcision';[15] faced with media uproar, he clarified that his comments were not antisemitic but simply a 'vulgar joke against a dickhead'.[16]

Still, Corsaro had raised a point that has often exercised his former *camerati*: should they occupy the terrain of a free market right, and does this mean ending the MSI tradition? From the outset, Fratelli d'Italia insisted on its right-wing identity rather than a transversal populism, but also hinted at a more state-interventionist version of the neoliberal principles it accepted during the Berlusconi governments. The historic MSI spanned a range of stances, from praise for Salò-era 'socialisation' to the 'anti-bourgeois' hues of the Rautian left and the influences of the Reaganite New Right. In its early period, Fratelli d'Italia fused parts of each tradition, with its 2014 European election campaign leaning into anti-austerity policies as well as tax cuts.[17] It called for the 'controlled dismantling of the Eurozone' as the 'first condition to bring Europe out of recession and Italy out of crisis', alongside a national investment plan free of deficit constraints. Even this proposal included major conditions: it was not posed as an 'Italexit' but a collective agreement to be made by all member states. After the

2016 Brexit referendum, then Marine Le Pen's abandonment of her calls for France to quit the euro, the idea was dropped entirely.[18] Fratelli d'Italia instead took up the mantle of a 'European conservative party' which combines tax-cutting, free market economics with a peculiar focus on culture wars, national identity and redeeming its neofascist forefathers. In this it also exploits a certain political vacuum on the centre-right. In a series of technocratic and grand coalition cabinets since 2011, Berlusconi recast his party as an 'anti-populist' force able to forge alliances with the Democrats; this has in turn helped Meloni to claim a central role in the right-wing alliance and be 'monogamous'[19] in matters of coalition-making.

This also points to a wider reality: as far as a broad right-wing electorate and civil society is concerned, Fratelli d'Italia no longer needs to prove its legitimacy; indeed, it can even draw political capital from mocking the idea that it any longer needs to bend to the demands of antifascism. Conservative pundits such as *Libero* editor Alessandro Sallusti often accuse Democrats of refusing to accept that anyone 'not on the Left' can be anything other than 'fascist', and Meloni similarly speaks of the left's arrogance in imposing terms of political legitimacy.[20] Addressing an activist audience at the party's Atreju winter school in December 2021, which it dubbed 'the conservatives' Christmas', Meloni promised that Fratelli d'Italia would 'never be a party that seeks its enemies' approval'[21] – an apparent jibe at Fini's supposed treachery in bending the party to the codes of official antifascism.[22] There are surely some on the centre-right who find Fratelli d'Italia's leadership unpalatable: Berlusconi's party has repeatedly suffered splits by ministers who would rather join centrist pacts than commit to a permanent alliance with Meloni and Salvini. Yet the tendency for right-wing voters and even activists to circulate between these parties – illustrated by the rapid succession of first the Lega's and then Fratelli d'Italia's dominance within the *centrodestra* coalition – would tend to suggest that there is little in the way of a specific 'antifascist' barrier to support for Meloni's party among Italians who back its longstanding allies. Rather, its success lies in the fact that over the last three decades the MSI tradition has become an established part of the broad right, including through a strong cross-fertilisation of ideas and personnel.

In 2015, the departing Corsaro damned Fratelli d'Italia's mixed messaging on economic issues for alienating a more liberal figure like Guido Crosetto. The latter has, in recent years, come to play an important public relations role for the party, improving its ties with business and softening its identitarian edges for a wider electorate. Up to the September 2022 election he was often presented in TV debates as a 'surrogate' – a sympathetic observer rather than party representative – and indeed a sign of its truly 'centre-right' credentials, given that he is not from the neofascist tradition. From 2001, Crosetto was an MP for Berlusconi's Forza Italia, distinguished in the crisis period by his sharper Euroscepticism. He was, moreover, one of few figures from this camp to join the 2012 split that created Fratelli d'Italia, before becoming president of the Italian Federation of Aerospace, Defence and Security Businesses (AIAD). Through his on–off engagement in the party's core structures, he has often intervened on its behalf in TV debates, typically with a view to asserting its 'liberal' credentials. Illustrative of this was another intervention, also in October 2021, where he called on Meloni to do more to thwart possible accusations of neofascism. Even if such charges are the stuff of electoral propaganda, he argued, she nonetheless ought to 'take these arrows out of the hands of her opponents, who ultimately do not let her talk about her proposals and force her onto the defensive'.[23] In this same interview, he explained that Fratelli d'Italia is a party both of 'those who went through [the turn that dissolved the MSI at] Fiuggi and followed Fini' and 'others from the Right that I represented, a more liberal-democratic one'.[24] Following the Marbella speech, Crosetto downplayed the importance of this ally, insisting that Meloni has to be in 'dialogue' with other 'conservatives' but should restrain her 'shouting'.[25]

ALLIES ABROAD

It is easy to characterise this party in terms of a residual or inherited extremism: its militant base retains a strong link to the history of World War II and it remains obsessed with breaking down the remaining bastions of antifascism in Italian public life. Even outside of its historical references and recycling of neofascist personnel, we see this genealogy in its latter-day conspiracy theories and the belief that its mission is to prevent a Marxist-led destruction of white, Christian Europe. But the force of this politics is that it does not belong to the past: for the postfascist current has already been integrating its base and its ideas into a broader right-wing project for some three decades. In the First Republic, the MSI often dreamt of an outside intervention that would break it out of its marginal position in Italian politics. But with the collapse of the old antifascist culture, Fratelli d'Italia's activists have little remaining need to search for 'legitimisation', including from established centre-right media. Rather, they can make alliances on their own terms. While the postfascist party's representatives often bristle at the disrespect they earn from leftist commentators, they are not the victims of any official *cordon sanitaire*. Rather, it is a normalised part of Italian democracy, which has succeeded in redefining 'conservatism' in a way that can integrate fascist references and personnel. In a twenty-first-century political landscape marked by disaffection with established parties and institutions, its rise promises not a 'return to the past' but a new identity politics geared towards the present.

For historian Giuseppe Parlato, the postwar MSI's militant identity was defined by neofascism, but its more fundamental political raison d'être was anticommunism.[26] Today's Fratelli d'Italia exhibits a similar distinction between its own militants' specific attachment to the MSI tradition and an electoral offer aimed at a broader right-wing electorate. Yet there are also important differences, some inherited from the Alleanza Nazionale era. One is the simple fact that, even compared to the MSI in its final years,

Fratelli d'Italia is much more governed by its leader's electoral tactics and has a less dynamic internal life. Moreover, while its own element of 'social' economic policies has drastically diminished, its enemy is not communism per se, so much as the spectre of communism projected onto various progressive causes, leftists and even liberals. This can also integrate a specific 'human rights' discourse, for instance in attacks on the 'communist dictatorship' in Venezuela, or the defence of Taiwanese sovereignty from Chinese claims.[27] Yet, beyond its often vitriolic attacks on the 'Stalinist' partisans of World War II, the party above all mobilises on the basis of defending the white, Christian family – and the overtaxed Italian small-business owner – from what it paints as an overmighty progressive ideology. It defines itself as 'conservative' while specifically taking this to mean a rejection of liberal and egalitarian conceptions of citizenship, grouped together under the idea of 'cultural Marxism'. In its denunciation of 'LGBT dictatorship' and the refugee solidarity NGOs that want to ethnically substitute European citizens, it conflates 'progressivism' and 'totalitarianism' in a manner familiar to observers of Viktor Orbán's Fidesz in Hungary, or Poland's Law and Justice party.

Fratelli d'Italia has repeatedly praised these parties, citing them as models for its own politics. We see this in the *Trieste Theses* mentioned in Chapter 1. The right-wing governments of these central European states are, it claims, 'symbols of the defence of real, historical Europe' as against those who would destroy the nation state and replace Europe's citizens with outsiders.[28] The post-Eastern Bloc reference point also makes it possible to present the 'national conservative' agenda in terms of fighting for freedom against a Communist establishment, even if – as in the Italian case – it was one's own ideological forefathers who imposed dictatorship, whereas the Communists helped to restore democracy. Yet, while Meloni has long entertained warm relations with Hungarian premier Orbán – a critic of 'great replacement' and 'ethnic mixing' – even these ties are combined with connections to a larger conservative tradition. Telling, in this sense, was Meloni's participation at the National Conservatism conference in Rome in February 2020, organised by Yoram Hazony, author of *The Virtue of Nationalism*. While this event was addressed by Orbán, and sponsored by the government-financed Danube Institute, it claimed the spiritual patronage of John Paul II and Ronald Reagan. While damning, in passing, the 'European progressive mainstream' for its attacks on the Hungarian and Polish governments, Meloni's speech framed her politics in terms of an homage to these two icons of 1980s anticommunism.

Meloni's NatCon intervention again worked to set her own party within a broader conservative camp, while also dramatising the latter's mission of defending civilisation from a totalitarian progressive agenda. Citing Pope Wojtyła, to the effect that 'there is no Europe without Christianity', Meloni's insisted that this 'Christian, patriot, and ... critic of mass immigration' would surely 'be on the EU's blacklist as a dangerous subversive'.[29] While it is unclear which specific 'blacklist' she was referring to, she added that it would just as surely have included Reagan. While a certain distrust of Yankee materialism pervaded postwar MSI culture, this anticommunist and scold of US progressives was the kind of American it could admire.[30] Also notable in this bid for conservative credentials was her evocation of low-tax, free-marketeer economic policies, upheld by the 1980s Republican leader as by Donald Trump. Citing Reagan's metaphor of the 'three-legged stool' of conservatism, she insisted on the combination of (first) 'the patriotic soul (which today would be called "sovereignist")'; (second) 'economic freedom', since 'over-taxation stifles and forces the state to build up a system of controls similar to that of the totalitarian regimes'; and (third) the 'social soul', referring not to welfare policy but rather the need 'to protect religious and moral values, the noblest purpose of all political action'. In a speech of explicit 'sovereigntist' temper, she roundly condemned 'globalists' of all stripes: 'we did not fight against, and defeat, communism in order to replace it with a new internationalist regime'.[31]

Yet, despite this rhetorical grandstanding, Fratelli d'Italia accepts the main Euro-Atlantic institutions, in practice accommodating to Italy's junior role within the Western camp. Even insofar as its nationalist grievances attack other forces in Italy as unpatriotic, this basic framework is assumed. The *Trieste Theses* themselves cite Galli della Loggia's judgement that 'from the crisis situation that began [with Fascism's military defeat] in 1943, no political subject could afford to pursue the national interest and that alone';[32] Italy's governments would instead have to choose between various foreign designs for its integration into the international scene. Yet this, adds the *Trieste Theses*, has led Italy's ruling class to lose their 'sense of the Fatherland', falling in behind the agendas of others in international forums rather than assert the national interest. The document thus extolls De Gaulle's vision of a 'confederal Europe' based on strong nation states. It cites, as examples of this approach, Hungary and Poland, each of them non-eurozone countries who continually confront EU rules on judicial independence and migrant rights.[33] Fratelli d'Italia propaganda has often denounced the 'Soviet-style European bureaucracy'. Yet, even in this 2017 document the prospect of euro exit was placed as a second possibility after an internal 'recalibration', posed in the vaguest terms. Indeed, even when Fratelli d'Italia does make gestures towards the idea of reforming EU institutions, such ideas are couched in vague and thus consensual terms ('making the European Central Bank work for nation-states'). The clear aim is to express discontent at the results of the euro and the relative weakening of Italy's economic position, while then falling back on reassurances it will not risk a split.

So, what are 'national conservatives'? One basis for identifying this current lies in the group in the European Parliament called European Conservatives and Reformists (ECR). This alliance was originally founded at the initiative of David Cameron's UK Conservative Party, to separate this increasingly Eurosceptic party from the European People's Party (EPP), which includes parties like the German Christian Democrats and Italy's Forza Italia.

Upon its first incarnation in 2009, the ECR included mostly central-eastern European parties such as Poland's ruling Law and Justice and the Czech Republic's Civic Democrats. Compared to the British Tories, the other forces involved tended to be both more stridently anti-immigrant and more committed to membership of the European Union, albeit remaining critical of federalism. Having emerged as a split from Berlusconi's party, the residual Fratelli d'Italia group in Brussels began life in the EPP but quit in advance of the 2014 elections: Carlo Fidanza MEP damned this bloc as the 'servants of Merkel'.[34] In November 2018, it joined the ECR, and in doing so also allied with Raffaele Fitto, a former Christian Democrat and Berlusconian who was vice-president of this group. By the time this happened, Britain had already voted to leave the European Union; the Tories did no campaigning for the May 2019 European elections, in which they scored 8.8 per cent. This brief overlap with the Conservatives, before the formalisation of Brexit in January 2020, nonetheless remains a key plank of Fratelli d'Italia's boast that Meloni's role as ECR president starting in September 2020 represents the leadership of one of the 'three great political families that built Europe'.[35]

Indicative of the alliances that have allowed the party to build its international networks is its relationship with Vox, today the third-largest party in Spain. Founded in December 2013, this is a split from the Partido Popular (PP), heir to the conservative Alianza Popular created after the death of dictator Francisco Franco. Amid mounting tensions over Spain's territorial integrity and the release of imprisoned ex-terrorists from the Basque Country, Vox was created on the promise to recentralise Spain and abolish its autonomous regional governments. Headed by former PP right-winger Santiago Abascal, it integrates various ex-Francoite and small fascist circles, but more broadly is remarkable for raising the pitch of nationalist identity politics. One prong of this is its Catholic-hued Islamophobia, calling for a 'Reconquista' from creeping Muslim influence. Staunchly monarchist and hostile to left-wing memory culture investigating Spain's Francoite and colonial past, it also has a special interest in the country's former possessions, calling for a regeneration of the 'Iberosphere'. Normally, this does not mean sending vessels across the Atlantic. Yet, as well as seeking closer ties with far-right leaders such as Brazilian president Jair Bolsonaro, in November 2021 Vox MEP Hermann Tertsch led a delegation to Miami that included Spanish congress member Víctor González and Fratelli d'Italia MEP Carlo Fidanza. While they failed in their initial plan to head to Havana to join anti-government protests, they met with Cuban exile leaders as well as US Republican Party officials like deputy governor Jeanette Nuñez.[36]

Among the ECR parties, Meloni has especially close relations with Vox. Abascal has spoken at the Italian postfascist party's Atreju activist summit, and Meloni has returned the favour, with both an October 2021 intervention at its Viva21 meet-up in Madrid (entitled 'feel Spanish again') and a rally for the party in Marbella, Andalusia in June 2022 during its regional election campaign. These events highlighted the similarities in their politics. At the Viva21 event she railed against 'LGBT pressure groups who want to tear down our sexual identity, using gender propaganda in schools, media, institutions and the media'.[37] In Marbella, she again took up this theme, insisting that 'gender ideology pursues not the much-vaunted fight against discrimination, or the overcoming of male–female differences: no, the undeclared but tragically obvious aim is the disappearance of women and the end of maternity'.[38] This served to illustrate how political correctness serves 'the attempt to give high minded motives to sinister interests: to destroy identity, the centrality of the human person, the achievements of our civilisation, to fatten the big multinationals of the indistinct, the synthetic, the wealth held by few on the backs of many'.[39] Later, Meloni emphasised that she directed her fire against 'LGBT lobbies' not 'the homosexual community'. Yet, if motherhood is being destroyed by the reign of the 'synthetic and the indistinct' – an assault on what the Italian transcript of her speech termed 'the borders of the family' – [40] then the 'men who are both father and mother, in a wide range between male and female' are its weapons.

The 'national conservative' milieu is defined by its dramatisation of political conflict: a defence of Western civilisation from its destruction by a conspiracy of elite and radical left forces. Indeed, these terms are often conflated in such a way that each of them can be used to describe liberal and social-democratic parties. Parties like Vox and Fratelli d'Italia thus combine their commitment to EU and international institutions with the allegation that they have been captured by the fusion of speculators, communists and minority lobby groups who plot the destruction of the nation. Speaking to a reporter at the Viva21 meeting, Meloni identified her key enemies as 'globalist ideology' and a 'French–German axis' in the EU which she accused of 'turning Europe into a Soviet state'. Vox leader Abascal, like Meloni a propagator of anti-Soros conspiracy theories, especially damns 'Agenda 2030' – the UN's sustainable development plan – as a plot to impose 'climate dictatorship', 'classroom indoctrination', the 'destruction of the family' and 'immigration crises'.[41] Addressing the Marbella Vox rally, Meloni did not specifically cite 'ethnic substitution', but confected an image of creeping 'Islamisation', mounting 'ethnic violence' against Italians and 'the culture of death'. Delivered in Spanish, her fiery speech concluded with the words: 'Yes to safe borders, no to mass immigration, yes to jobs for our people, no to international high finance, yes to people's sovereignty, no to the Brussels bureaucrats, yes to our civilisation – and no to those who want to destroy it!'[42] The acceptance of core planks of the Euro-Atlantic institutions and most of the canons of neoliberal economics is thus combined with a sharply anti-systemic rhetoric regarding its domestic opponents. In the 2022 election campaign, Meloni repeatedly claimed that the left is not only 'culturally hegemonic' but enjoys an undemocratic 'hegemony of power'.[43]

But are Fratelli d'Italia's rebranding exercises accurately descri-bed as 'mainstreaming'? This word is much more common in journalistic accounts than political science terms referring to its 'normalisation'. Yet the word 'mainstream' has two major limits as a description of this phenomenon. First is the fact that while the party defends its 'mainstream' status when under attack from the left (its legitimate standing) it proudly rejects the 'mainstream' (vaunting its anti-systemic credentials) when referring to its social policies. Meloni's appearance at CPAC (the Conservative Political Action Conference) in Miami in February 2022 illustrated her acceptance by the Republicans, that is, the main conservative party in what remains the world's most important economic and military power. Yet she told the conference that she didn't want to be close to the powerful: 'we prefer the public squares and we will not be part of their mainstream, because we are on the side of the people. You in America and us in Europe.' To this she added that the 'only way to be a rebel is to be a conservative', and she refused to be the kind of right that stays 'on a leash'.[44] This is combined with the other limit to the idea of 'mainstreaming', namely the openness of the US conservative movement to conspiracy theorists, which means that inclusion in such forums in no way implies conformity to some imagined fixed set of 'mainstream' or 'normal' conservative positions. We need only think of the fact that CPAC also hosts US Congresswoman Marjorie Taylor Greene, who often speaks of a planned 'genocide' against whites and promotes the claims of QAnon and Pizzagate, which each allege the existence of Satanist paedophile cabals which dominate national government.

Given the nativist trends, not only in a postfascist party like Fratelli d'Italia but in historic Anglophone conservative parties as well as formerly liberal-nationalist forces in the former Eastern Bloc, it today makes little sense to imagine any simple relationship by which one force exerts a pull of moderation on another. The EPP – the largest group in the European Parliament, with almost half a century of activity behind it – is more 'mainstream' than the ECR. Yet the fact that Meloni leads the 'European Conservatives' group in the Brussels parliament – having arrived there by quitting the EPP – is widely presented in mainstream media as a sign of the party's prestige and international acceptance as a 'conservative' party. This stands in contradiction with another tendency that is especially common in centre-left media, which finds, upon contact with individual other affiliates of this group, that they in fact highlight Fratelli d'Italia's ties to extremists in other countries. Indicative in this regard is Meloni's relationship with Spain's Vox, which Italian media widely term 'neo-Francoite' and racist. Indeed, 'the Marbella rally', referring to Meloni's Spanish-language address in June 2022, became a ubiquitous catchphrase in Italian media, much more so than previous interventions in Italy where she had used stronger wording to condemn the 'ethnic substitution' of Italians by non-Europeans. When Meloni was prodded by an interviewer into expressing regret over the rally, she insisted that only her speech register made it look bad: when she is 'too tired' she struggles to fit her 'passions' into a moderate 'tone', but she defended the 'substance' of what she had said.[45] Spain's *El País* inverted this relationship by speaking of Vox's alliance with an Italian 'ultraderechista' leader.[46]

Yet the obvious conclusion that Meloni's 'angry' message was embarrassing to her deserves to be questioned. While Crosetto warned that she should 'shout less', the antagonistic element of her public image surely helps reach some elements of society that are difficult to place on a conventional political axis. In Chapter 4, we referred to mobilisations such as the World Congress of Families and NoVaxxers, who are indeed proud of their resistance against mainstream media, the dominant 'single way of thinking' and the speech codes of established political parties. This is especially summed up by the slogan that is beloved of protestors against coronavirus restrictions: 'La gente come noi non molla mai' – 'folks like us don't give in'. This echoes an old fascist slogan, 'boia chi molla', but – also being a football chant – is less strongly politically coded and expresses a broad mood of defiance. For a postfascist politician like Meloni, the difficulty lies in channelling the mood of such anti-systemic and conspiracy theorist subcultures without binding herself to their specific 'scientific' claims. The art of her framing is thus to express a generic scepticism of the powerful – globalists, left wingers, NGOs, medical experts – in largely moral terms, without straying too close to a specific endorsement of alternative theories. She instead relies on counterpositions of the authentic masses and the elites who lord it over them: 'our civilisation' against 'those who would destroy it', 'liberty' against 'dictatorship', the call for a 25 April celebration that hopes for freedom from Covid-19 lockdowns rather than the Communist partisans of World War II.

BECOMING ANTIFASCISTS?

Meloni's memoir topped book charts, but it wasn't a hit with everyone. May 2021 saw a storm of controversy around Simon Levis Sullam, a professor at Venice's Ca' Foscari university known for his research on the Holocaust in Italy, after he posted a photo of the bestseller shelves at an outlet of chain bookstore Feltrinelli, with copies of Meloni's book turned upside down. The gesture – a nod to Mussolini being hung from his feet at Milan's Piazzale Loreto – might have seemed a trivial prank. Yet Fratelli d'Italia whipped up a storm of outrage which made national headlines for days.[47] Meloni's social media claimed that she was the target of 'red hatred' and that the photo was a 'simulation of her hanging'.[48] Stepping up the claim of victimhood, party news site *La Voce del patriota* proposed that antifascism's search for an 'ideological elimination of its enemy, where a physical one is not possible' is today the 'worst form of totalitarianism'.[49] Fratelli d'Italia members organised protests at the Jewish historian's campus; while the rector had quickly distanced herself from the professor, the party also called on the universities minister to launch disciplinary action against him.[50] This was not the only case of hounding masked as outrage at being 'cancelled': that same month, Meloni took to TV to publicly denounce a bookshop owner in the Roman suburb of Tor Bella Monaca for refusing to stock *Io Sono Giorgia*, claiming that she was being silenced, even as the book featured prominently in all national media. This dispute also became wrapped up with another story, surrounding the right-wing parties' candidate

for mayor of Rome, Enrico Michetti. He averred in a radio programme that Roman saluting was 'more hygienic' as a greeting, in
times of Covid-19, and moreover not a product of fascism but of
the Roman Empire.[51]

These incidents stirred discussion of the party's relationship
with fascism. For *Corriere della Sera* columnist Ernesto Galli della
Loggia, it was clear that Fratelli d'Italia ought to make a more
purposeful rejection of fascism: what *Secolo d'Italia* sarcastically
termed a 'Fiuggi 2.0'.[52] Galli della Loggia doubted the relevance
of contemporary antifascism: it had become 'nothing more than
the radical version of a left-wing ideological position', serving a
'shoddy political operation of delegitimising any position that is
disagreeable to itself'.[53] Yet one could only have 'a totally negative
judgement of fascism: of its ideal assumptions, its methods, its
choices, its results'; and a party of government had to say so: 'Our
history, the principles of our Constitution, and the international
alliances and friendships we wish to maintain demand it. The possibility of becoming the country's leadership class demands it.'[54]
Meloni, however, dismissed even this apparently goodwill call
to reason: she insisted that her party had already distanced itself
from fascism, whereas the left had not disavowed communism. It
was this, she claimed, that made Italy an 'anomaly in Europe'.[55]
This was not the end of the dispute. Later that month, Galli della
Loggia made another intervention, citing setbacks for Marine Le
Pen's party in France to show the far-right's problem of historical
legitimacy.[56] Meloni now claimed that Galli della Loggia himself
was trying to set up a false challenge to the party's good pedigree.
For her, Fiuggi had already damned Mussolini's Racial Laws and
alliance with Nazi Germany, so '[w]e believe that the time for
blood tests against Fratelli d'Italia and the Italian Right has long
since ended'.[57]

Fratelli d'Italia surely had made allies far beyond its original
postfascist milieu. What remains much less clear is how deeply
this has changed the party's internal culture – or indeed, whether
doing so is even necessary to its future electoral success. Indicative,

in this sense, were the party's responses to two scandals it faced in autumn 2021, which both prompted forces on the left wing of Italian politics to demand that it distance itself from neofascists. The first came on 30 September with the documentary *Lobby Nera*. A report alleging neo-Nazi links and money laundering in Fratelli d'Italia's Milan organisation, it was produced by online newspaper *Fanpage* and then rebroadcast by La7's *Piazzapulita*. Fratelli d'Italia and Lega politicians often abstain from interviews with either this website or the TV programme hosted by Corrado Formigli, which often expose them to a degree of critical scrutiny uncommon in other outlets. The second, on 9 October, came after militants from neofascist group Forza Nuova, including veterans of the terrorist group NAR, attacked the offices of the CGIL trade union at a demonstration against 'green passes', which regulated access to public spaces during the Covid-19 pandemic. In each case, Fratelli d'Italia fell back on stonewalling, choosing not to answer its critics but denounce them for using the scandals for political ends ahead of local elections planned for that month. Equally telling of the process that has allowed Fratelli d'Italia's mainstreaming was the reaction by right-wing figures from outside the party, suggesting that discussion of these incidents was irrelevant given that Meloni's party has long since proven its democratic credentials.

The film *Lobby Nera* centres on the Cuore Nero founder Roberto Jonghi Lavarini, whom we met in Chapter 4, as well as Carlo Fidanza, head of Fratelli d'Italia's group in the European Parliament. Ahead of local elections in Milan, in which this 'Black Baron' worked on its campaign, the *Fanpage* reporter posed as a businessman interested in supporting its candidates. Jonghi Lavarini boasts to him not only of his close ties with Lega and Fratelli d'Italia politicians, but also his role in a 'esoteric group with various masons, admirers of Hitler and former military personnel'.[58] The rest of the documentary bore out Jonghi Lavarini's closeness to the Milan Fratelli d'Italia organisation, including when he appears to propose that the undercover reporter should make an illicit campaign donation; the MEP Fidanza is also filmed referring to 'under-the-table' campaign financing. Apart from the impression of close collaboration with Jonghi Lavarini, Fidanza is also shown at a drinks evening Roman saluting, saying 'Heil Hitler' and joking about the 'use of having a Jewish friend'.[59] At one campaign event, the 'Black Baron' calls a candidate 'an old *camerata*, a Fascist of Approved Origin' – much as one might label a Prosecco – and introduces another as 'a patriot: we could use another word, but patriot will do for now'.[60] Fratelli d'Italia members habitually use the word 'patriot' rather than *camerata*. When Fidanza and other members of the campaign pose for a photo, rather than say 'cheese' they say the surname of Paolo Berizzi, a *Repubblica* journalist who is forced to live under police escort because of neofascist death threats.

While both men were placed under criminal investigation, Fratelli d'Italia blamed the reporters. Its official response bemoaned the film's broadcast 'hours before an important election', claiming that it could not judge an exposé 'blatantly meant to besmirch our honour' without seeing all 100 hours of footage first.[61] Meloni insisted she had already told Fidanza to 'stay away from those circles';[62] journalist Berizzi later circulated footage which depicted Meloni in the close company of Jonghi Lavarini on repeated occasions in 2017–18.[63] Fidanza announced his 'self-suspension' from his role in Brussels, but Meloni was reluctant to remove this ally from his position: she insisted that she was 'not afraid to drive people out' but wanted to know if this was a 'trap'.[64] The party announced no further sanctions for Fidanza, who despite his supposed 'suspension' continued to represent it even in international forums; less than two months later he met Republican officials on its behalf in Miami.[65] He continued working for Fratelli d'Italia in the European Parliament and, together with Meloni, led the ECR delegation to the February 2022 CPAC in Orlando.[66] Fidanza could also benefit from the indulgence of right wingers in Italy. Asked to comment on the affair in a TV panel, right-wing MP Vittorio Sgarbi refused to judge these 'hijinks' 'out of context' and abruptly changed the subject: the 'horrors of fascism should be set alongside the horrors of the *foibe*, of today's communism and Korea'.[67] *Libero* journalist Alessandro Giuli doubted the story had much to say about Fratelli d'Italia: Fidanza was a political 'moderate' who had sunk into 'dismal hijinks': there was a 'grey zone' in the party but it could not seriously be suggested that 'Italy's most popular party is a party of neofascists'.[68]

Faced with evidence of neofascist ties, Fratelli d'Italia's defenders often insist that such incidents should not be taken 'out of context' – the party has reformed itself, there is no chance of a 'return to the past' and thus all reference to fascism is anachronistic or indeed malicious propaganda. Illustrative, in this sense, was the protest against Covid-19 passes which took place in Rome just a few days later. The rally involved both Forza Nuova militants and no-vaxxers. These groups sacked the offices of the CGIL union, fighting with police as they broke their way into the building. Faced with shocking images of the assault, Meloni first claimed she didn't 'know where the attack came from'. Faced with criticism for this ambiguity – pushing her towards the admission that it was a neofascist attack, though antifascist violence was equally to be condemned[69] – Meloni then went on the counter-attack. She accused Interior Minister Luciana Lamorghese of having 'deliberately allowed' the attack to happen, in a new 'strategy of tension'.[70] *Secolo d'Italia* quoted remarks by Sgarbi claiming that just as *Fanpage* had 'infiltrated' a reporter to expose Fidanza, 'there were clearly people infiltrated into the protests, to make out that a group of people who have a different view of things are fascists'.[71] Yet there is no 'danger of fascism'; this was just being used to smear Meloni.[72] The centre-left then began moves to dissolve the Forza Nuova group through a vote in parliament. Fratelli d'Italia's Fabio Rampelli told Radio24 that his party had no problems with breaking up the organisation even if this was ultimately a 'propagandistic act', in which Forza Nuova served as 'the Democrats' best allies'.[73] While during the 2018 campaign Meloni had insisted 'CasaPound and Forza Nuova are not xenophobic parties',[74] this time the emphasis was on the lack of connection between the groups. Fratelli d'Italia ultimately abstained on the motion, while the right-wing parties put forward their own proposal to suppress 'all criminal organisations'. Forza Nuova leaders Giuliano Castellino and Roberto Fiore were jailed following the attack, but the organisation continues to exist despite the ban.[75]

BUSINESS RELATIONS

The Fratelli d'Italia programmatic conference at the end of April 2022 showcased the party's appeal to business – what Italian journalists call the 'party of GDP', that is, those interested in increasing Italy's economic output. Held in the city of both Salvini and Berlusconi – and capital of the Lega heartland region of Lombardy – the conference was entitled 'Energies to Be Liberated' and set out the party's agenda for restoring economic growth. While Meloni mocked the idea that her party lacked a high-quality 'leadership class', this event was also notable for the attempt to integrate a wider panorama of figures into its front rank. Speakers from outside the MSI tradition included Crosetto – also head of the defence and aerospace contractors' group AIAD, part of employers' association Confindustria – Mani Pulite-era magistrate Carlo Nordio and Giulio Tremonti, who was finance minister throughout most of Berlusconi's nine years in government. Tremonti's presence was of special interest given his past conflicts with the incumbent prime minister, Mario Draghi. The former European Central Bank chief had played a key role in the downfall of the previous centre-right coalition in 2011, joining his ECB predecessor Jean-Claude Trichet in writing an open letter to Rome which demanded that the Italian government implement wide-scale privatisations and labour market reforms in exchange for continued European support during the sovereign debt crisis. As investor confidence in the government collapsed, sending the spread between German and Italian bond yields soaring, the ECB abstained from the bond buybacks that might have saved it, thus helping the creation of Monti's administration.

While the conference advertised Fratelli d'Italia's commitment to free market economics and even its ability to integrate former Christian Democrats, this was also consistently framed as a strident rejection of liberalism, 'globalist elites' and what Tremonti called the 'International Republic of Money'. Both the financial collapse and the Covid-19 pandemic have pushed in the direction of more national capitalisms, in which the state interventionism typical of neoliberalism – creating the social conditions for businesses to survive, for instance through reducing labour costs – is allied with a harder protectionist edge. But it also illustrated the longer-term radicalisation of the 'centre-right' in Italy: for not only former MSI members but Tremonti himself connected these themes to a general discourse on civilisational values. In his speech, Berlusconi's long-time finance minister denounced the 'artificial and spectral world, alternative to the natural and political one ... [with the] triumph of the net giants over states and therefore peoples'.[76] He connected this to the 'demographic collapse starting with the conversion of human sex from responsibility to pleasure and as a consequence, the mutation of the traditional family into a horizontal family, the appearance of terminal individualism'. Citing the idea of *pensiero unico* – the liberal orthodoxy of recent decades – Tremonti insisted that recent 'crises have swept away the single thought. They have broken the software of globalisation.' To this, he counterposed a more national free market capitalism built on revived manufacturing, for instance by 'lifting taxation on all investments made by industry to restructure' as well as stripping back regulation.[77]

Fratelli d'Italia is often considered to be 'welfare-chauvinist': a party that defends welfare but only for nationals and the nuclear family. It surely does claim that migrants are putting pressure on schools and hospitals, and sometimes speaks of increasing the availability of public childcare. Yet the perspective offered at this conference was anything but 'welfarist'. In 2019, the Five Star Movement introduced a 'citizens' income' (RdC), a package of benefits for jobless Italians comparable to Job Seeker's Allowance in the United Kingdom, including the fact that it is conditional on actively seeking work. The scheme offers up to €780 per month to around a million households; Fratelli d'Italia boasts of being the only party which has consistently voted against it. A document distributed at the conference,[78] called 'Notes for a Conservative Programme', featured a section on the labour market 'curated' by Crosetto, which promised to go further in making benefits conditional. It floated the idea of an artificial intelligence system that would 'register the list of young people who finish high school and university each year and attach them to firms, job agencies and employment hubs, activating a competitive system ... The young person will no longer be able to choose to work or not, but is bound to accept the job offer, for themselves, for their family and for the country, on pain of losing all benefits, with the application of a sanctions system.'[79] Crosetto termed this a 'cultural provocation, ideas put out for reflection's sake',[80] and it was not included in the party's 2022 election programme.

This focus on reinvigorating a national capitalism as a response to civilisational decline – what Fratelli d'Italia leaders call its 'productivist' politics – is even apparent in its approach to green issues, where it rejects statist plans for ecological transition or tax disincentives to polluters. It has often damned the left for imposing its ownership over ecological issues, denouncing the 'gretins' (merging the first name of activist Greta Thunberg with the word 'cretins') who want to impose a 'new communism' through plans for a Green New Deal. At the conference, ecology spokesman Nicola Procaccini made a verbal distinction between this left-wing 'environmentalist' ideology and ecology, understood as a spiritual disposition towards life itself: what Meloni has called 'man's role as defender of Creation'.[81] For Procaccini, '[t]he big difference between left-wing environmentalism and right-wing ecology also lies in our spirituality versus their materialism. For us, life is sacred in all its forms: it is what leads us to fight for the life of a seal pup, but all the more so for the young pup in a woman's womb.'[82] For Procaccini, environmentalism was a 'replacement' for communism, driven by its hatred of business: '174 years after Marx's *Communist*

Manifesto, another spectre lurks in Europe, that of environmentalism in its degenerated form, which retains the same founding elements of that Marxist idea, namely materialism, internationalism, hatred of corporations and economies, and a certain violence in the way they assert their ideas against those who do not think like them.'[83] The party has called for tax cuts for Italian auto manufacturers, in order to help them compete with the greater polluters (i.e. Chinese electric car firms).

Yet, the most important speaker was Meloni herself, a leader now coasting towards national government and able to showcase her party to Milan business leaders. There had been no 'second Fiuggi', no repudiation of the MSI tradition. Fratelli d'Italia may not have wanted to be part of the mainstream, yet it had become a party with whom others could do business. It was a party that even proudly boasted that it no longer needed to keep apologising for its fascist grandfathers, when it was talking about its offer to those whose interests it might serve. Closing the programmatic conference, Meloni did not avoid the subject of fascism, but chose to bring it up herself, in her own speech, without provocation. She told a story about the way her party gets treated by the media – a way of showing that the issue is now to be sneered at. 'A journalist asked a delegate, so is this dark shirt you're wearing a tribute to the Blackshirts?'[84] What better example of the malicious media, the intolerant antifascists, the attempts to 'cancel' the party of patriots? Meloni opened her eyes wide in mock astonishment, slowly revolved her head to the left, then to the right, and threw her arms behind her back. She brought her palms together, then vigorously shook them up and down in a gesture meaning 'what the fuck are you on about?' Her delighted audience cheered, ever louder, many standing up in an ovation. She said, to her press critics, '[d]o you realise how out of this world you are, how ridiculous you are – I'm saying even in terms of your own professionalism?' She did not say which journalist had asked the question. But Meloni had her moment. The old MSI youth activist marched towards power not with Blackshirts and salutes but to the laughter of men in suits and ties.

Conclusion
After Antifascism

On 5 April 2022, the Senate passed a bill creating Italy's latest national Remembrance Day. The new annual commemoration honours the Alpini, the mountain infantry formed after Italian unification, which most distinguished themselves in the battles fought on snow and ice during World War I. The Alpini's role as an elite fighting force enjoys broad social recognition, and the Senate vote to honour them passed near unanimously, with only a single abstention.[1] However, the bill, originally tabled by members of the Lega during its spell in government in 2018–19, also established a remarkable connection between this memorial day and the period of Fascist rule.[2] The bill proclaimed its intention 'to preserve the memory of the heroism shown by the Alpine Army Corps in the Battle of Nikolayevka during World War II, as well as to promote the values of the defence of sovereignty and the national interest and the ethics of civic participation, solidarity and volunteerism, which the Alpini embody'.[3] For this reason, the memorial day would be held on 26 January, in reference to the anniversary of Nikolayevka – that is, part of the Battle of Stalingrad, during the invasion of the Soviet Union led by Nazi Germany and Fascist Italy. Surrounded by Red Army forces at the end of the failed conquest of the city, the Alpini together with German troops mounted a frontal assault, broke out of their encirclement and retreated in relatively good order. This is what they are to be celebrated for.

Some Alpini complained about the choice of date: a group of 39 officers wrote to President Sergio Mattarella to call it an 'unjust' decision, noting that 'in Nikolayevka the Alpini were commanded to retreat from an attack on a foreign country'.[4] Yet the national

MUSSOLINI'S GRANDCHILDREN

Alpini association welcomed the memorial day; in January, Fratelli d'Italia had proposed a similar bill in the Piedmont region, in that case insisting that the link to Nikolayevka was the choice of a 105-year-old veteran.[5] The Alpini's bleak fate in Russia is hardly an unknown story: however, it has historically been blamed on the Fascist regime that sent unequipped men to die in Hitler's war;[6] one veteran who documented his experience, Nuto Revelli, famously hailed the partisans in Italy who had 'fought against the Nazi-fascists on behalf of their brothers, sons and friends who had died in Russia'.[7] Yet, now these same events were heaped together with the 'national interest'. The Senate vote also came at a time when the Soviet Union's fight for its own 'sovereignty' was buried by newer history: for the bill was passed just five weeks after Vladimir Putin had invaded Ukraine. For writer Tomaso Montanari, the bill celebrated a 'mad war of aggression against a nation we now want to think of as an "enemy" again. So, instead of contesting the bloodthirsty nationalism of the despot Putin, invader of Ukraine, we resurrect the ghosts of our own.'[8]

Right-wing parties in former Eastern Bloc countries have often used contemporary Russian imperialism to redeem their own historical nationalists, including even Nazi-collaborationists, and such a practice is not limited to these states alone. The lack of communism in contemporary Russia, and its near absence from the European political space, has not halted the use of anticommunism as an apparent 'corrective' to antifascism. In 2019, the European Parliament passed a motion condemning communism as equivalent to Nazism and, in this spirit, referred to Soviet monuments in eastern Europe as examples of totalitarian symbolism. Russia's invasion of Ukraine, cynically drawing on the language of 'de-Nazification', provided the pretext for authorities in countries including Poland and Lithuania to tear down socialist-era statues, including those commemorating Red Army soldiers. These were monuments, they insisted, not just to men who died in uniform but also to the Soviet Union itself; and the dominant public memory culture in these states no longer treats 1945 as a moment of liberation. While there were never Soviet tanks on Italian streets, right wingers here dream of imposing a comparable shift in public commemoration of this period. It is a hope expressed in the call to strip Josip Broz Tito of his honorary Italian citizenship, and the claim that Italians, too, count among the victims of communism, patriots buried by an overbearing, communist-inspired, antifascist hatred. Fratelli d'Italia aims not to rehabilitate Mussolini but the men and women who died in Fascist uniforms, and those who kept the fascist movement alive even after the war.

Antifascists long sought to redeem Italian patriotism by presenting Fascism as a betrayal of the *Patria*, which had made its sons into cannon fodder for Nazi Germany. Today's right-wing memory politics seek to liberate national-patriotic history from fascism and antifascism altogether. The Senate bill did not celebrate the Fascist regime or its invasion of the Soviet Union. Rather, the real development of events – the Fascist regime that led the Alpini to Stalingrad – is simply missing, much like the Italian war on Yugoslavia in the tributes to *foibe* victims. It becomes a story about Italians and the foreign enemy who tried to kill them. This is the principal form that historical revisionism takes: not a recovery of the symbols of fascism so much as their airbrushing out of national and nationalist history; neither an exaltation nor a critical investigation of fascism, but the implicit claim that it can be ignored. As against the injunction to remember – the call 'never again' – this way of talking about fascism and antifascism speaks the language of 'pacification', 'making peace' between political sides, and thus erasing all conflict around fascism. A hundred years since Mussolini first came to power, he remains an almost ever present image in Italian public life. Yet, in everyday politics, fascism is ever more spoken of as a distant past, rather than a living history: antifascism becomes the concern of a minority, largely on the left wing of politics, while the right coalesces behind a leader who claims that antifascism is a militant danger to contemporary 'patriots'.

In July 2022, I got a taste of this treatment of antifascism when I wrote a piece for the *New York Times* about the rise of Meloni. In it I insisted that the radicalisation of the Italian right is not just a national story: for across Europe, the barriers between centre-right and far-right forces are collapsing. The Italian story may have been the 'original', given that it happened in the 1990s, but the basic phenomenon is today spreading across the Western world. A radicalised right is able not only to adopt the language or ideas of former fascist and collaborationist parties, but to make alliances with them and even accept their leadership. I emphasised that this is not a return to the past but the future. It reflects an electoral battleground in which political forces ever less able to satisfy the material needs of the broad majority, or promise paths to future prosperity, instead polarise around questions of identity, culture and what is called the defence of civilisation. It is an environment in which both the world of 1945 and the antifascist parties rooted in it are on the path to disappearance. In this same article I also noted one of the particular forms this takes: Meloni's allegiance to the Western camp, a nationalism that does not aim to break Italy from Europe or the NATO alliance but claims to strengthen its place within it. During the election, she was asked to insist on this international positioning more often than about her party's fascist roots or use of 'great replacement theory'.

My article briefly made waves in Italian media, not least as it was published on the same day that the election was called. The title had read 'The Future Is Italy – And It's Bleak', an assessment which was unduly translated by press agency ANSA, *La Stampa* and various TV presenters as 'Italy Has a Bleak Future'.[9] The piece was widely reported as having insinuated that Fratelli d'Italia pursues a return to fascism, and much of the uproar in response sought to deny such an obviously false assertion. But the interest in it mainly derived from the perception of where the article had come from. Given Bernie Sanders' defeat in the 2020 Democratic Party primary, the political circles in which I move are not especially influential on the State Department. Yet the column was widely presented as an expression of an American or even US government standpoint; a piece in *La Repubblica* cited it as an example of what 'Washington' thought about the prospect of a Meloni government.[10] Some apparent Fratelli d'Italia supporters on social media alleged 'foreign interference' in the election process itself. Asked why Americans were posing questions about his party, former Defence Minister La Russa pointed out that I did not represent Washington: 'I don't know if the Americans are asking it. The Americans have certainly noted our always pro-Western, pro-Atlanticist position, of absolute support for Ukraine.'[11]

Meloni made this same argument when *La Stampa* asked her for her response to my article: she insisted that, '[a]s demonstrated by [the party's] position on Ukraine there is nothing to fear'.[12] Meloni referred to the article as a 'put-up job', the result of 'Italian left-wing think tanks going around saying that if Meloni wins, Italy will be sucked into a black hole'.[13] For Daniela Santanchè – a politician who had recently used the term with regard to herself – fascism was a question of 'the last century' alone, which historians ought to address as such; people like myself talk about antifascism because we 'make money off it'.[14] Asked to comment on my *New York Times* piece, La Russa had also seen conspiracy afoot, with the hidden hand behind the antifascist attack detected in the article: 'We have specific pieces of evidence to claim that very Italian elements, think-tanks as they are called, are working so foreign papers will help them – desperately – to not lose.'[15] While this would not hurt his party's vote, he insisted it 'was a way of damaging Italy'.[16] He insisted that 'Italian cultural, political and journalistic circles are working in cahoots with foreign papers to tell them what to say'; this would 'not lose [Fratelli d'Italia] any votes, but it is a way to damage Italy'.[17] At the time of writing, the senator had yet to publish his evidence.

Meloni became prime minister on 22 October 2022, as leader of a cabinet uniting postfascists from Fratelli d'Italia, Lega leaders well known for their racist outbursts and figures from both the former Christian Democrats and Berlusconi's centre-right. Italy's most right-wing government since 1945 was not the recreation of Mussolini's regime, or the dawn of a new one, but the image of the modern right. It was made up of parties that are radical in their attacks on their domestic opponents, conspiracy theorist in their understanding of the relations between supposed 'global elites' and the 'radical left', and willing to wage war on migrants in defence of national identity. Yet there were also signs of the limits to its ambitions: Meloni's government promised to do almost nothing to alter Italy's international position, including its place in the eurozone and current support for Ukraine; it also more or less openly accepted that Italy is to remain a land of small businesses with poor productivity and low wages. It is quite plausible that this alliance will not hold; that Meloni's partners will chafe against her leadership or that they will all find themselves faced with unmanageable crises. More radical plans for tax cuts and the removal of welfare benefits may not survive contact with reality. But what Meloni had already made clear was that postfascism is not just a matter of a 'return to the past'. The far right is in power in new times, writing new history for the bearers of the tricolore flame.

Appendix
Voting Patterns in General Elections

Table 1   Votes for Chamber of Deputies in general elections

	Total votes	%	MPs in lower house
MSI			
1948	526,882	2.0	6/574
1953	1,582,154	5.8	29/590
1958	1,407,718	4.8	24/596
1963	1,570,281	5.1	27/630
1968	1,414,036	4.4	24/630
1972 (as MSI-DN)	2,894,722	8.7	56/630
1976	2,238,339	6.1	35/630
1979	1,930,639	5.3	30/630
1983	2,511,487	6.8	42/630
1987	2,281,126	5.9	35/630
1992	2,107,037	5.4	34/630
1994	5,214,133	13.5	109/630
Alleanza Nazionale			
1996	5,870,491	15.7	92/630
2001	4,463,205	12.2	99/630
2006	4,707,126	12.3	72/630
Fratelli d'Italia			
2013	666,765	2.0	9/630
2018	1,426,564	4.3	31/630
2022	7,302,517	26.0	118/400

Fratelli d'Italia rose sharply from 2013 till 2022, but Alleanza Nazionale had already scored several million votes in the mid-1990s.

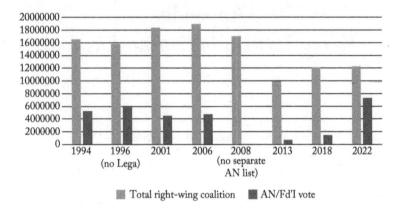

Figure 1 Total votes for right-wing coalition (lower house) in general elections, 1994–2022

This graph shows that the right-wing coalition is not at historically high vote numbers, but a larger share of it went to Fratelli d'Italia in 2022, beating even Alleanza Nazionale's best scores in the mid-1990s.

Notes

INTRODUCTION

1. Veronica Cursi, 'Rachele Mussolini, chi è la nipote del Duce più votata a Roma', *Il Messaggero*, 6 October 2021.
2. 'Caio Mussolini, dopocena a base di dottrina del fascismo: il ristorante lo caccia', *Il Messaggero*, 10 April 2019.
3. Tom Kington, 'Lazio sign Benito's great-grandson Romano Mussolini to bolster their right', *The Times*, 3 February 2021.
4. Giorgia Meloni, 'Fascismo consegnato da decenni alla storia, condannando infami leggi anti-ebraiche', *Corriere della Sera*, YouTube, 12 August 2022.
5. For instance, Allison Pearson, 'Giorgia Meloni isn't far-right – she just says what we all think', *Telegraph*, 28 September 2022.
6. Almirante made these comments at the 1956 MSI congress: see Nicola Rao, *La Fiamma e la Celtica*, Milan: Sperling & Kupfer, 2010, p. 79. 'We should present ourselves for what we really are: that is, the fascists of the RSI [Repubblica Sociale Italiana] … There is just one ambiguity, that of being fascists in a democracy. We alone are estranged [from it] and that is to our honour, but also an almighty difficulty for this democracy, this postwar Italy. Our courage, since 1946, consisted in inserting ourselves into it as the MSI, as a party operating in this democracy'.
7. As recounted by Gianfranco Fini, cited in Enzo Palmesano, *Gianfranco Fini: sfida a Berlusconi*, Rome: Alberti 2010, p. 40.
8. More often referred to within party circles as a break-out of 'the ghetto'.
9. Giorgia Meloni, *Io sono Giorgia: Le mie radici, le mie idee*, Milan: Rizzoli, 2021, Kindle edition, position 17.
10. Marco Tarchi, *La rivoluzione impossibile: dai Campi Hobbit alla nuova destra*, Florence: Vallecchi, 2010.
11. Interviewed in Nicholas Farrell, 'Is Giorgia Meloni the most dangerous woman in Europe?', *The Spectator*, 20 August 2022.
12. Giorgia Meloni, Facebook post, 9 March 2014, during the party's first congress at Fiuggi.

13. 'Congresso Fdi-An, il discorso di apertura di Giorgia Meloni', Fratelli d'Italia, YouTube, 8 March 2014.

14. Giorgia Meloni, *Io sono Giorgia*, position 194.

15. Giorgia Meloni, Facebook post, 3 January 2019.

16. Giorgia Meloni, *Io Sono Giorgia*, position 157. She also cites this in the interview, Edoardo Sylos Labini, 'Giorgia Meloni, la donna sincera che difende sempre tutto quello che ama', *Culturaidentità*, 1 March 2019, and in her speech to the NatCon conference in Rome, 'Giorgia Meloni: god, homeland, family – NatCon Rome 2020', National Conservatism, YouTube, 22 February 2020.

17. Giorgia Meloni, *Io Sono Giorgia*, position 178.

18. 'MEM & J – Io Sono Giorgia (Giorgia Meloni Remix)', YouTube, uploaded 27 October 2019.

19. For instance, regularly referring to 'ten years of the left-wing in government without winning elections'.

20. Michele Barbero, in 'Is Italy returning to its Fascist past?', *Al Jazeera*, 23 September 2022.

21. Cyrille Beyer, 'Giorgia Meloni en 1996: "Je crois que Mussolini était un bon politicien"', *INA*, 1 September 2022.

22. 'Grana per Meloni a Civitavecchia: manifesti della X Mas nella sede di Fratelli d'Italia e croci celtiche', *La Repubblica*, 27 July 2022.

23. Redazione, 'Affile, inaugurato sacrario per soldato di Salò tra polemiche e contestazioni', *RomaToday*, 13 August 2012.

24. See Chapter 5.

25. Ignazio La Russa and Daniela Santanchè, respectively (see Chapter 4).

26. 'Giorgia Meloni avverte: "No ai nostalgici da operetta, sono i traditori della nostra causa"', *Libero*, 28 July 2022.

27. Cited (and video included in) Alberto Consoli, '"Siete penosi, per due mesi non parlate di storia": Mieli distrugge la campagna sul pericolo fascista', *Secolo d'Italia*, 28 July 2022.

28. Speaking at the party's Atreju meetup: see 'Discorso epico di Giorgia Meloni dal palco di Atreju21', Fratelli d'Italia, YouTube, 12 December 2021.

29. Meloni defended the naming of a 'street' in the party's Atreju event after Fascist hierarch Italo Balbo, one of the four key organisers of the March on the Rome and colonial governor of Libya. She dedicated two 13 January 2018 Facebook posts to this dispute; in one she characterised Balbo as a 'great Italian patriot'. In remarks directed against Democratic MP Emanuele Fiano, who has called for tightened laws on Fascist symbolism, she said, 'either you throw me in jail and burn all the books that in various ways talk about people who had anything

to do with fascism, such as Marinetti, Gentile or Balbo himself, or it will become clear that the nonsense you have been spouting all these years about the crime of apologia for fascism was just a blatant ploy to shut up your political opponents in the election campaign'. She called this a 'dictatorship' in a speech to party activists: see 'Fiano (PD) risponde a Giorgia Meloni: non c'era apologia di fascismo nel dedicare una via ad Italo Balbo', *Omnibus*, La7, 15 January 2018.

30. Robert Paxton, *The Anatomy of Fascism*, New York: Knopf, 2004, p. 39.
31. Roger Griffin, 'The "post-Fascism" of the Alleanza Nazionale: a case study in ideological morphology', *Journal of Political Ideologies*, 1, 2, 1996, pp. 123–45.
32. Ibid., p. 142.
33. The historian Giuseppe Parlato emphasises this distinction between the party's historically grounded identity and its anticommunist political rationale in the present: see his 'Delegitimation and anti-communism in Italian neofascism', *Journal of Modern Italian Studies*, 22, 1, 2017, pp. 43–56.
34. See interview with Gregorio Sorgonà (by David Broder), 'How Italy's far right fell in love with the United States', *Jacobin*, 29 July 2022. It discusses his recent book, Gregorio Sorgonà, *La scoperta della destra: il movimento sociale italiano e gli Stati Uniti*, Rome: Viella, 2019.
35. Meloni, *Io Sono Giorgia*, position 300.
36. Meloni, *Io Sono Giorgia*, positions 296–7.
37. Rossana Rossanda, 'Il discorso sulla DC', *Il manifesto*, 28 March 1978.
38. Carlo Marini, 'Meloni ricorda Giorgio Almirante: A 34 anni dalla morte, la destra italiana non dimentica', *Secolo d'Italia*, 22 May 2022.
39. 'MSI: comizio in occasione dell'Anniversario del 25 Aprile', Radio Radicale, 25 April 1992.
40. Paolo Berizzi, 'Neofascismo, ad Ascoli Piceno Fratelli d'Italia celebra la marcia su Roma con una cena-evento', *La Repubblica*, 29 October 2019.

CHAPTER 1

1. For an excellent recent study of the city's postwar history, as a cosmo-politan city having to find its place in a nation state, see Dominique Kirchner Reill, *The fiume crisis: life in the wake of the Habsburg Empire*, Cambridge, MA: Harvard University Press, 2020.
2. Annamaria Vinci, *Sentinelle della patria: il fascismo al confine orientale 1918-1941*, Bari: Laterza 2011.

3. Carlo Schiffrer, *Sguardo storico sui rapporti fra italiani e slavi nella Venezia Giulia*, Rome: Stabilimento Tipografico Colombo, 1946, cited in Annamaria Vinci, *Sentinelle della patria*.

4. Elio Apih, *Italia, Fascismo e antifascismo nella Venezia Giulia (1918–1943)*, p. 15, notes the existence of nationalist irregular forces even before World War I; Renzo de Felice would define the Narodni dom attack one of the first instances of Fascist squadrism proper, in *Mussolini il rivoluzionario, 1883–1920*, Turin: Einaudi, 1965, p. 624.

5. Annamaria Vinci, *Sentinelle della patria*.

6. 'Solenne commemorazione delle vittime del comunismo partigiano', *Corriere della Sera*, 20 January 1944, available at diecifebbraio.info.

7. 'The sinews of peace', the speech given at Westminster College, Fulton, Missouri, on 5 March 1946.

8. Fabiano Capano, 'Cold-War Trieste: metamorphosing ideas of Italian nationhood, 1945–1975', *Modern Italy*, 2016, 21, 1, pp. 51–66.

9. The *Tesi di Trieste* are available at the party leader's homepage: www.giorgiameloni.it/tesitrieste/.

10. In his provocatively titled *Autobiografia di un Fucilatore* (Milan: Edizioni del Borghese 1973, p. 70), MSI founder Giorgio Almirante claims that those who volunteered after 1940 were inspired 'out of the conviction that this was a matter of completing the work of the Risorgimento'.

11. See the overview of this theme in Claudio Pavone, *Dal Risorgimento alla Resistenza*, Rome: Edizioni dell'asino, 2015.

12. *Tesi di Trieste*.

13. Ibid.

14. Ibid.

15. Ibid.

16. Ibid.

17. Ibid.

18. Ibid.

19. Jean Raspail, *The camp of the saints*, New York: Scribner, 1975.

20. *Tesi di Trieste*.

21. The relevant passage in the *Doctrine of Fascism* reads: 'It is not the nation which generates the State; that is an antiquated naturalistic concept which afforded a basis for nineteenth-century propaganda for of national governments. Rather, the nation is created by the State, which gives the people, conscious of its own moral unity, a will and thus a real existence.' The difference is less between the two passages of Gentile, than the fact that the Fratelli d'Italia citation cuts out the word State and replaces it with an ellipse.

22. *Tesi di Trieste*.

23. Ibid.
24. 'Fanno polemica persino sulla statua di D'Annunzio: la Meloni li zittisce', *Secolo d'Italia*, 12 September 2019; she has also claimed that D'Annunzio has 'nothing to envy Che Guevara': 'Giorgia Meloni inaugura gli aforismi su Facebook, Huffpost, 8 August 2016.
25. Ibid.
26. As noted by Franco Ferrari, 'Italy's poll leader says it's "conservative" – but its ideology has clear fascist elements', *Jacobin*, 16 August 2022.
27. Vittoria Belmonte, 'Dio, patria, famiglia: per Repubblica Meloni cita il fascismo, ma il motto risale a Mazzini', *Secolo d'Italia*, 31 March 2019. In fact, while Mazzini does list these themes (while also linking them to a fourth term, 'humanity') in his *Doveri dell'uomo*, the slogan with just the three belongs to Giovanni Giurati, *segretario* of the National Fascist Party, and dates to 1931.
28. For a summary, see Thomas Chatterton Williams, 'The French origins of "you will not replace us"', *New Yorker*, 27 November 2017.
29. *Tesi di Trieste.*
30. Ignazio La Russa, Twitter, 11 February 2018.
31. The motion is republished at www.isbrec.it/wp-content/uploads/2021/02/Mozione-giunta-regionale-Veneto.pdf.
32. Davide Maria de Luca, 'Fratelli d'Italia vuole equiparare le foibe alla Shoah', *Domani*, 28 May 2021.
33. For the 9 February 2021 Veneto region motion, see www.isbrec.it/wp-content/uploads/2021/02/Mozione-giunta-regionale-Veneto.pdf.
34. Eric Gobetti, *E allora le foibe?*, Rome: Laterza 2021.
35. Ibid.
36. One important first contribution was the collective volume Cristiana Colummi et al. (eds), *Storia di un esodo: Istria 1945–1956*, Trieste: Istituto Regionale per la Storia del Movimento di Liberazione nel Friuli Venezia Giulia, 1980. This was a study of the exiles from this region, beginning in the war period itself, which thus also addressed the question of the *foibe*. The preface by Giovanni Miccoli identified the need for the left to break out of its 'cautious and suspicious' attitude toward difficult historical problems, identified with a 'substantially paternalistic' approach to how it spoke to the masses (ibid., p. vii). Colummi's contribution addressed postwar literature on the *foibe*, citing a 1973 article by Guido Miglia which set the 'barbarism' and 'often even personal vendettas' behind the foibe in the context of twenty years of fascism and denationalisation of Slavic populations (ibid., p. 42). She criticises the idea that the *foibe* were the 'concrete

example of a deliberate will to extermination and genocide' as a 'political mystification' (ibid., p. 38).

37. Andrea Cossu, 'Memory, symbolic conflict and changes in the national calendar in the Italian Second Republic', *Modern Italy*, 15, 1, 2010, pp. 3–19. For an English-language reconstruction which draws heavily on Allied military responses to the events, see Elysa McConnell, 'International disputes in the Italian-Yugoslavian borderlands', *Les Cahiers Sirice*, 22, 2019, pp. 117–34; in Italian, see Gorazd Bazc, 'Gli angloamericani e le "foibe"', in Jože Pirjevec, *Foibe: una storia d'Italia*, Turin: Einaudi, 2009.

38. The historiographical 'state of the art' is well summarised in Raoul Pupo, 'Le foibe fra storiografia a uso pubblico', *Passato e Presente*, 84, 2011, pp. 145–63. See his *Il lungo esodo – Istria: le persecuzioni, le foibe, l'esilio*, Milan: Rizzoli, 2005; Jože Pirjevec, *Foibe: una storia d'Italia*, Turin: Einaudi, 2009.

39. 'Foibe, la cerimonia a Basovizza – Salvini: bimbi nelle foibe e ad Auschwitz sono uguali', *Sky tg24*, 10 February 2019; 'Giorno del Ricordo, Meloni, Salvini e Gasparri alla foiba di Basovizza', *Vista Agenzia Televisiva Nazionale*, YouTube, 10 February 2020. On 10 February 2022, he tweeted this phrasing with a short video about the Day of Memory, ending with the text 'Never Again Guilty for Being Italians' juxtaposed with the Lega's logo.

40. On this, see Eric Gobetti, *E allora le foibe?*, Rome: Laterza 2021.

41. The 'offending' booklet is available at www.irsml.eu/vademecum_giorno_ricordo/Vademecum_10_febbraio_IrsrecFVG_2019.pdf, and the motion is reproduced in Nicoletta Bourbaki, 'A giocare con il nero perdi sempre', Medium post, 29 March 2019.

42. The law is published online at https://presidenza.governo.it/ufficio_cerimoniale/normativa/legge_20040330_92.pdf.

43. There is no official list of all the medal recipients, but Sandi Volk has compiled one based on individual official statements and news reports. While in some cases there is no evident relationship between their job and the occupation regime, a large majority are police, soldiers, militia members or Fascist party members. See the list at www.diecifebbraio.info/wp-content/uploads/2021/01/premiati-2020.pdf.

44. 'Via la medaglia al fascista Mori: grazie all'Anpi rivive l'odio di 70 anni fa', *Secolo d'Italia*, 16 March 2015.

45. 'Ritirata l'onorificenza a Paride Mori, soddisfazione del Pd', *La Repubblica*, 24 April 2015.

46. Federazione delle Associazioni degli Esuli Istriani, Fiumiani e Dalmati, 'Onorificenza a Paride Mori', 25 March 2015.

47. For an overview of worsening relations between the parties and their connection to the territorial dispute, see Karlo Ruzicic-Kessler, 'Togliatti, Tito and the shadow of Moscow 1944/45–1948: Post-war territorial disputes and the communist world', *Journal of European Integration History*, 20, 2, 2014, pp. 181–201. See also Geoffrey Swain, 'The Cominform: Tito's International?', *The Historical Journal*, 35, 3, 1992, pp. 641–63, see p. 657 for the clash between the parties at the September 1947 Cominform congress.

48. Cited in Pirjevec, *Foibe: Una storia d'Italia*, p. 204.

49. See my obituary, David Broder, 'The Fascists' historian', *Jacobin*, 14 January 2020; 'Giampaolo Pansa e la storia non condivisa', *Internazionale*, 25 January 2020.

50. Bruno Vespa, *Storia d'Italia, da Mussolini a Berlusconi*, Milan: Mondadori, 2005, pp. 9–10.

51. Ibid., p. 10.

52. Ibid.

53. Four works entitled *Il sangue dei vinti*, *Sconosciuto 1945*, *La grande bugia* and *I vinti non dimenticano*.

54. Giampaolo Pansa, *I gendarmi della memoria*, Milan: Sperling & Kupfer, 2007.

55. Notably his *Il triangolo della morte: la politica della strage in Emilia durante e dopo la guerra civile*, Milan: Mursia, 1992 and *Storia della guerra civile in Italia, 1943–1945*, Milan: FPE, 1965–6.

56. Claudio Pavone, *A civil war*, London: Verso Books, 2013, translated by Peter Levy with the assistance of David Broder. Pavone had in fact used the term before, and as he notes (see chapter 5 of his book) it was often used, if not ubiquitously, within Resistance-era antifascist press.

57. In the introduction to the English translation, Stanislao Pugliese compares this to 'Nixon going to China': Pavone, *A civil war*, p. x.

58. See ibid., pp. 271–2: he criticises 'a bland, reassuring vision of the Resistance, where all trace of civil war has been scrubbed out', '[t]he anti-Fascist unity embodied in the system of [National Liberation Committees], which is still the legitimising source of the Italian Republic and of what has been called its "arco costituzionale", is thus reinterpreted as mere anti-German unity, almost as if the Republic was founded on opposition to Germany and not to Fascism'.

59. Giampaolo Pansa, *I vinti non dimenticano: I crimini ignorati della nostra guerra civile*, Milan: Rizzoli, 2010. Also typical in this regard is his novel *I Figli dell'Aquila*, Milan: Sperling & Kupfer, 2002, in which the hero, the young Bruno, is stirred to fight for the Salò Republic out of patriotism and the will to redeem Italy from the cowardice of Badoglio and the king. This account also 'humanises' the German

soldiers on Italian soil: 'They found themselves in a foreign, enemy land. They knew they were headed for defeat, the Fatherland was distant, their families disappeared under the Allied bombs. Inevitably, they had no regard for anyone.' Cited in Giuseppe Spina, 'Lettera a Giampaolo Pansa', in Giampaolo Pansa, *Non è Storia senza i vinti: La memoria negata della Guerra civile*, Milan: Rizzoli, 2022.

60. The comparison was explicitly made in a 2022 education ministry circular. See 'Foibe, circolare del ministero dell'Istruzione: "Italiani categoria umana da nullificare come gli ebrei"', *La Stampa*, 10 February 2022. It stated that '[t]he human category [the *foibe* killings] wanted to bend and culturally nullify was Italians. Shortly before, it had happened, on a European scale, to another category, Jews.'

61. Guido Franzinetti offers this interesting insight into the reasons why not only the MSI but also the ex-Partito Comunista Italiano (PCI), the other party unable to hold governmental power in the First Republic, could take up this issue as its own, in the years when it dropped its residual 'Communist' identity. Cited in Raoul Pupo, 'Le foibe fra storiografia a uso pubblico', p. 152. Franzinetti writes that '[p]aradoxically, at the end of the Cold War the PCI found itself with more political and ideological baggage than the MSI's own ('Le riscoperte delle "foibe"', in Jože Pirjevec, *Foibe: Una storia d'Italia*, p. 320), adding that the 'Holocaustisation' of the *foibe* itself helped the centre-left to move toward recognition of it (ibid., pp. 323–4).

62. 'Gasparri: ora spero di vedere una seria fiction sulle foibe', *La Stampa*, 18 April 2002. I owe this reference to Damiano Garofalo, 'La memorializzazione delle Foibe e il paradigma della Shoah', *Officina della Storia*, www.officinadellastoria.eu/it/2016/07/06/la-memorializzazione-delle-foibe-e-il-paradigma-della-shoah/.

63. For Raoul Pupo, a scholar of this period, it would 'be difficult to speak negatively enough' about the film. See his 'Le foibe fra storiografia a uso pubblico', p. 158.

64. Gianluca Modolo, 'Film sulle foibe in tv, le associazioni degli esuli contro Fratelli d'Italia: "Giù le mani dal nostro dramma"', *La Repubblica*, 1 February 2019.

65. As Gobetti notes in *E allora le foibe?*, the difference with the earlier miniseries is that in this case the victim with whom viewers are meant to sympathise appears not simply as an Italian, but as a Fascist.

66. 'Il fumetto "Foiba Rossa" sarà distribuito nelle scuole secondarie di Verona', *Verona Sera*, 7 February 2019; 'Piemonte, in tutte le scuole il fumetto sulle foibe ma è polemica: "Così si sdogana il fascismo"'. *La Repubblica*, 12 February 2020; 'Umbria, polemica sul fumetto Foiba

Rossa distribuito alle scuole – Studenti: "Casa editrice legata a partiti neofascisti'", *Corriere dell'Umbria*, 15 February 2020.

67. The article is entitled 'Profughi', *l'Unità*, Milan edition, 30 November 1946.
68. Ibid.
69. The collective dismantles this version of events: see 'L'Unità e gli esuli', https://nicolettabourbaki.medium.com/unita-e-gli-esuli-f669dee e3b3b, 14 January 2019; the article from the PCI daily is reproduced there.
70. Ibid.
71. See Chapter 3.
72. This claim closely resembled historian Renzo de Felice's assertion in a 1988 interview that 'one can be antifascist and not democratic. This … applies also to the Italian Communists': 'La Costituzione non è certo il Colosseo', *Corriere della Sera*, 7 January 1988.
73. 'Solo Salvini e Meloni ricordano più le foibe della Shoah sui social', *Pagella Politica*, 11 February 2022.
74. 'Pericolosa deriva da fermare: Giorgia Meloni affossa Tomaso Montanari "così i talebani sono nati nelle università"', *Il Tempo*, 28 August 2021.
75. Sergio Luzzatto, *La crisi dell'antifascismo*, Turin: Einaudi, 2004, p. 8.
76. Ibid., pp. 58 *et seq.*
77. See Chapter 5.
78. Interviewed in Carmelo Caruso, 'Non sono fascisti: sono selvaggi – Usata per tutto la parola fascismo si svuota', *Il Foglio*, 13 October 2021.
79. Ibid.
80. 'DiMartedì, Paolo Mieli smentisce la sinistra: "Pericolo di fascismo? Una assurdità, cosa passerà alla storia"', *Libero Quotidiano*, 27 October 2021; the clip of his intervention on La7's *DiMartedì* is available on YouTube.
81. Renzo de Felice, *Mussolini*, Turin, Einaudi: 1964–97.
82. See the reconstruction in Francesco Germinario, *Da Salò al Governo*, Turin: Bollati Boringhieri, 2005, p. 83.
83. Francesco Germinario, *L'Altra memoria: l'estrema destra, Salò e la Resistenza*, Turin: Bollati Boringhieri, 1999.
84. Pasquale Chessa (interviewer) and Renzo de Felice, *Rosso e Nero*, Milan: Baldini e Castoldi, 1995, pp. 61–5, 68–9.
85. Ibid., pp. 55–7.
86. As part of two interviews by Giuliano Ferrara: 'Perché deve cadere la retorica dell'antifascismo', *Corriere della Sera*, 27 December 1987; followed by 'La Costituzione non è certo il Colosseo', 7 January 1988.

87. John Foot, *Italy's divided memory*, New York: Palgrave Macmillan, 2009.

88. Alberto Asor Rosa in Simonetta Fiori (interviewer), *Il grande silenzio: Intervista sugli intellettuali*, Bari: Laterza, 2011.

89. 'I ragazzi di Salò'. The statement was by Luciano Violante, elected president of the Chamber of Deputies in 1996.

90. Stanislao Pugliese, 'Introduction', in Claudio Pavone, *A civil war*.

91. Cited in Fabrizio Boschi, 'I Mussolini querelano la Rai, "Violata la tomba di famiglia"', *Il Giornale*, 13 December 2017.

92. Alessandra Menzani, 'Raitre profana la tomba di Mussolini: cosa si sono spinti i fare i "rossi" in diretta', *Libero*, 17 December 2017.

93. Ibid.

94. Alessandra Mussolini on *Non è l'Arena*, La7, 17 December 2017.

95. Luca Sablone, 'L'offensiva di FdI: "Al bando il comunismo per legge"', *Il Giornale*, 7 June 2021.

96. Enrico Tata, 'Caso Civitavecchia, Giorgia Meloni: "nostalgici da operetta sono traditori di Fratelli d'Italia"', *Fanpage*, 28 July 2022.

97. 'Gerardo Picardo intervista Giano Accame', in Pansa, *Non è Storia senza i vinti*, p. 116.

98. La Russa, 'A trent'anni dalla caduta del muro di Berlino la sinistra non ha fatto i conti con il comunismo', fratelliditaliasenato.it.

99. For a study of this theme see Giuseppe Parlato, 'Delegitimation and anticommunism in Italian neofascism', *Journal of Modern Italian Studies*, 22, 1, 2017, pp. 43–56.

100. See Antonio di Francesco, 'Ignazio la Russa: "noi abbiamo chiuso con il fascismo al tempo di Almirante"', *La Verità*, 11 October 2021.

101. Charlotte Matteini, 'Il Giorno del ricordo dedicato alle vittime delle Foibe, tra celebrazioni e polemiche politiche', *Fanpage*, 10 February 2017.

102. Milena Desanctis, 'Meloni: "in Italia la libertà, mentre la celebriamo, non è più scontata. Aiutateci ad abolire il coprifuoco"', *Secolo d'Italia*, 25 April 2021.

103. '25 aprile, Meloni: libertà significa difendere sovranità dei popoli', giorgiameloni.it, 25 April 2022; '25 aprile, Meloni attenta a non scontentare i fascisti', *Globalist*, 25 April 2022.

104. 'La Russa: "Il 25 Aprile diventi il giorno del ricordo delle vittime di tutte le guerre del Coronavirus"', *Corriere della Sera*, 18 April 2020.

105. Alexander D. Barder, *Global race war: international politics and racial hierarchy*, Oxford: Oxford University Press, 2021, pp. 211 *et seq.*

106. Interview by Gad Lerner, '"Le grand remplacement", il manifesto ideologico delle destre sovraniste', *L'Approdo*, Rai, 14 June 2019.

107. In an 18 April 2020 Facebook post she accused 'the Left of try[ing] to exploit the COVID-19 crisis to amnesty irregular migrants and substitute the Italian workforce with a low-cost foreign one'.

108. Alessandra Muglia, 'Il killer di Christchurch: "Combatto contro gli invasori, mi ispiro a Breivik e Luca Trainii"', *Corriere della Sera*, 15 March 2019.

109. 'Sparatoria razzista a Macerata, scontri tra Forza Nuova e la polizia', *Corriere della Sera*, 8 February 2018.

110. Piera Matteucci, 'Raid razzista a Macerata, Salvini: "Colpa di chi ci riempie di clandestini"', Renzi: "Ora calma e responsabilità"', *La Repubblica*, 3 February 2018.

111. Sergio Rame, 'Meloni: "Casapound e Forza Nuova non sono partiti xenofobi"', *Il Giornale*, 10 February 2018.

112. 'Macerata, scontri in piazza tra polizia e manifestanti di Forza Nuova', *La Repubblica*, YouTube, 9 February 2018.

113. Giorgia Meloni, Twitter, 31 October 2018. See also the press conference cited in '4 Novembre, il video celebrativo di Giorgia Meloni tra Grande guerra e sovranismo: "Oggi come ieri non passa lo straniero"', *Il Fatto Quotidiano*, 1 November 2018.

114. Giorgia Meloni, Twitter, 8 January 2018.

115. Giorgia Meloni, Twitter, 24 March 2019.

116. 'La Ue è complice dell'invasione dell'Europa e del progetto di sostituzione etnica: Mogherini si dimetta', giorgiameloni.it, 3 February 2017.

117. Ibid.

118. The bill was ultimately felled in the Senate without a vote taking place, due to the lack of quorum.

119. 'Ius soli, il centrodestra unito in piazza: "In Italia disegno di sostituzione etnica"', *alanews*, YouTube, 21 June 2017.

120. *Tesi di Trieste*.

121. Meloni speaking on La7's *L'Aria che tira*, 26 November 2019: she explained that NGOs care about refugees from Africa but not from Venezuela because 'there is a plan to bring in people different from our identity'.

122. Matteo Salvini, *In Onda*, La 7, 3 July 2018.

123. 'Il voto che unisce l'Italia: il programma', text available at www.bollettinoadapt.it/wp-content/uploads/2018/02/Fratelli-dItalia.pdf.

124. *Tesi di Trieste*.

125. 'Bimbi stranieri in classe: consiglio comunale approva tetto del 30%', *Il Gazzettino*, 27 November 2018.

CHAPTER 2

1. 'Funerali Assunta Almirante: l'uscita del feretro', 28 April 2022, YouTube.
2. 'Saluti romani e slogan fascisti ai funerali di Assunta Almirante', *Fanpage*, 28 April 2022.
3. *Io Sono Giorgia*, position 255.
4. Carlo Marini, 'Meloni ricorda Giorgio Almirante: A 34 anni dalla morte, la destra italiana non dimentica', *Secolo d'Italia*, 22 May 2022.
5. *Io Sono Giorgia*, position 179.
6. The words 'believe and fight' are strikingly reminiscent of the Mussolinian slogan 'believe, obey, fight'.
7. *Io Sono Giorgia*, position 118.
8. A 26 January 1986 speech, reported in Mario Tortello, 'Almirante: rifarò il segretario', *La Stampa*, 24 March 1986, cited in Aldo Grandi, *Almirante: biografia di un fascista*, Reggio Emilia: Diarkos, 2021, p. 409.
9. 'Almirante risfodera la nostalgia per celebrare i 40 anni del Msi', *Corriere della Sera*, 27 January 1986, cited in ibid.
10. Cited in Marta Bravi, 'La Russa sfida il sindaco: "I mazzi di fiori uguali per fascisti e partigiani"', *Il Giornale*, 6 November 2016.
11. Ibid. He here made specific reference to tributes to playwright and actor Dario Fo, upon his death the previous month; Fo's youthful enrolment in the Salò Republic's armed forces was in fact the source of a series of controversies including a major defamation case in 1978–9.
12. The title of Marco Tarchi's book, *Esuli in patria: I fascisti nell'Italia repubblicana*, Parma: Guanda, 1995.
13. Piero Ignazi, *Il polo escluso: profilo storico del Movimento Sociale Italiano*, Bologna: il Mulino, 1998.
14. Intervention at the 1963 MSI congress cited in Conti, *L'anima nera*, p. 35.
15. See Valentina Pisany (ed.), *La difesa della razza: antologia 1938–1943*, Milan: Bompiani, 2007.
16. 'Il fascismo e i problemi della razza', published in *Il Giornale d'Italia*, 14 July 1938, text available at anpi.it.
17. Cited in 'Giorgio Almirante e la razza: ecco cosa scrisse nel 1942', *Corriere della Sera*, 14 June 2018.
18. Giorgio Almirante, *Autobiografia di un fucilatore*, Milan: Edizioni del Borghese, 1974, pp. 124–5.

19. Reconstructed in Nicola Rao, *Neofascisti! La Destra italiana da Salò a Fiuggi nel ricordo dei protagonisti*, Rome: Settimo Sigillo, 1999, pp. 5–8.
20. Almirante, *Autobiografia di un fucilatore*, p. 128.
21. Arianna Streccioni, *A destra della destra dentro e fuori l'Msi, dai Far a Terza posizione*, Roma: Settimo Sigillo, 2008, p. 17.
22. Giuseppe Parlato, *Fascisti senza Mussolini le origini del neofascismo in Italia, 1943–1948*, Bologna: il Mulino, 2008, p. 241.
23. Giuseppe Parlato, 'L'esordio di Almirante', in Parlato and Andrea Ungari (eds), *Le destre nell'Italia del secondo dopoguerra: dal qualunquismo ad Alleanza nazionale*, Soveria Mannelli: Rubbettino Editore, 2021, p. 90.
24. Ibid.
25. Ibid., p. 101.
26. Antonio Carioti, *Il 'Sessantotto nero' dei giovani neofascisti nel dopoguerra, 1945–1951*, Roma: Mursia, 2008, p. 71.
27. The case is reconstructed in Mimmo Franzinelli, *L'Amnistia Togliatti: 1946 – Colpo di spugna sui crimini fascisti*, Milan: Mondadori, 2016.
28. As discussed in Mimmo Franzinelli, *Il fascismo è finito il 25 aprile 1945*, Bari: Laterza, 2022.
29. Giulio Andreotti, *Concerto a sei voci: Roma 1944–1945 – I primi governi dell'Italia liberata*, Milan: Boroli, 2007, p. 17.
30. Cesare Bermani, *Il nemico interno*, Rome: Odradek, 1997.
31. See Davide Conti, *Gli uomini di Mussolini : prefetti, questori e criminali di guerra dal fascismo alla Repubblica italiana*, Turin: Einaudi, 2018; Franzinelli, *Il fascismo è finito il 25 aprile 1945*.
32. Francesco Germinario, *L'Altra memoria: l'estrema destra, Salò e la Resistenza*, Turin: Bollati Boringhieri, 1999. See my review at David Broder, 'The memory of the defeated', *Jacobin*, 28 April 2018.
33. Illustrative in this case are the examples cited by Germinario in *L'Altra memoria*, for instance Enrico de Boccard's novel *Donne e mitra*, in which the fictional Ismaele Cohen is driven by patriotism to fight for the Repubblica Sociale Italiana, even though his Jewishness set him against it.
34. On liberal conceptions of pluralism and its limits, see Federico Mazzei, *Liberalismo e democrazia protetta: un dibattito alle origini dell'Italia repubblicana*, Soveria Mennelli: Rubbettino, 2011.
35. On contemporary debates on its application, see Chapter 4.
36. See Sandro Setta, *L'Uomo qualunque, 1944–1948*, Bari: Laterza, 1975.
37. Germinario, *L'Altra memoria*, pp. 81 et seq.
38. Cited in Piero Ignazi, *Il Polo escluso: profilo storico del Movimento sociale italiano*, Bologna: Il Mulino, 1998, p. 68.

39. Parlato, 'L'esordio di Almirante', pp. 131–3.
40. Giuseppe Parlato, 'Guareschi, Trieste e la Destra Possibile', in *Le destre nell'Italia del secondo dopoguerra*, p. 137.
41. Nicola Tonietto, *La genesi del neofascismo in Italia: dal periodo clandestino alle manifestazioni per Trieste italiana – 1943–1953*, Florence: Le Monnier, 2019. See also Parlato, 'Guareschi, Trieste e la Destra Possibile'.
42. As borne out by the diplomatic correspondence with US ambassador Clare Boothe Luce: see *Foreign relations of the United States 1952–1954: Diplomatic Papers*, Vol. 8, Washington: Government Printing Office, 1988, pp. 239 *et seq*.
43. See Parlato, 'Guareschi, Trieste e la Destra Possibile', pp. 144–7.
44. As reconstructed in Sergio Luzzatto, *Il Corpo del Duce*, Turin: Einaudi, 2019, pp. 278–85.
45. Ibid.
46. Ibid., p. 285.
47. Andrea Ungari, 'I progetti di "Grande Destra"', in *Le destre nell'Italia del secondo dopoguerra*, p. 182.
48. Guido Crainz, *Storia del miracolo italiano culture, identità, trasformazioni fra anni cinquanta e sessanta*, Rome: Donzelli, 2005, p. 172.
49. Gregorio Sorgonà suggested this in an interview with the author, 25 June 2022.
50. See the reconstruction in Philip Cooke, *Luglio 1960: Tambroni e la repressione fallita*, Milan: Teti, 2000.
51. Ibid., p. 76. See also Manuela Consonni, *L'eclisse dell'antifascismo Resistenza, questione ebraica e cultura politica in Italia dal 1943 al 1989*, Bari: Laterza, 2015.
52. The most famous example of this phenomenon taking place was in the Sicilian regional government led by Silvio Milazzo in 1958–9; the Christian Democrat formed an administration reliant on both the PCI and MSI, earning him expulsion from his own party.
53. Roberto Chiarini, 'Il Msi: il problema storico di una destra illegittima', *Democrazia e diritto*, 34, 1, January–March 1994, p. 95, cited in Ungari, 'I progetti di "Grande Destra"', p. 183.
54. E.g. 'Trecento giuristi chiedono che il MSI sia posto fuori legge', *l'Unità*, 29 June 1960; Giorgio Amendola, 'La forza del popolo: l'MSI deve essere messo fuori legge!', *l'Unità*, 3 July 1960; Flavio Michelini, 'Ardente assemblea delle forze antifasciste a Genova', *l'Unità*, 4 July 1960.
55. Pierluigi Totaro, 'L'azione politica di Aldo Moro per l'autonomia e l'unità della Dc nella crisi del 1960', *Studi Storici*, 46, 2, 2005, pp. 437–513.

56. This also fed the idea of the Resistance as an 'unfinished revolution', for example in Renzo Del Carria, *Proletari senza rivoluzione*, Rome: Oriente, 1970. See Steve Wright, 'Missed opportunities – new left readings of the Italian Resistance', in Alastair Davidson and Steve Wright (eds), *'Never give in': the Italian Resistance and politics*, New York: Peter Lang, 1998.

57. '"Non votate come vorrebbero votaste le Brigate Rosse" Appelli finali per il voto del Referendum del 1974 sul divorzio', *Radio Radicale*, 13 May 2021.

58. For a sympathetic account by the central figure behind the camps, see Marco Tarchi, *La rivoluzione impossibile: dai Campi Hobbit alla nuova destra*, Florence: Vallecchi, 2010.

59. See Francesco Cassata, *A destra del fascismo: profilo politico di Julius Evola*, Turin: Bollati Boringhieri, 2003; Loredana Guerrieri, 'La giovane destra neofascista italiana e il '68: il gruppo de "L'Orologio"', *Storicamente*, 5, 14.

60. Francesco Germinario, *Da Salò al governo: immaginario e cultura politica della destra italiana*, Turin: Bollati Boringhieri, 2005, p. 69.

61. *Tesi di Trieste*.

62. Gregorio Sorgonà, *La scoperta della destra: il Movimento sociale italiano e gli Stati Uniti*, Rome: Viella, 2019, pp. 45 *et seq.*

63. Conti, *L'anima nera*, pp. 149 *et seq.*

64. Clemente Graziani, *La Guerra rivoluzionaria*, Rome: La litograf, 1963.

65. Mario Tedeschi, 'Il PCI prepara il terrorismo organizzato', *L'Italiano*, 7 July 1961, cited in Pier Paolo Alfei, 'La guerra rivoluzionaria nella Destra italiana (1950–1969)', laureate thesis in contemporary history, Università di Macerata, 2015–16, p. 89.

66. Franco Ferraresi, *Threats to Democracy: The Radical Right in Italy after the War*, Princeton, NJ: Princeton University Press, 1996, p. 53.

67. Cited in Alfei, 'La guerra rivoluzionaria nella Destra italiana', p. 93.

68. Ibid., p. 94.

69. Davide Conti, *L'Anima nera della Repubblica*, Bari: Laterza, 2013, pp. 53–6.

70. Ferraresi, *Threats to democracy*, pp. 69–70.

71. See Andrea Mammone, *Transnational neofascism in France and Italy*, Cambridge: Cambridge University Press, 2015, pp. 106–8.

72. Enrico de Boccard, 'Lineamenti ed interpretazione storica della guerra rivoluzionaria'; the text of this and the other contributions is available at stragi.it.

73. Cited in Aldo Giannuli et al., *Dopo le bombe Piazza Fontana e l'uso pubblico della storia*, Milan: Mimesis, 2019.

74. Cited in David Ward, *Contemporary Italian narrative and 1970s terrorism: stranger than fact*, London: Palgrave Macmillan, 2017, p. 13.

75. Anna Cento Bull interviewed him in 2005 and summarises his comments in this phrase. See her *Italian neofascism: the strategy of tension and the politics of nonreconciliation*, Oxford: Berghahn, 2007, p. 34.

76. See the interview and profile of the MSI leader by Melton S. Davis, 'Almirante is no Mussolini yet', *New York Times*, 6 June 1971.

77. Stefano delle Chiaie, 'Almirante, un guitto', *La Repubblica*, 2 December 1984, cited in Grandi, *Almirante*, pp. 398–400; see also p. 293.

78. Nino Tripodi, 'Europa senza volto', *Secolo d'Italia*, 7 October 1972, cited in Sorgonà, *La scoperta della destra*, p. 59.

79. Ferraresi, *Threats to democracy*, pp. 117–24.

80. See his reflections collected in Enrico Berlinguer, *I comunisti italiani e il Cile*, Rome: Riuniti, 1973.

81. Italicus, 'Le pentole vuote di Santiago', *Secolo d'Italia*, 15 October 1972, cited in Sorgonà, *La Scoperta della destra*, p. 58.

82. This regime was deemed 'in appearance absolute but in reality the will of the majority ... attracted neither by Anglo-Saxon democracy or the party-ocracy'. Francesco Cavalletti, 'Miope faziosità verso la Spagna', *Secolo d'Italia*, 6 January 1974, cited in Sorgonà, *La Scoperta della destra*, p. 58.

83. Italicus, 'La tigre de Alliende', *Secolo d'Italia*, 18 May 1973, cited in Sorgonà, *La Scoperta della destra*, p. 61.

84. 'Per la libertà in Chile, i militari destituiscono Allende', *Secolo d'Italia*, 12 September 1973.

85. 'Dopo tre anni di tiranni comunista, il Cile ... ha scelto la libertà', *Secolo d'Italia*, 13 September 1973, cited in Sorgonà, *La Scoperta della destra*, p. 62.

86. See my interview of Sorgonà: 'How Italy's far right fell in love with the United States', *Jacobin Magazine*, 29 July 2022.

87. For another such case, see Amy King, 'Antagonistic martyrdom: memory of the 1973 Rogo di Primavalle', *Modern Italy*, 25, 1, 2020, pp. 33–48.

88. See Luciano Cheles, '"Nostalgia dell'avvenire": the propaganda of the Italian far right between tradition and innovation', in Cheles et al. (eds), *The far right in western and eastern Europe*, London: Longman, 1995, p. 55.

89. 'Presentazione del libro "Cuori neri" di Luca Telese', *Radio Radicale*, 3 September 2006. Meloni commented that while the stories of murdered MSI members related in Luca Telese's book *Cuori neri* were a powerful 'glue' for her political side, 'our community has done for

these young men exactly what it has done with the history of the *foibe*', that is, 'transforming them into a shared inheritance to teach that it must not happen again'.

90. Meloni cited Ramelli's case during her speech to the Chamber of Deputies. Upon the vote of confidence in her government on 25 October 2022, she said that '[t]he Italian democratic right has always acted in the full light of day and in full force in our republican institutions, even in the darkest years of criminalisation and political violence, when in the name of militant anti-fascism innocent young men were murdered with spanners'. Cited in Alessandra Benignetti, '"Innocenti uccisi in nome dell'antifascismo": Meloni ricorda le vittime degli anni di piombo', *Il Giornale*, 25 October 2022.

91. Cited in Pierluigi Zavaroni, *Caduti e memoria nella lotta politica: le morti violente della stagione dei movimenti*, Bologna: FrancoAngeli, 2010, pp. 137–8.

92. Ibid.

93. 'Adesso anche a Lodi c'è via Ramelli: il sindaco Casanova scopre la targa', *Il Cittadino*, 29 April 2021.

94. See the useful study of this combination, Elia Rosati, 'L'eterno Presente! La trincea della memoria storica del neofascismo italiano, il caso Sergio Ramelli', *Zapruder*, 42, January–April 2017, pp. 40–53.

95. Walter Veltroni, 'Sergio Ramelli, il ragazzo con il Ciao che venne ucciso perchè "fascista"', *Corriere della Sera*, 16 February 2020.

96. In 2015, Ignazio La Russa, the Fratelli d'Italia leader who had once acted as a lawyer for Ramelli's family, addressed a meeting on 'forty years of antifascist hatred' – see '"40 anni di odio antifascista": a Milano incontro in memoria di Sergio Ramelli', *Secolo d'Italia*, 17 June 2015.

97. On this, see Giovanni Tizian, 'Strage di Bologna, Meloni e Fratelli d'Italia sono i negazionisti della matrice fascista', *Domani*, 2 August 2022. While four neofascist terrorists have been handed definitive convictions, Meloni's social media posts marking the anniversary have consistently referred to an unresolved judicial process ('Strage di Bologna, Meloni: Una ferita aperta per tutta la Nazione', giorgiameloni.it, 2 August 2022). On 2 August 2021, she thus tweeted: 'more than 40 years since the Bologna massacre, amidst shadows and red-herrings, we continue to remember all the victims and call for justice'. In 2018, Fratelli d'Italia MP Paola Frassinetti told parliament that the attack was not attributable to the far right, citing to this effect words from former president Francesco Cossiga (see Chapter 3); 'Governo Meloni, quando nel 2018 la neo sottosegretaria di FdI Frassinetti diceva: "La strage di Bologna non ha matrice fascista"', *Il Fatto Quotidiano*, 1 November 2022.

98. Conti, *L'Anima nera*, p. 139.
99. See Sorgonà, *La scoperta della destra*, pp. 37–47; he notes (p. 44) that the MSI's own memoranda to US Republican officials were 'impregnated with a simplistic and erroneous idea that Italian politics was a sort of function of the [US] Embassy on [Rome's] Via Veneto', in effect hoping for relations with the Nixon administration that could grant this small party a legitimacy that they lacked in domestic politics.
100. See Giorgio Galli, *La crisi italiana e la destra internazionale*, Milan: Mondadori, 1974.
101. A connection noted by Alessandro Campi in the collective volume *Pinuccio Tatarella: passione e intelligenza al servizio dell'Italia*, Rome: Giubilei Regnani, 2019, p. 109.
102. Cited in Grandi, *Almirante*, p. 379.
103. Cited in ibid., p. 397.
104. Clemente Pistilli, 'Terracini, il Comune vuole piazza Almirante-Berlinguer', *La Repubblica*, 29 July 2020.
105. 'Pannella al congresso del Msi ("il fascismo è qui!") 1982', *Radio Radicale*, 20 February 1985.
106. See Cheles, 'Nostalgia dell'avvenire', pp. 72, 74.

CHAPTER 3

1. Alessandro Fulloni, 'Le monetine tirate a Craxi? Fu un'idea di Buontempo', *Corriere della Sera*, 30 April 2013.
2. Eugenio Scalfari, 'Come ai tempi del caso Moro', *La Repubblica*, 30 April 1993. He added that 'never since 1945 has Italian democracy run greater dangers', a view echoed in Ferdinando Adornato, 'Attenti, Rischiamo Weimar', *La Repubblica*, 1 May 1993.
3. 'MSI: comizio in occasione dell'Anniversario del 25 Aprile', *Radio Radicale*, 25 April 1992.
4. 'Gli applausi del MSI a Cossiga', *La Repubblica*, 19 March 1991.
5. Ibid.
6. Discussed in Antonio Carioti, 'From the ghetto to "Palazzo Chigi": the ascent of the National Alliance', *Italian Politics*, 2006, pp. 57–78.
7. Cited in Marco Tarchi, *Dal MSI ad AN organizzazione e strategie*, Bologna: Il Mulino, 1997, p. 118.
8. Cited in 'Berlusconi, il gran giorno', *La Stampa*, 26 January 1994.
9. Piero Ignazi, *Postfascisti? Dal Movimento sociale italiano ad Alleanza nazionale*, Bologna: Il Mulino, 1994, pp. 89 *et seq.* This sense of Fini's return marking an 'indisputable victory' over Rauti's current also appears in Ungari, 'Da Fini a Fini', p. 226.

10. Cited in 'Berlusconi dice che fu lui a portare i fascisti al governo', *Il Post*, 29 September 2019.

11. Ibid.

12. Cibited in Ungari, 'Da Fini a Fini', p. 238.

13. On this, see Broder, *First they took Rome*, London: Verso Books, 2020.

14. Cited in 'Berlusconi, il gran giorno', *La Stampa*, 26 January 1994.

15. Ibid.

16. 'Il migliore resta Mussolini', *La Stampa*, 1 April 1994.

17. 'Ecco il 25 aprile in "nero"', *La Stampa*, 21 April 1994; 'Fina, una Messa per Dimenticare', *La Repubblica*, 26 April 1994.

18. Alan Cowell, 'Leader of Italian neo-fascists praises Mussolini', *New York Times*, 2 April 1994.

19. Both Di Rupo and Tatarella were interviewed about the incident for *l'Unità*: 'Di Rupo "Sono valori portanti non banalità"'; 'Tatarella, "Non sono fascista. E Salò …"', in the 31 May 1994 edition; Di Rupo said that the MSI's politics had to be fought 'fundamentally, beyond normal political fighting'.

20. John Tagliabue, 'Italian coalition trips on old Yugoslavia issue', *New York Times*, 25 April 1994; 'Bad memories in Italy', *New York Times*, 2 June 1994.

21. Cited in Federico Fubini, 'Quando Fini Sognava Istria e Dalmazia', *Limes*, 5 January 1996.

22. Cited in William Drozdiak, 'Italian neo-fascists move toward center, but Europe still frets', *Washington Post*, 20 May 1994.

23. Ibid.

24. Historian of Italian communism Grant Amyot suggested in 1990 that its looming 'social-democratisation' could be termed a Bad Godesberg: see his 'The PCI and Occhetto's new course: the Italian road to reform', *Italian Politics*, 4, 1990, pp. 146–61, p. 160.

25. Roger Griffin, 'The "post-fascism" of the Alleanza Nazionale: a case-study in ideological morphology', *Journal of Political Ideologies*, 1, 2, 1996, pp. 123–45.

26. Germinario, *Da Salò al Governo*, p. 71.

27. Nicola Rao, *La fiamma e la celtica*, Milan: Sperling & Kupfer, 2010, p. 310.

28. As Andrea Ungari notes ('Da Fini a Fini', in *Le Destre nell'Italia del secondo dopoguerra*, p. 230), the theme had already been taken up by Gennaro Malgieri in *Secolo d'Italia*'s 31 December 1992 issue.

29. 'Parapiglia nel MSI: una pioggia di no sulla "cosa nera"', *La Repubblica*, 27 April 1994. The paper's headline compared the mooted change in the MSI to that which had already taken place in the ex-PCI, known as the 'cosa'.

30. Ibid.
31. 'Alleanza nazionale? È subito rissa nel MSI', *Corriere della Sera*, 26 April 1993.
32. 'Parapiglia nel MSI'.
33. 'Fini: la seconda Repubblica nascerà dallo scontro tra destra e sinistra', *Secolo d'Italia*, 24 July 1993, cited in Ungari, 'Da Fini a Fini', p. 234.
34. Cited in Ungari, 'Da Fini a Fini', p. 238.
35. See Melton S. Davis, 'Almirante is no Mussolini yet', *New York Times*, 6 June 1971.
36. Ungari, 'Da Fini a Fini', p. 239.
37. *Pensiamo l'Italia – il Domani c'è già. Valori, idee e progetti per l'Alleanza Nazionale: Tesi politiche approvate dal Congresso di Fiuggi*, Rome: Alleanza Nazionale, 1995.
38. Carioti, who makes this argument, moreover cites a remarkable Freudian slip in *Secolo d'Italia*: an image of the party leader pointing at the old emblem combined with the words 'Alleanza Nazionale' was captioned 'Gianfranco Fini shows the new symbol of the MSI'. Carioti, 'From the Ghetto to "Palazzo Chigi"'.
39. 'Pensiamo l'Italia – Il domani c'è già'.
40. Ibid.
41. Ibid.
42. As noted by Carioti, 'From the Ghetto to "Palazzo Chigi"'.
43. 'Pensiamo l'Italia – Il domani c'è già'.
44. Ibid.
45. Ibid.
46. Ibid.
47. Ibid.
48. Ibid.
49. Ibid.
50. 'La Mussolini contro Fini "Nessuna pacificazione"', *La Stampa*, 8 January 1994.
51. 'An non siederà con Le Pen', *La Stampa*, 2 June 1994; see also 'Fini: An offrì i suoi avvocati contro Priebke', *La Stampa*, 15 January 1996.
52. 'Su Priebke Msi spaccato', *La Stampa*, 16 June 1994.
53. Ibid.
54. 'Il fascismo? Buono fino al '38', *La Stampa*, 3 June 1994.
55. Ibid.
56. Ibid.
57. Ibid.
58. 'Egregio Indro Montanelli scusi il mio italiano', *Corriere della Sera*, 17 April 1996.

59. Vittorio Sgarbi, 'Priebke doveva essere assolto', *La Stampa*, 3 August 1996.

60. Ibid.

61. 'Lo sdegno tiepido di An "E" finita all'italiana'', *La Stampa*, 2 August 1996.

62. 'Elezioni? Siamo pronti', *La Stampa*, 5 December 1995.

63. Cited in Marco Bracconi, 'Priebke, Haider e i Serenissimi La carriera del deputato Serena', *La Repubblica*, 19 November 2003.

64. Marco Tarchi, 'What's left of the Italian right?', *Studia Politica*, 13, 4, pp. 693–709.

65. Piero Ignazi, 'Strappi a destra: le trasformazioni di Alleanza nazionale', *Il Mulino*, 1, 2004, pp. 67–76, see table on p. 72.

66. 'Fini ha deciso: "No al partito unico"'; 'Meglio sulle barricate', *La Stampa*, 25 April 1996.

67. 'L'ira di Fini si abbatte sul Cavaliere', *La Stampa*, 31 May 1999.

68. As summarised by Fabio Martini in 'Scatta l'ora dell'Elefante', *La Stampa*, 11 March 1999.

69. Marco Tarchi, 'The political culture of the Alleanza Nazionale: an analysis of the party's programmatic documents (1995–2002)', *Journal of Modern Italian Studies*, 8, 2, 2003, pp. 135–81.

70. Ibid.

71. Cited in Marco Bracconi, 'Priebke, Haider e i Serenissimi La carriera del deputato Serena', *La Repubblica*, 19 November 2003.

72. Gianfranco Fini, *Il Ventennio: Io, Berlusconi e la Destra Tradita*, Milan: Rizzoli, 2013, p. 140. Fini approvingly cites the political scientist Angelo Panebianco's judgement that such a move was necessary for the party, many of whose militants had seen the turn at Fiuggi 'more as a matter of necessity (the price to be paid to make the party competitive) than a moral and political obligation'.

73. 'Fini in Israele: "Le leggi razziali furono infami"', *Corriere della Sera*, 24 November 2003.

74. Ibid.

75. Ibid.

76. Historian Simon Levis Sullam notes how the focus on the 'righteous' Perlasca, a fascist representing 'absolute good', has been used to obfuscate the record of those who were 'unrighteous': see 'Gli Usi dei Giusti e l'Oblio degli Ingiusti', *La Rassegna Mensile di Israeli*, 83, 1, January–April 2017, p. 194. Perlasca is cited in a similar key in Meloni's *Io Sono Giorgia*, a book which otherwise avoids any reference to the regime era.

77. 'Fini: il fascismo fu il male assoluto', *La Repubblica*, 24 November 2003.

78. Pierluigi Battista, 'Storia di una fake news politica mai smentita: Gianfranco Fini e una frase mai detta', *HuffPost*, 29 June 2021.

79. Barbara Jerkov, '"Ma la fiamma non si tocca: è il nostro legame con il Msi', *La Repubblica*, 25 November 2003.

80. 'Fini: una scelta di coerenza', *Secolo d'Italia*, 28 November 2003, cited in Giovanni Cantoni, 'Per la purificazione della memoria storica del popolo italiano', *Cristianità*, 320, 2003.

81. The full video is available at www.ina.fr/ina-eclaire-actu/video/ cac96016828/zoom-elections-en-italie.

82. Stéphanie Dechezelles, 'Boia chi molla! Les nouvelles générations néofascistes italiennes face à l'(in)action violente', *Cultures et Conflits*, 81–2, pp. 101–23.

83. On this current, see Guido Caldiron, 'Fascistopoli: la Roma di Alemanno', *MicroMega*, 4, 2013, pp. 41–55.

84. Cited in '"Pregiudizi sul mio cognome" Alessandra Mussolini lascia An', *La Repubblica*, 27 November 2003.

85. 'An, nasce la Lista Storace e si allontana la scissione', *La Repubblica*, 3 December 2003; Amedeo La Mattina, 'Migliaia con Storace, "vogliamo il congresso"', *La Stampa*, 4 December 2003.

86. 'Ad Arezzo An applaude Fini: diciamogli grazie', *Corriere della Sera*, 29 November 2003.

87. Ibid.

88. Ibid.

89. See Francesco Boezi, *Fenomeno Meloni: viaggio nella 'Generazione Atreju'*, Verona: Gondolin, 2020.

90. Meloni, *Io Sono Giorgia*, position 79.

91. Boezi, *Fenomeno Meloni*, p. 30.

92. Roberto Chiarini, 'Profilo storico-critico del MSI', *Il Politico*, 54, 3, July–September 1989, pp. 369–89, p. 387 *et seq*; Ignazi, *Postfascisti?*, pp. 76–80.

93. Ibid.

94. 'Fecondazione: Gasparri, astensione in difesa diritto vita', *Adnkronos*, 24 May 2005.

95. Cited in Adalberto Baldoni, *Storia della Destra: dal postfascismo al Popolo della Libertà*, Florence: Vallecchi, 2009, p. 323.

96. 'Assemblea di AN', quotidiano.net, 3 July 2005.

97. 'Politica e schieramenti: l'Assemblea di AN', *Corriere della Sera*, 3 July 2005.

98. 'An nel caos, è la resa dei conti Fini revoca gli incarichi del partito', *La Repubblica*, 18 July 2005.

99. 'Bufera in An, Fini revoca tutti gli incarichi', *Corriere della Sera*, 19 July 2005.

100. 'Santanchè-Mussolini, scontro a distanza', *Corriere della Sera*, 26 March 2008.

101. 'Fascismo, Alemanno corregge il tiro La Russa rilancia: omaggio ai soldati Rsi', *Corriere della Sera*, 8 September 2008.

102. Ernesto Menicucci, 'Male assoluto le leggi razziali non definisco così il fascismo', *Corriere della Sera*, 7 September 2008.

103. 'Fini: "Destra si riconosca nei valori antifascisti"', *La Repubblica*, 13 September 2008.

104. Ibid.

105. Ibid.

106. Ibid.

107. Giorgia Meloni, 'La lettera sul web: noi crediamo nella Costituzione, ora basta offrire armi alla sinistra', *Il Giornale*, 18 September 2008.

108. Ibid.

109. Fabio Luppino, 'Ruby, Berlusconi e gli alleati', *HuffPost*, 15 January 2022.

110. Francesco Bei, 'Lo strappo definitivo di Gianfranco "Rimanere così non è più dignitoso"', *La Repubblica*, 15 April 2010.

111. 'Nasce il partito di Futuro e Libertà Fini: "Non An in piccolo, Pdl in grande"', *La Repubblica*, 5 October 2010.

112. *L'Aria che tira*, La7, 14 March 2014.

113. 'Gli esponenti di FdI-An non votarono il Fiscal Compact', fratelli-italia.it, 8 April 2014. In this letter to *Il Tempo*, Fratelli d'Italia's Carlo Fidanza rejected Matteo Salvini's claim that this party had supported the Fiscal Compact in 2012.

CHAPTER 4

1. 'La sfida di uscire dal ghetto senza diventare "moderati"', *Libero*, 31 August 2021.

2. Gianni Alemanno, 'La verità su Paolo di Nella', Facebook post, 10 February 2020.

3. Ibid.

4. They divorced in 2018.

5. John Hooper, 'Cries of "Duce! Duce!" salute Rome's new mayor', *The Guardian*, 30 April 2008; 'Right back: a former neo-fascist will be the next mayor of Rome', *The Economist*, 1 May 2008; and in a later alleged incident involving two councillors, Nick Squires, 'Italian politicians "made fascist salutes" during tribute to Jews', *The Telegraph*, 17 October 2008.

6. Giulio Meotti, 'Alemanno votato dal ghetto', *Il Foglio*, 29 April 2008; Guy Dunmore, 'Fascists and Jews united for Rome mayor', *Finan-*

cial Times, 4 May 2008; 'Campidoglio, issata ieri la bandiera d'Israele', *Corriere della Sera*, 8 May 2008.

7. 'Shoah, polemica di Storace: "Il museo è uno sperpero di denaro pubblico"', *Roma Today*, 19 January 2009. 'Shoah: Alemanno e Pacifici replicano a Storace', *Roma Today*, 20 January 2009.

8. 'Foibe, agli studenti con Alemanno un opuscolo sui comunisti assassini', *La Repubblica*, 15 February 2009.

9. 'Alemanno nei luoghi della memoria "La Resistenza non si discute"', *La Repubblica*, 5 May 2008.

10. 'Le leggi razziali un male assoluto', *La Stampa*, 7 September 2008.

11. Lorenzo Galeazzi, 'Affile celebra il gerarca fascista: il sindaco: "Esempio per i giovani"', *Il Fatto Quotidiano*, 12 August 2012.

12. Cited in Wu Ming, 'Affile in Blu', *Internazionale*, 23 April 2013.

13. Patrizia Maciocchi, 'Il mausoleo a Rodolfo Graziani non basta per l'apologia del fascismo, annullata la condanna di sindaco e assessori', *Il Sole*, 24–26 March 2021.

14. See Caldiron, 'Fascistopoli. La Roma di Alemanno'.

15. See for instance the debate in 'Piazzapulita – Io ti odio (Puntata 09/11/2017)', La7 Attualità, YouTube, 9 November 2017.

16. Federica Frazzetta, *L'onda nera frastagliata: l'estrema destra nell'Italia del nuovo millennio*, Milan: Meltemi, 2022.

17. Pierre Milza, *Europa estrema: il radicalismo di destra dal 1945 ad oggi*, Rome: Carocci, 2003, p. 9. I owe this reference to Stefano Bartolini, 'I "nipoti del Duce" tra eredità, novità, persistenze e sviluppi all'alba del nuovo secolo', *Quaderni di Farestoria dell'Istituto Storico della Resistenza e della Società Contemporanea di Pistoia*, 10, 3.

18. Ibid.

19. In his *La rivoluzione impossibile: dai Campi Hobbit alla nuova Destra*, Florence: Vallecchi, 2010. Tarchi comments amusedly on the stuffy reactions from party leaders worried that it was not a properly political occasion.

20. 'Infame ska', on the group's 1999 debut studio album, *Dittatura del sorriso*.

21. 'William Butler Yeats' [sic], 'Una terribile bellezza è nata', Casapound. it, undated.

22. 'Cinghiamattanza', from the group's fourth studio album, *La ballata dello stoccafisso*, 2007.

23. Interview with 'Deddo', in Domenico di Tullio, *Centri sociali di Destra: occupazioni e culture non conformi*, Rome, Castelvecchi, 2006, p. 104.

24. As reported in Mariagrazia Gerina, 'Ecco "CasalePound", così Alemanno sistema gli amici nel parco', *L'Unità*, 12 January 2012. The council logo even appeared on CasaPound posters, as the sponsor

of a conference: 'Il Comune appoggia un convegno di Casapound e scoppia la polemica', *RomaToday*, 15 April 2009.

25. Cited in 'Scontri di Cuneo, CasaPound si appella alla Costituzione', *FascinAzione*, 5 March 2011.

26. Interview with Gabriele Adinolfi, cited in di Tullio, *Centri sociali di Destra*, p. 18.

27. Sean Mantesso, 'The ghost of Benito Mussolini lingers as far-right popularity surges in Italy', *ABC*, 25 May 2019; 'Fascism in Italy: the hipster fascists trying to bring Mussolini back into the mainstream', *Channel 4 News*, YouTube, 2 March 2018.

28. Valerio Renzi, 'Gianluca Iannone di CasaPound condannato in appello per lo schiaffo al giornalista Filippo Rossi', *Fanpage*, 24 September 2019, with reference to a physical assault on a journalist; 'Aggressione di Casapound a Milano, l'editore di Altaforte Polacchi condannato a un anno per lesioni', *La Repubblica*, 11 February 2020. Altaforte publisher and CasaPound activist Maurizio Zatelli assaulted a member of partisans' association ANPI and a migrants' rights activist when they interrupted a meeting with Milan mayor Beppe Sala at the city hall.

29. This so-called 'Angels and Demons' case centred on allegations that social workers manipulated children to make abuse claims in order to remove them from their parents. Despite the vast bubble of media coverage, based on a vast array of wild claims, CasaPound alleged that the story had been hushed up, through banners reading 'Parlateci di Bibbiano' (tell us about Bibbiano), highlighting the letters P and D in an effort to associate the case with the locally ruling Partito Democratico. This meme was adopted by institutional right-wing politicians, while pop stars like Laura Pausini and Nek each called on Italians to inform themselves about the supposedly hushed-up case. See David Broder, 'The fascist movement at the centre of Italy's culture war', *New Statesman*, 6 August 2019.

30. 'Attività', on casaggi.blogspot.com.

31. 'Casaggì: sospesi fra nazismo e destra istituzionale', *Patria Indipendente*, 6 March 2020. It links to the article 'Fascismo e abrogazione della dodicesima disposizione transitoria', *Casaggì*, 7 April 2011, which continues: 'Fascism does not need to be refounded: it is there, it is alive and will always be in the historical memory of this people. Not only does it live in the palaces, the testimonies and the cultural heritage of our country, but it is something that in its essence, in its mystique, lives on regardless: it is a movement of the soul, a way of being in the world, a sneer of defiance that carries timeless and eternal values. Our Fascism has never been condemned by any court: it is the honour of the fighters of the Italian Social Republic, the marble of

our cities, the most important social achievements of the twentieth century, the cultural and anthropological avant-garde, the hymn to life and the buoyant will to be an example.'

32. Ibid.
33. Silvio Berlusconi blocked the candidacies of both Tilgher and Fiore but made an alliance with these minor parties. Reported in Fabrizio Rancone, 'Tilgher e Fiore: altri sono impresentabili', *Corriere della Sera*, 17 February 2006.
34. 'Con la Fiamma tricolore c'è Iannone: allievo di Boccacci, leader di CasaPound', *L'Unità*, 6 March 2006.
35. Giacomo Russo Spena, 'Fascismo liquido', *Il manifesto*, 7 September 2008, available at insorgenze.net.
36. Castellino belonged to a long series of groups (La Destra, Movimento Sociale Europeo, Forza Nuova), became a leading no-vax activist during the Covid–19 pandemic and was jailed after the October 2021 assault on the CGIL trade union headquarters in Rome. On his chequered career, see Valerio Renzi, 'Giuliano Castellino: romanzo nero del più trasformista dei fascisti romani', *Fanpage*, 21 October 2021.
37. As explained in 'Roberto Cappiello: per una politica d'immigrazione seria e controllata', *Piu Culture*, 31 May 2016; 'Gli esponenti di CasaPound nelle liste che sostengono Michetti a Roma', *Il Post*, 10 September 2021.
38. Alessandro Capriccioli, 'Roma, Casapound spiazza tutti', *L'Espresso*, 8 February 2012.
39. La Redazione [de Il Primato Nazionale], 'Cosa dice veramente la Costituzione sull'economia? Lo ha capito solo CasaPound', *Il Primato Nazionale*, 19 February 2018, www.ilprimatonazionale.it/approfondimenti/programma-casapound-applicare-costituzione-79981/.
40. 'Ecco perché l'Unione Europea odia le Costituzioni e la sovranità delle nazioni', *Il Primato Nazionale*, 8 November 2018.
41. Ibid.
42. Diego Fusaro, 'Bimbi costretti a scrivere lettere d'amore gay: benvenuti nel gender-totalitarismo', *Il Primato Nazionale*, 3 October 2018; 'L'immigrazione è un inganno: e l'unico comunista che l'ha capito è Marco Rizzo', *Il Primato Nazionale*, 10 January 2019. This latter article praises Marco Rizzo, leader of the Stalinist Partito Comunista, as the only left-wing leader who recognises the ill effects of immigration.
43. Adolfo Spezzaferro, '"La Costituzione è antifascista": l'ignoranza social contro il Salone del libro', *Il Primato Nazionale*, 4 May 2019.
44. Adolfo Spezzaferro, 'Compagni, basta riempirvi la bocca di Costituzione (o almeno leggetevela)', *Il Primato Nazionale*, 13 October 2021.

45. It might be added that the articles appearing in such a publication as the lifestyle supplement of *Corriere della Sera* – Andrea Rossi, 'Siamo tutti un po' fascisti? Forse', *Style Magazine*, 17 January 2018; Erika Riggi, 'Nuovi fascismi: como sono cambiati i ragazzi di Casa Pound', *Style Magazine*, 15 February 2018 – have often been less trivialising than supposed political analyses of 'hipster fascists'.

46. CasaPound, 'FAQ: Ovvero le Frequently Asked Questions, "domande poste frequentemente" sul nostro movimento', casapounditalia.org.

47. Ibid.

48. Cited in Emma Bubola, 'I numeri di CasaPound: 20 arresti e 359 denunce in 5 anni', *Open*, 1 May 2019.

49. 'Il programma', text from casapounditalia.org. On 'totalitarian' immigration plans see the interview with Great Replacement theorist Renaud Camus: Adriano Scianca, '"Il nuovo comunismo è venuto per sostituire i popoli": parla Renaud Camus', *Il Primato Nazionale*, 6 February 2016; Adriano Scianca, 'Ius soli, lo "sbrocco" di Unicef racconta l'isteria totalitaria dei progressisti', *Il Primato Nazionale*, 27 December 2017.

50. Roberto Maggiori, 'L'aggressore di Emmanuel con Casapound', *Radio Popolare*, 11 July 2016.

51. 'I fascisti di Casapound in piazza con la Lega: "Salvini è il nostro leader"', *Il Fatto Quotidiano*, YouTube, 28 February 2015.

52. 'Renzi a casa! Roma 28 Febbraio 2015', *Lega Salvini Premier*, 28 February 2015.

53. See Chapter 5.

54. Marco Fattorini, 'Il patto del Brancaccio, a Roma nasce la destra di Salvini e Casapound', *Linkiesta*, 12 May 2015.

55. The show was presented by Gianluigi Paragone. In the 2022 general election, he led a small vaccine-sceptic, anti-euro party called Italexit, whose lists included CasaPound activists. The social centre was also apparently key to its effort to gather signatures from members of the public, such that it could run in the election: see Redazione ANSA, 'Italexit candida militanti Casapound e no vax', *ANSA*, 21 August 2022.

56. The exchange took place on *La Gabbia*, La7, 8 March 2015.

57. La Redazione [de Il Primato Nazionale], 'Legge Fiano, tanti cari saluti: lo scioglimento delle Camere la affonda', *Il Primato Nazionale*, 29 December 2017.

58. The process is reconstructed at www.cortecostituzionale.it/action-SchedaPronuncia.do?anno=1958&numero=74; for a fuller panorama of interpretations see Alessandra Galluccio, 'Il Saluto Fascista è Reato? L'attuale panorama normativo e giurisprudenziale ricostruito dal

tribunale di Milano, in una sentenza di Condanna', Diritto Penale Contemporandeo, 29 April 2019, https://archiviodpc.dirittopenaleuomo. org/d/6644-il-saluto-fascista-e-reato-l-attuale-panorama-normativo-e-giurisprudenziale-ricostruito-dal-tribuna.

59. Text taken from http://documenti.camera.it/leg17/dossier/pdf/ GI0485a.pdf.

60. Paolo Berizzi, 'La spiaggia fascista di Chioggia: "Qui, a casa mia, vige il regime"', *La Repubblica*, 9 July 2017; 'Spiaggia di Chioggia dedicata a Mussolini: arriva la legge che vieta l'apologia di fascismo', globalist. it, 9 July 2017.

61. As noted in Vittorio Prada, 'Il cuore nero dell'Italia: la vexata quaestio dell'apologia del fascismo', *Horizonte*, 6, 2018.

62. Cited in ibid.

63. 'Apologia di fascismo, Santanchè (Fi): "Ho una bellissima testa del duce in legno sul mio comodino"', *Il Fatto Quotidiano*, 18 July 2017. The exchange had taken place on La7's *L'Aria che Tira*.

64. 'Sallusti: essere fascista non è reato, la legge di Fiano è illiberale', *In Onda*, La7, available on YouTube, 16 July 2017; 'Mussolini (FI) a Verini (PD): la legge Fiano è una minchiata colossale', *Omnibus*, La7, YouTube, 14 July 2017.

65. 'Già mercoledì: l'intervista a Giampaolo Pansa sul suo nuovo libro Il mio viaggio tra i vinti', Già Mercoledì, YouTube, 23 September 2017.

66. 'Ronde di CasaPound in spiaggia a Ostia', *Corriere della Sera*, 10 July 2017.

67. 'Giorgia Meloni ridicolizza la Legge Fiano', intervention at Atreju 2017, YouTube, 24 September 2017.

68. 'La Russa fa il saluto romano alla Camera', Vista Agenzia Televisiva Nazionale, YouTube, 13 September 2017.

69. Cited in David Barra, 'Ray-Ban, giacche di pelle e saluti romani: breve storia dei 'sanbabilini"', *Vice*, 18 December 2017.

70. Mario Capanna, *Formidabili quegli anni*, Milan: Garzanti, 2007, p. 116, cited in Pierluigi Zavaroni, *Caduti e memoria nella lotta politica: le morti violente della stagione dei movimenti*, Bologna: FrancoAngeli, 2010, p. 74.

71. 'La Destra Fiamma apre la sua campagna elettorale!', Roberto Jonghi Lavarini blog post, 1 March 2008.

72. 'Inni al Duce e croci celtiche Santanché: sono fascista', *La Repubblica*, 30 March 2008.

73. 'ITALIAinFORMA intervista Roberto Jonghi Lavarini', text from Roberto Jonghi Lavarini blog post, 26 January 2011.

74. Ibid.

75. 'Cuore Nero – I neofascisti di Milano si raccontano', *Mag Zine*, YouTube, 27 November 2012.

76. Ibid.

77. 'Viaggio nel Cuore Nero di Milano', YouTube, 17 October 2008.

78. 'Cuore Nero – I neofascisti di Milano si raccontano', *Mag Zine*, YouTube, 27 November 2012. In a more recent interview, he claims '5 percent of Italians, according to sociologists and political scientists have the same ideas as me, a positive historical judgment about certain periods close to us, say from 1922 to 1945, and this is an inescapable fact'. He asserts that the majority of this 5 per cent vote for Fratelli d'Italia: see Umberto Baccolo, interviewer, 'La Verità di Roberto Jonghi Lavarini contro le lobby del pensiero unico dominante', *Consul Press*, 22 November 2021. A poll shortly before the 2022 election, based on 1,500 voters, found that 7.7 per cent of Italians think fascist ideas can contribute to democracy, but the figure was 20.5 per cent among Fratelli d'Italia supporters and 29 per cent among Lega supporters. See Lisa Zanotti and Carlos Meléndez, 'Survey evidence: are Fratelli d'Italia voters less democratic than supporters of other Italian parties?', London School of Economics blog, 28 September 2022.

79. He cites his inspiration from Dugin's 'Fourth Theory' in 'Intervista a Roberto Jonghi Lavarini: "La vecchia Destra con la nuova Lega"', *Consul Press*, 28 February 2019. 'The bipolar ideological world is over. Communism is dead and financial capitalism is in deep crisis. We need to think about a new multipolar and also multi-cultural international system. Geopolitically, Europe is already part of Eurasia and in Putin's Russia there are, not only extraordinary opportunities for Italian businesses, but firm cultural and spiritual landmarks. *Ex oriente lux*: Moscow has truly returned to being Third Rome, a beacon of light and civilization.'

80. 'Adunata del Popolo della Libertà a Milano', Roberto Jonghi Lavarini blog post, 11 November 2010.

81. 'La nostra DESTRA nel PDL', Roberto Jonghi Lavarini blog post, 17 November 2010.

82. Ibid.

83. 'DESTRA-PDL: incontro politico-conviviale a Milano', Roberto Jonghi Lavarini blog post, 18 November 2010.

84. Paola di Caro, 'Meloni furiosa per l'inchiesta di Fanpage su Fidanza: "Ma come si fa, per 30 voti? Io impazzisco"', *Corriere della Sera*, 2 October 2021.

85. Alessandro Catto, *Radical chic: Conoscere e sconfiggere il pensiero unico globalista*, Viareggio: La Vela, 2017.

86. 'ROBERTO JONGHI LAVARINI: fare fronte contro i radical chic', Il reporter indignato, YouTube, 27 January 2018.
87. Ibid.
88. Ibid.
89. Ibid.
90. Ibid.
91. Ibid.
92. Backstair, 'Lealtà azione: la destra istituzionale ci mette il nome, l'estrema destra la militanza e i voti', *Fanpage*, 7 October 2021.
93. 'Gaggiano, aperta la sede di Lealtà e Azione per il Sud Milano', *Il Fatto Quotidiano*, 6 September 2021.
94. 'Cooxazione – distribuzione pacchi alimentare per le famiglie in difficoltà', Lealta Azione, 13 December 2017.
95. Carmen La Gatta, 'Raduno di Lealtà Azione, all'inaugurazione anche parlamentari Lega e FdI', *Il Fatto Quotidiano*, 7 July 2018.
96. Ibid.
97. Ibid.
98. See the video at 'Milano 29 aprile 2015 Sergio Ramelli', YouTube, 25 May 2015.
99. Conti, *L'Anima nera della Repubblica*, p. 178.
100. Paolo Berizzi, È gradita la camicia nera*: Verona, la città laboratorio dell'estrema destra tra l'Italia e L'Europa*, Milan: Rizzoli, 2021.
101. Cited in Paolo Barcella, *La Lega: una storia – nodi dell'Italia contemporanea*, Rome: Carocci, 2022.
102. Cited in Guido Caldiron, *La Destra Plurale*, Rome: Manifestolibri, 2001, p. 124.
103. The idea that northerners are polenta-eaters is itself a stereotype encouraged by southerners' mocking description of them as *polentoni*: 'polenta heads'.
104. For an interesting perspective on the class dynamics of this vote, see Barcella, *La Lega*. See the English-language review at Pietro Bianchi, 'Italy's Lega is a party of and for business', *Jacobin*, 27 September 2022.
105. Barcella, *La Lega*.
106. Concetto Vecchio, 'Verona, sindaco Tosi condannato per razzismo', *La Repubblica*, 21 October 2008.
107. Massimo Rossignati, 'Andrea Miglioranzi a Verona lo conoscono tutti: fosse solo', *Il Gazzettino*, 5 June 2020.
108. 'Fascisti? A Verona', *La Stampa*, 6 May 2008.
109. 'L'infiltrazione neofascista delle curve', Carmilla online, 5 February 2007, cited from *Fascisteria: I protagonisti, i movimenti e i misteri dell'eversione nera in Italia (1945–2000)*, Rome: Castelvecchi, 2001.

110. Giulia Siviero, 'Verona, dove comanda l'estrema destra', *Il Post*, 1 May 2018.

111. 'Fascisti? A Verona', *La Stampa*, 6 May 2008.

112. Ibid.

113. 'L'ironico capo ultrà del Verona: "Balotelli non è del tutto italiano – E anche noi abbiamo un negro"', *Il Napolista*, 4 November 2019.

114. Interviewed at 'Chi è Luca Castellini, l'ultrà del Verona ed esponente di Forza Nuova', *Fanpage*, YouTube, 4 November 2019.

115. Ibid.

116. 'Castellini a processo per frasi su Hitler e Balotelli: Aned e Circolo Pink parti civili', *Verona Sera*, 27 January 2021.

117. The video appears at www.facebook.com/roberto.lorenzetti.siseco/videos/10214341716248143/.

118. Andrea L. P. Pirro, 'Far right: the significance of an umbrella concept', *Nations and Nationalism*, 27 June 2022, speculates about a possible local-level rapprochement based on the common repertoires of action visible in the research of Piero Castelli Gattinara, 'Europeans, shut the borders! Anti-refugee mobilisation in Italy and France', in Donatella della Porta (ed.), *Solidarity mobilizations in the 'refugee crisis'*, London: Palgrave, 2018, pp. 271–97. Castelli Gattinara interviewed Lega and Forza Nuova activists, who described their involvement in 'citizen' initiatives to whistleblow on refugee NGOs, albeit also claiming to report abuses by the 'migrant business'.

119. Claudio Bozza, 'Il senatore veneto in uno scatto con il capo di Forza Nuova nella città scaligera che ha attaccato Balotelli', *Corriere della Sera*, 5 November 2019.

120. Hélène Barthélemy, 'The American anti-LGBT movement goes to Italy', Southern Poverty Law Center, 19 December 2018.

121. See Giulia Siviero, 'Italian neo-fascists prepare to join World Congress of Families events', *OpenDemocracy*, 29 March 2019.

122. 'Family event in Italy's "city of love" hides violent ties', *SourceMaterial*, 29 March 2019; Ferruccio Pinotti and Elena Tebano, 'Tutti i legami tra Pro Vita e Forza Nuova', *Corriere della Sera*, 10 July 2017.

123. Giulia Siviero, 'Italian neo-fascists prepare to join World Congress of Families events'.

124. Full speech available at 'Giorgia Meloni's electrifying speech at the World Congress of Families, English subtitles', YouTube, 17 April 2019.

125. Giulia Siviero, 'Verona in nero: raduno di Casapound in tandem con il "family day" del Comune', *Il manifesto*, 7 September 2019.

126. La Russa (FdI): 'Un fronte unico per il sovranismo', Il Primato Nazionale, 8 September 2019.

127. Nicola Mattei, 'La Russa (FdI): "Un fronte unico per il sovranismo"', *Il Primato Nazionale*, 8 September 2019.
128. Ibid.
129. Ibid.
130. 'Di Stefano: "CasaPound avanguardia di pensiero per il sovranismo"', *Il Primato Nazionale*, 8 September 2019.
131. Ibid.
132. Alberto Speciale, 'AMIA Verona, Andrea Miglioranzi: la Cassazione rigetta l'appello e conferma la pena 14 mesi di reclusione', *Veneto News*, 30 December 2020.
133. 'Andrea Miglioranzi e Gigi Pisa con Fratelli D'Italia: la conferenza stampa al Liston 12', Gruppo Verona Network, 22 May 2019.
134. Luca Ciuffoni, 'Tosi: "Sboarina inefficiente nel gestire Amia" – L'azienda: "I numeri smentiscono l'ex sindaco"', *Verona Sera*, 5 January 2022.

CHAPTER 5

1. For a fuller investigation of this theme, I refer the reader to Broder, *First they took Rome*.
2. Ibid.
3. Jacopo Iacoboni, *L'esperimento : inchiesta sul Movimento 5 Stelle*, Bari: Laterza, 2018. See my interview with the author, 'The experiment', *Jacobin*, 2 March 2018.
4. Grillo ai fascisti di Casapound, 'Se volete benvenuti nel M5S', *La Repubblica*, 11 January 2013.
5. Data on the 2013 and 2018 votes are compared in Marco Maraffi, 'Le basi sociali del voto 2018: fra continuità e cambiamento', in Itanes, *Vox populi, Il voto ad alta voce del 2018*, Bologna: il Mulino, 2018.
6. See Moreno Mancosu and Riccardo Ladini, 'The red and the black: neo-fascist inheritance in the electoral success of the Lega in Tuscany, Umbria, and Marche', *Journal of Modern Italian Studies*, 25, 2, 2020, pp. 197–216, on the recent strength of the Lega in areas with previously high MSI votes.
7. SWG Radar, 'Speciale elezioni 2022', 26 September 2022.
8. 'Il ricordo della figlia Isabella, l'orazione funebre di Malgieri', *Secolo d'Italia*, 5 November 2012.
9. For a reconstruction of this affair see 'Ritorni di fiamma: la disputa sull'uso del simbolo di Alleanza Nazionale, tra fondazioni e scissioni', federalismi.it, 25 March 2015.
10. Andrea Indini, 'Fini sputa sulla destra: "A Fiuggi bambini viziati che scimmiottano la storia"', *Il Giornale*, 7 March 2014.

11. 'Congresso Fdi-An, il discorso di apertura di Giorgia Meloni', Fratelli d'Italia, YouTube, 8 March 2014.

12. 'Meloni replica a Fini: "Io mascotte di Salvini? Se mi critica vuol dire che sono nel giusto"', *Il Fatto Quotidiano*, YouTube, 26 February 2015.

13. Viola Longo, 'Corsaro lascia Fratelli d'Italia: in una lettera tutte le ragioni della sua scelta', *Secolo d'Italia*, 4 March 2015.

14. Ibid.

15. Sebastiano Messina, 'Il vergognoso post di Corsaro contro Fiano: "Con le sopracciglia copre i segni della circoncisione"', *La Repubblica*, 12 July 2017.

16. Video at 'Corsaro: "Frase su Fiano? Nessun riferimento antisemita, voleva solo dire che è una testa di c ... "', *Il Fatto Quotidiano*, 12 July 2017.

17. 'In Europa a Testa Alta', from fratelli-italia.it.

18. In a 2 March 2021 interview, Meloni defended this line, insisting that the euro could not be considered 'irreversible': *L'Aria di Tira*, La7.

19. 'Enrico Letta e Giorgia Meloni alla presentazione del nuovo libro di Bruno Vespa', hyperbros.com, YouTube, 17 October 2021.

20. Giada Oricchio, 'Otto e mezzo, Sallusti zittisce lo studio La7 sul caso Meloni: "Tutto ciò che non è di sinistra, è fascista"', *Il Tempo*, 16 June 2022; 'Meloni: Capezzone smaschera le assurde pretese della sinistra', Fratelli d'Italia, YouTube, 14 October 2021.

21. 'Diretta live Atreju 2021 – Settima giornata: Conclude Giorgia Meloni', Fratelli d'Italia, YouTube, 12 December 2021.

22. See Chapter 3.

23. 'L'aria che tira, Guido Crosetto: "Fascismo? Frecce in mano agli avversari, un problema che la Meloni deve porsi"', *Libero Quotidiano*, 12 October 2021. The interview is available on YouTube.

24. Ibid.

25. 'Crosetto: "Meloni sbaglia a urlare troppo, tra poco contro di lei si muoverà la magistratura"', *Il Fatto Quotidiano*, 16 June 2022.

26. 'Delegitimation and anticommunism in Italian neofascism', *Journal of Modern Italian Studies*, 22, 1, 2017, pp. 43–56.

27. On *foibe* Remembrance Day 2019, Forza Italia's Antonio Tajani would draw a parallel between the communist dictatorships of the past and contemporary Venezuela, using a speech in Basovizza to warn: 'We must not let a wicked dictatorship in Venezuela repeat what happened here.' Cited in 'Foibe, il giorno del ricordo: Salvini e Tajani a Basovizza – Il ministro: "Non esistono martiri di serie A e di serie B"', *Il Fatto Quotidiano*, 10 February 2019.

28. *Tesi di Trieste.*

29. 'Giorgia Meloni: God, homeland, family – NatCon Rome 2020', National Conservatism, YouTube, 22 February 2020.
30. Ibid.
31. Ibid.
32. *Tesi di Trieste*.
33. Ibid.
34. Alfonso Bianchi, 'Daul caccia Fratelli d'Italia dal Ppe. E loro: "Siamo noi che non vogliamo starci"', *EU News*, 16 April 2014.
35. Guido Crosetto, interviewed in Claudio Trabona, 'Crosetto in missione tra gli industriali: "Noi qui al 30 per cento? Un successo così aiuterebbe la Meloni a governare con coraggio"', *Corriere del Veneto*, 8 September 2022.
36. 'City of Miami (USA) honours ECR MEPs for their commitment to freedom in Cuba', ecrgroup.eu, 25 November 2021.
37. 'Giorgia Meloni en VIVA21: "Todo lo que nos identifica está siendo atacado"', *VOX España*, YouTube, 14 October 2021.
38. 'Una grande Giorgia Meloni interviene a Marbella, in Spagna, insieme ad Abascal e agli amici di Vox', Fratelli d'Italia, YouTube, 14 June 2022.
39. Ibid.
40. 'Una grande Giorgia Meloni interviene a Marbella, in Spagna, insieme ad Abascal e agli amici di Vox', Fratelli d'Italia, YouTube, 14 June 2022.
41. 'Lo que se oculta tras la Agenda 2030', *VOX España*, YouTube, 5 October 2020.
42. Giorgia Meloni and VIVA21, 'Todo lo que nos identifica está siendo atacado', *VOX España*, YouTube, 14 October 2021.
43. As cited, for instance, in Massimo Balsamo, '"Sono disperati" ... : la Meloni asfalta Letta e la sinistra', *Il Giornale*, 31 August 2022.
44. 'President Giorgia Meloni speech at CPAC 2022', ECR Party, YouTube, 26 February 2022.
45. Francesco Olivo, 'Giorgia Meloni: "Governa chi vince alle urne – con Vox ho sbagliato i toni e su Kiev non cambio linea"', *La Stampa*, 23 July 2022.
46. Miguel González, 'Vox se trae a la líder de la ultraderecha italiana para apoyar la campaña de Olona', *El País*, 7 June 2022.
47. 'Il prof e la foto choc della Meloni: a testa in giù', *Il Giornale*, 28 May 2021.
48. 'FdI, Meloni: Normale che un docente universitario scherzi su miei libri ribaltati per simulare il fatto che io venga appesa?', giorgiameloni. it, 28 May 2021.
49. 'Meloni a testa in giù: e se l'antifascismo fosse il peggiore dei totalitarismi?', *La Voce del Patriota*, 29 May 2021.

50. 'Libro di Giorgia Meloni esposto a testa in giù in libreria – FdI: "Allusione a piazzale Loreto"', *Corriere della Sera*, 28 May 2021.

51. Marina de Ghantuz Cubbe, 'Michetti, "il saluto romano è più igienico": le nostalgie fasciste dell'avvocato-tribuno del centrodestra', *La Repubblica*, 27 May 2021.

52. Adele Sirocchi, 'Galli della Loggia rilancia l'antifascismo: a FdI serve una Fiuggi 2 – Crosetto replica: un'assurdità', *Secolo d'Italia*, 3 June 2021.

53. Ernesto Galli della Loggia, 'Passato e aspirazioni: la destra e la storia che pesa', *Corriere della Sera*, 1 June 2021.

54. Ibid.

55. Giorgia Meloni, 'Meloni: Il rapporto con il passato? Noi contro i totalitarismi – I problemi sono a sinistra', *Corriere della Sera*, 2 June 2021.

56. 'Destra e populismo: la lezione che viene dalla Francia', *Corriere della Sera*, 29 June 2021.

57. Giorgia Meloni, 'Non abbiamo bisogno di esami del sangue, siamo il movimento dei patrioti italiani', *Corriere della Sera*, 1 July 2021.

58. 'Lobby Nera: inchiesta sulla destra neofascista', *Fanpage*, rebroadcast on 'Lobby Nera', *PiazzaPulita*, La7, 30 September 2021.

59. Ibid.

60. Ibid.

61. A Milan court ruled that the programme was indeed reflective of the content of all 100 hours of footage: see 'Inchiesta Lobby Nera di Fanpage.it, la procura: "Video fedeli alle 100 ore di girato"', *Fanpage*, 11 October 2021.

62. 'Lobby nera, Giorgia Meloni: "Io, arrabbiata con Fidanza – in Fdi niente spazio per nostalgie"', *Il Messaggero*, 7 October 2021.

63. Paolo Berizzi, 'Giorgia Meloni e il "barone nero" il capo della "lobby nera" condannato per apologia di fascismo e odio razziale', *La Repubblica*, 26 July 2022.

64. Paola Di Caro, 'Meloni furiosa per l'inchiesta di Fanpage su Fidanza: "Ma come si fa, per 30 voti? Io impazzisco"', *Corriere della Sera*, 2 October 2021.

65. 'City of Miami (USA) honours ECR MEPs for their commitment to freedom in Cuba'.

66. 'Giorgia Meloni al CPAC 2022, La Festa dei Conservatori Americani', *La Nostra Europa*, March 2022. This publication is Fidanza's own newsletter; his attendance went unmentioned in the Italian press. He also attended Meloni's Marbella rally in June 2022: he is visible in the audience at 'Una grande Giorgia Meloni interviene a Marbella, in Spagna, insieme ad Abascal e agli amici di Vox', Fratelli d'Italia, YouTube, 14 June 2022.

67. *L'Aria che tira*, La7, 4 October 2021.

68. *Otto e Mezzo*, La7, 4 October 2021.

69. Adriana de Conto, 'Meloni: "Sta succedendo di tutto, menzogne e killeraggio: è la tecnica della sinistra"', *Secolo d'Italia*, 12 October 2021.

70. Cited in Giacomo Salvini, 'Meloni contro Lamorgese per i contestatori ai comizi: "Strategia della tensione"', *Il Fatto Quotidiano*, 19 September 2022.

71. Vittorio Sgarbi, 'Vogliono depotenziare Meloni e isolare Michetti: Per questo la identificano col fascismo', *Secolo d'Italia*, 11 October 2021. The remarks were cited from Adnkronos.

72. Ibid.

73. Gisella Ruccia, 'Fratelli d'Italia, Rampelli: "Non c'è mai stata una relazione tra noi e Forza Nuova – Sciogliere il partito? Decide la magistratura"', *Il Fatto Quotidiano*, 12 October 2021.

74. Tg24 interview, cited in Sergio Rame, 'Meloni: "Casapound e Forza Nuova non sono partiti xenofobi"', *Il Giornale*, 10 February 2018. She made these comments during a tense situation following the terrorist attack by Luca Traini, a former Lega candidate, who opened fire on African immigrants in Macerata, in Le Marche region, injuring six people, as well as shooting at the front of the local Democratic Party office in a drive-by attack. He claimed this was 'revenge' for a young woman killed in Rome, whose parents then condemned his actions as well as the political use of her death. The night before she made the comments, Forza Nuova militants had defied a ban on protests in the city and gathered to Roman salute and chant 'Forza – Nuova – National Pride'.

75. 'Escluse le liste di Forza Nuova – Roberto Fiore: "Sistema banditesco, pronti i ricorsi"', *HuffPost*, 24 August 2022.

76. 'L'intervento del professor Giulio Tremonti alla conferenza programmatica di Fratelli d'Italia', Fratelli d'Italia, YouTube, 7 May 2022.

77. Ibid.

78. *Secolo d'Italia*, 30 April 2022.

79. 'Appunti per un Programma Conservatore', 30 April 2022.

80. 'Lavoro obbligatorio nel programma di Fdi? Crosetto', *Avvenire*, 7 May 2022.

81. 'Giorgia Meloni: "L'ecologia è un elemento fondamentale dell'identità politica dei conservatori. Coniugare ambiente e crescita"', giorgiameloni.it, 3 June 2021.

82. 'L'intervento di Nicola Procaccini, deputato europeo e resp. dipartimento ambiente ed energia di FdI', Fratelli d'Italia, YouTube, 6 May 2022.

83. Ibid.

84. "'Chiarezza, Regole, Orgoglio": Giorgia Meloni chiude la 3 giorni della conferenza programmatica FdI', Fratelli d'Italia, YouTube, 1 May 2022.

CONCLUSION

1. Domenico Gallo, 'La Giornata della Memoria ... perduta!', *MicroMega*, 15 April 2022.
2. Atto Senato n. 1371, senato.it.
3. Ibid.
4. 'Giornata nazionale degli Alpini, la lettera di 39 ufficiali a Mattarella: "Cambiare data, quella scelta è ingiusta ed errata"', *Il Fatto Quotidiano*, 8 May 2022.
5. "'Giornata degli alpini" il 16 gennaio Scontro in Regione sulla legge di FdI', *La Repubblica*, 20 February 2022.
6. Most famously in Nuto Revelli, *La guerra dei poveri*, Turin: Einaudi, 2014 [1962].
7. Nuto Revelli, 'Nikolajewka: la vittoria della disperazione', *La Stampa*, 22 January 1963, text from improntadeglialpini.it.
8. "'Eroi contro i russi", l'insulto revisionista ai nostri Alpini', *Il Fatto Quotidiano*, 11 April 2022.
9. Antonio Bravetti, 'New York Times e Guardian contro Giorgia Meloni: "Il futuro dell'Italia è desolante"', *La Stampa*, 25 July 2022. Michela Suglia, 'Berlusconi vede Meloni, presto un vertice: e cerca la rivincita in Senato', ANSA, 23 July 2022.
10. Paolo Mastrolilli, 'Caso Meloni, negli Usa cresce la preoccupazione per una "post-fascista" verso Palazzo Chigi', *La Repubblica*, 23 July 2022.
11. *Mezz'ora in più*, RAI, 24 July 2022.
12. Bravetti, 'New York Times e Guardian contro Giorgia Meloni'.
13. Ibid.
14. Daniela Santanchè, *L'Aria Che Tira*, La7, 29 July 2022.
15. *Mezz'ora in più*, RAI, 24 July 2022.
16. Ibid.
17. Ibid.

Index

Thanks to our Patreon subscriber:

Ciaran Kane

Who has shown generosity and comradeship in support of our publishing.